Praise for

UNICORN TEAM

"When you're ready to leap, Jen Kem offers you insight, practical thought models, and most of all, confidence. Go build your team."
— **Seth Godin**, *New York Times* best-selling author of *Tribes*, speaker, and thought leader

"*Unicorn Team* is a powerful call to action for leaders to rethink how they bring ideas to life. The Unicorn Innovation Model is a transformative tool for any organization."
— **Mike Michalowicz**, author of *Profit First*

"With tangible insights, game-changing strategies, and her own inimitable voice, Jen Kem reveals how to tap into your most intensely extraordinary qualities to create rare ideas that truly matter."
— **Sally Hogshead**, *New York Times* best-selling author of *Fascinate*

"A must-read for anyone looking to lead with purpose and drive innovation. Jen's practical framework and compelling stories make this book an indispensable resource."
— **Nicole Walters**, *New York Times* best-selling author of *Nothing Is Missing* and host of *The Nicole Walters Podcast*

"This is the new leadership playbook for all executives and entrepreneurs who want to drive innovation in the modern era."
— **Rory Vaden**, co-founder of Brand Builders Group and *New York Times* best-selling author of *Take the Stairs*

"If you want to build a million-dollar business, you need a team . . . but not just any team. A Unicorn Team. This book shows you how."
— **Rachel Rodgers**, CEO and founder of Hello Seven and *Wall Street Journal* best-selling author of *We Should All Be Millionaires*

"An essential guide for leaders who want to build something legendary, for innovators who refuse to settle for mediocre, and for anyone ready to change the game. Bold, insightful, and full of heart, this book is a must-read for anyone serious about innovation and leadership."
— **Michael Port**, *New York Times* and *Wall Street Journal* best-selling author of *Steal the Show*

"Jen Kem provides a revolutionary framework for leaders to rally the right people and rapidly bring visionary ideas to market. This book is a game-changer for anyone with big dreams."
— **Farnoosh Torabi**, financial expert, author of
A Healthy State of Panic, and host of the *So Money* podcast

"*Unicorn Team* is a magical blueprint for turning your unique brilliance into both power and profit. Jen Kem's innovative insights show you how to create and lead with authenticity and make a significant impact."
— **SARK**, author of *Succulent Wild Woman* and artist

"*Unicorn Team* gives you the ability to tap into the YOU that's uniquely special and clarify how your ideas are worth rallying around—so that your ideas change the world in a real way."
— **Neeta Bhushan**, best-selling author of *That Sucked, Now What?*,
host of the *Brave Table* podcast, and founder of Highest Self Institute

"Harness your inner Unicorn leader, surround yourself with an exceptional team, and watch people rally around your ideas."
— **Pamela Slim**, author of *Body of Work* and *The Widest Net*

"If you have an idea that you know will change the world, this is a complete guide to helping you bring it to life in a powerful way."
— **Randy Garn**, *New York Times* best-selling author
of *Prosper* and founder of Prosper Inc.

"*Unicorn Team* stands out when it comes to books on leadership, business growth, and teams. It's a strategic guide for companies large and lean to optimize their innovation, collaboration, and execution cycles."
— **Jadah Sellner**, best-selling author of *She Builds* and
Simple Green Smoothies and host of the *Lead with Love* podcast

"A glimpse into the new consciousness the world is emerging into. The old game is broken, and this book is a blueprint on how to turn your mission into the most impactful game you can play for purpose and profit while changing the world."
— **Gordy Bal**, *Wall Street Journal* best-selling author of
The New Millionaire's Playbook, entrepreneur, and investor

"Jen is a rare mix of no-nonsense real talk and a giant caring heart. *Unicorn Team* will not only inspire you but give you a practical road map to make your ideas happen."
— **Denise Duffield-Thomas**, best-selling author of *Lucky Bitch* and *Get Rich, Lucky Bitch!*, money mindset expert, and entrepreneur

"*Unicorn Team* helps you tap into what makes you uniquely YOU and shows you how to rally people around your ideas in a way that sparks meaningful change. A must-read for anyone with big dreams and the drive to bring them to life."
— **Jen Gottlieb**, co-founder of Super Connector Media and best-selling author of *BE SEEN*

"Jen Kem's book is a blueprint for how to harness the unique magic of teams. The Unicorn Innovation Model is all-encompassing in terms of process and self-knowledge, turning diverse talents into unstoppable, high-performing teams that are innovative and collaborative."
— **Lisa Sun**, founder and CEO of GRAVITAS and national best-selling author of *Gravitas*

"*Unicorn Team* provides a road map for a truly innovative approach to leadership and teamwork—essential for anyone looking to change the world with their BIG ideas."
— **Yanik Silver**, best-selling author of *Moonlighting on the Internet* and *Evolved Enterprise* and founder of Maverick1000

"Packed with practical strategies and inspiring examples, *Unicorn Team* is a must-read for anyone ready to lead with purpose, inspire innovation, and create lasting impact."
— **Sheena Yap Chan**, *Wall Street Journal* best-selling author of *The Tao of Self-Confidence*

UNICORN TEAM

THE NINE LEADERSHIP TYPES YOU
NEED TO LAUNCH YOUR BIG
IDEAS WITH SPEED AND SUCCESS

JEN KEM

HAY HOUSE LLC
Carlsbad, California • New York City
London • Sydney • New Delhi

Copyright © 2025 by Jennifer A. Kem

Published in the United States by: Hay House LLC: www.hayhouse.com® • *Published in Australia by:* Hay House Australia Publishing Pty Ltd: www.hayhouse.com.au • *Published in the United Kingdom by:* Hay House UK Ltd: www.hayhouse.co.uk • *Published in India by:* Hay House Publishers (India) Pvt Ltd: www.hayhouse.co.in

Indexer: J S Editorial, LLC • *Interior design:* Karim J. Garcia
Cover design: theBookDesigners

Cataloging-in-Publication Data is on file at the Library of Congress

Hardcover ISBN: 978-1-4019-8027-6
E-book ISBN: 978-1-4019-8028-3
Audiobook ISBN: 978-1-4019-8029-0

10 9 8 7 6 5 4 3 2 1
1st edition, February 2025

Printed in the United States of America

This product uses responsibly sourced papers and/or recycled materials. For more information, see www.hayhouse.com.

To my real-life Unicorn Team:
Mikaela,
Jordan,
and
Noah

CONTENTS

AUTHOR'S NOTE

Kendra Scott started her jewelry business with $500 in her spare bedroom. Today, she's one of the wealthiest women in the world, a billionaire mogul with 100 retail stores and 2,000 employees,[1] and 1 of just 12 women in history to be inducted into the Texas Business Hall of Fame. She went on to establish the Kendra Scott Women's Entrepreneurial Leadership Institute[2] at the University of Texas, an incubator where young female students can share their business ideas and be taken seriously.

Shannan Penna made homemade protein bars in her kitchen and shared them with family and friends, who were blown away by the creative flavors and how shockingly delicious they were. Just a few short years later, she sold her company, Quest Nutrition, for 10 figures. Now she's living her best life, investing in luxury real estate,[3] running a sanctuary to provide compassionate care for shelter dogs that have terminal cancer,[4] and using her wealth to fund research that studies the connection between diet and chronic diseases.

Alon Matas struggled with his mental health and felt frustrated by how difficult and time-consuming it can be to find the right therapist. This sparked a billion-dollar idea: What if you could answer a few questions on your phone and get matched with a great provider, and then do video sessions from the privacy of your home? Therapy without the hassle and stress. His company, BetterHelp, is now the largest online counseling company in the world, with over 30,000 therapists and millions of customers served. Driven by the belief that therapy should be a basic human right accessible to all, BetterHelp has provided over $65 million in financial aid[5] to cover therapy for low-income individuals.

There are ordinary people, products, and companies. And then, there are the people that took ordinary ideas and transformed them into the extraordinary ones we admire today. The Unicorns.

Unicorns are the ones who have the greatest impact on society. The ones who change the way we live, work, and communicate; the way we find love, stay connected with friends, and raise our children; the way we experience the world around us. They expand our reality and improve our lives in ways that we could have never imagined on our own.

They create the brands that shape culture. Brands with that type of impact and influence start with a big idea.

Scribbled in a notebook or on a cocktail napkin, you may have a great idea that you want to bring to life. The next Kendra Scott jewelry, Quest Nutrition, BetterHelp; or the next Starbucks, Disney, or Martha Stewart Living. Or your great idea might not be a business you want to launch but instead an idea that will improve the company you work for or community you live in.

But this great idea will remain exactly that—a scribble on a napkin and nothing more—if you attempt to do it by yourself. This book fixes that problem. Unicorns need other Unicorns to make exciting ideas happen.

THIS IS A BOOK ABOUT UNICORNS.

In these pages, you'll learn how to become a Unicorn—the most innovative, inspiring, and powerful version of yourself, the kind of leader that people want to work for and with. You'll learn how to surround yourself with fellow Unicorns—brilliant people who possess the strengths that you lack and who help you achieve 1,000 times more than you ever could alone. Work alone and you will fail. Work with an underwhelming team and you will also fail (while wasting more resources in the process).

To achieve Unicorn-level greatness, you need the right people working on the right idea and using the right process. You'll learn the essential roles and energies of the nine Unicorn Leadership

Types that you need to bring your ideas to market in order to awe your audience and create buzz for your products and offers.

THIS IS A BOOK ABOUT BIG IDEAS.

I'm going to explain why most great ideas never become a reality—and how to make sure that yours does.

Whether your idea is a way for women to design personalized jewelry with a few clicks on their phones, a protein bar that actually tastes good, or a revolutionary new approach to counseling that helps millions of people improve their mental well-being, you'll discover how to rally the right people around your idea and bring it to life.

Sometimes the best ideas to rally around aren't even yours—and you might like that even better.

THIS IS A BOOK ABOUT LEADERS AND TEAMS.

Big ideas don't happen without powerhouse teams. However, most teams are dysfunctional. Many teams waste an enormous amount of time, energy, and money trying to solve the wrong problem instead of the right one. Many teams are horrendous at communicating, achieve mediocre results, get discouraged, and ultimately splinter apart. You will learn why these headaches happen and how to fix it.

I'll share timeless truths about how human beings can work together better—truths that remain constant even amid the rise of AI, remote work, and other cultural shifts. Even as technology advances, some things remain the same. Humans are still humans. Teams are still teams. We still need to collaborate to make great things happen.

Innovation will always involve people.

THIS IS A BOOK ABOUT CHOICES AND DECISIONS.

We live in a world where we've simplified things that aren't always so simple (like managing other humans) and where the loudest person on social media influences you to make a dogmatic, paint-yourself-in-a-corner decision instead of one that gives you the fluidity and flexibility to really win.

You'll learn how to use a delightfully modular and proven framework that helps you prioritize what really matters. You'll use what your big idea and the right people who rally around it really need, and then ignore the rest.

Applying the Unicorn Team methodology is like having free rein to play with Lego° blocks that you get to design, build, and then erect a whole new reality.

MOST OF ALL, THIS IS A BOOK ABOUT WINNING.

If you want to bring exciting ideas into the world and win in business, you can't do it alone. You need a team. But not just any team. A Unicorn Team. A team that collaborates so fluidly and harmoniously, watching this team work is like watching elite athletes sprint across the field at the Super Bowl. Poetry in motion. A team with such a stellar reputation that the world's best, brightest, and most talented individuals practically beg to join.

No matter what size company you are or what stage of business you're in, consider this your go-to innovation playbook to create a culture where you and your Unicorn Team test your ideas in your own lab and play big together and win—with predictability and without wasting precious time, money, and, most of all, energy. Get your best idea out into the world with astonishing speed and success. I'm handing the Unicorn keys over to you.

—Jen

INTRODUCTION

How a Scrappy Underdog
Changed the World

On Sunday, February 2, 2020, I went to see the San Francisco 49ers play the Kansas City Chiefs at the Super Bowl. Sitting in the stands in Miami, surrounded by thousands of die-hard 49ers fans, I watched my beloved team crumble in the fourth quarter and lose. I felt tears gather in the corners of my eyes, and my stomach dropped. This was a personal tragedy. In fact, I was sure it would be the most devastating moment of the year. Ha.

On Friday, March 13, I picked up my son from elementary school and didn't drop him off again for 340 days, along with every other parent who had school-aged children. Practically overnight, new phrases entered our collective vocabulary. "Social distancing." "Super-spreader." "Flatten the curve." Late-night talk show hosts delivered monologues live from their kitchen tables with family members operating the camera gear and family pets running across the screen. Nothing was normal anymore.

While people like you and I were figuring out how to use this thing called Zoom (and turning our homes into multipurpose offices, schools, and gyms), pharmaceutical companies were sprinting to develop a vaccine for COVID-19.

The billion-dollar question: Which company could do it the fastest?

The stakes were extremely high. Half a million people had already died. Millions more were expected to follow. Hospitals were overwhelmed and running out of beds for sick patients—setting up temporary triage centers outdoors and turning refrigerated trailers into morgues because they didn't have enough space for the bodies piling up. During a deadly surge, one hospital in California received a shipment of 5,000 body bags.[1] You don't need a crystal ball to know that's a very bad sign.

We needed a solution. Frankly, we needed a miracle. And we needed it now.

RACE FOR A CURE

As the global crisis and fear both mounted, two companies took on the race for a vaccine.

One company was Pfizer. You know them as the makers of pharmaceuticals like Advil, ChapStick, Preparation H, Neosporin, EpiPen, and one of its most famous prescription medications, Viagra. Pfizer had already produced 350 successful medications and other products and was poised to be the first to market with a vaccine. A giant, behemoth biotech company, 150 years old, with 96,000 employees[2] and $51 billion in annual revenue in 2019,[3] they, along with Johnson & Johnson (another household name), were the obvious front-runners to win the race.

And then there was Moderna. The David to Pfizer's Goliath. Moderna, a relatively new company, just 10 years old, was the underdog. With 800 employees (a skeleton crew compared to Pfizer's workforce) and zero commercial products on the market, they decided to put their hat in the ring.

At the time, Moderna was a biotech company working on treatments for illnesses like cancer and cystic fibrosis. They were doing important work and gaining traction, raising $2 billion in venture capital funding.[4] While $2 billion is nothing to scoff at, remember, it's peanuts compared to what Pfizer raked in every year. Moderna had never brought a product directly to the marketplace. Their first attempt would be mRNA-1273.[5]

It often takes 5 to 10 years, or more, to create an effective vaccine.[6]

Moderna got the job done in 42 days.

Just a few weeks after the genetic code of the virus was released, Moderna shipped a box containing a few hundred vials of the experimental vaccine to the National Institute of Allergy and Infectious Diseases. This made Moderna the first company to deliver a potential vaccine for clinical trials. Soon after, they became the first approved to do a small, early-stage trial on actual humans.

During the trial, zero people developed severe COVID-19 symptoms. Not a single one. And the Moderna vaccine was 95 percent effective, far higher than many scientists expected. Long story short: it worked—and it worked shockingly well. Pulling this off, on such a wildly fast timeline, was a feat deemed "absolutely remarkable"[7] by one vaccine expert who advises the FDA.

BILLIONS EARNED . . . AND THE QUEEN OF COUNTRY MUSIC'S SEAL OF APPROVAL

In December 2020, the U.S. Food and Drug Administration (FDA) authorized the Moderna COVID-19 vaccine under an emergency-use authorization. The Internet went ablaze when Dolly Parton proudly got her Moderna shot, singing her classic song "Jolene" but changing the lyrics to "Vaccine, vaccine, vaccine . . ." offering her seal of approval for this medication and encouraging her fans to do the same. (Sidebar: Parton used her own money to help fund the vaccine development, a charitable gift that Dr. Naji Abumrad says "made the research toward the vaccine go 10 times faster."[8]) Thanks to mRNA-1273, commonly known as Spikevax,[9] Moderna's annual revenue exploded astronomically from less than $1 billion in 2020 to $18.4 billion in 2021 and then $19.2 billion in 2022.[10]

How did a scrappy 10-year-old business pull this off? A working vaccine *and* one of the world's most beloved entertainers endorsing your product and giving her blessing on social media? That's the kind of positive PR that no amount of money can buy. Sure, Pfizer rolled out their own vaccine too, but Moderna did it faster and with significantly fewer resources.

Who was the leader behind this unlikely achievement?

Tracey Franklin, the 39-year-old chief of human resources. Franklin had been with Moderna for only one year and suddenly found herself facing the biggest professional challenge of her life.

She had to keep morale high while the world was falling apart; support team members through their stress, loss, and grief; and navigate complicated psychological and emotional dynamics (including the public's general mistrust of new medications, particularly fast-tracked vaccines), all while leading the Moderna team through the most daunting project of their lives. No big deal.

While most people in charge of HR aren't known as innovators, Franklin was first in line to put the idea of getting into the vaccine game in front of the leadership team and the board of directors.

She viewed it as a win-win. By pivoting into vaccine development, Moderna could keep people employed while the economy was volatile (win) and hopefully save countless lives (even bigger win). In a moment of visionary courage, the board agreed to go with the ambitious plan. "We literally decided overnight," the company's co-founder Noubar Afeyan says, "to try and do this."[11]

Describing this time in her career, the word that Franklin uses is *ownership*.[12] She was no longer a typical HR specialist, responsible for hiring and training, following the traditional playbook. Moderna's company values are "bold," "collaborative," "curious," and "relentless,"[13] and Franklin found a way to make these values burn strongly in each team member's heart. She took ownership of delivering the massive results that she had promised, laying out the timeline, which was unheard of and inspired people to believe that it could be done. And she led the business in a new direction and impacted the health of people around the world.

And Franklin is a Unicorn—an extraordinarily smart, skilled, driven person who consistently exceeds expectations. But there's no way she could have accomplished this miracle by herself. To overcome all the obstacles and achieve a nearly impossible goal, she needed to create a Unicorn Team. You can too, and that's what this book is about.

CREATING YOUR VERY OWN UNICORN TEAM

While Moderna's success may seem like magic, luck, the result of one brilliant person's leadership, or a one-time fluke, it is not. What this company did is actually a repeatable process that you can do too, with any business goal you want to achieve. I call it the Unicorn Innovation Model™.

You may not be a biotech executive like Franklin. Instead, you might be the founder of an app that helps people sit less and walk more. Leader of a team of software engineers. Social media marketing manager for a hotel chain. Or maybe you're a solopreneur running a business of one.

Whoever you are, you want to play bigger, to win, and to surround yourself with winners. You look out into the world and notice that 97 percent of individuals (and businesses) are struggling and only 3 percent consistently excel. You want to be part of this elite 3 percent. Unicorn status. Like Moderna and other case studies you'll hear about in this book, you want to be the one that reaches the top. This is doable. It all starts with rallying the right team around your ideas and goals.

However, and I suspect you'll agree with me here, most teams are dysfunctional. Many teams waste an enormous amount of time, energy, and money trying to solve the wrong problem instead of the right one. Many teams are horrendous at communicating, achieve mediocre results, get discouraged, don't enjoy working together, and head into each Monday filled with dread. Some teams splinter apart after a big disagreement or lawsuit. Others wither on the vine, slogging along without accomplishing anything noteworthy.

We have to do better.

Even amid the rise of AI, remote work, and other cultural shifts, humans are still humans. Teams are still teams. We still need to collaborate to make great things happen.

Bottom line: Innovation will always involve people.

WHO I AM . . . AND WHY YOU
SHOULD TAKE MY ADVICE

For decades, I've been a brand strategist for clients including Coca-Cola, Verizon, the Oprah Winfrey Network (OWN), *The Steve Harvey Show*, and other big-name brands and boot-strapped start-up founders that have redefined their industries.

I help my clients bring new offers to market quickly and become the undisputed leaders in their fields—the Unicorns that others aspire to be. I've been the Fixer that brands call when they're in trouble, bleeding revenue, losing top talent, or struggling to move forward with an initiative that's mission critical.

Whenever a client—whether their business generates 6, 7, 8, 9, or 10 figures per year—describes a frustrating dilemma to me, the first thing I say is, "Let's talk about your people." Often they protest and insist, "Oh, it's not a team thing. I want you to help me with my *brand* and I want the *business* to scale and grow." But trust me, the problem is almost always a people problem—and you can't eliminate those problems just by replacing them with AI, automation, or outsourcing the work. And you definitely can't fix it by avoiding the people altogether.

Remember, brands innovate. And innovation is innately human. So that must be addressed first.

That's why my framework—the Unicorn Innovation Model—was formed, after 20 years of working with real people, brands, and businesses in all phases of their growth. This is how I help my clients to pick the right idea and assemble the right people who rally to make it happen.

WHAT'S AHEAD

You might be a college student with entrepreneurial ambitions, a small business owner who is hungry for greater success, or an executive who wants to lead their company from good to great to

Unicorn status. Whoever you are, whatever phase of business you're in—whether your budget is a hundred bucks or billions, or if you have thousands of employees or none aside from yourself—you can use the Unicorn Innovation Model to make big things happen faster.

Previously, I've shared this model with my clients in private engagements, but I've never made it public until now.

As you keep reading, you'll find answers to the following questions:

1. What is a Unicorn Team, and how do I create one?

2. What if I need a Unicorn Team but don't have the budget to hire anyone right now? (Or what if I can't offer the competitive salaries and perks that other, bigger businesses can?)

3. Can I transform my current team into a Unicorn Team, or do I need to go out and find new people?

4. How do I get all the Unicorns on my team working together and collaborating successfully?

5. Once I've got the Unicorn Team of my dreams, how do I motivate people to stay long term instead of quitting and prancing away to other opportunities?

This book is a one-on-one conversation between you and me about your Unicorn Team. Why you need one, how to create it, and why this is the most important business move you'll ever make.

Creating your Unicorn Team will allow you to:

- Achieve *flow state* as a team and work together fluidly and successfully

- Create an innovation culture and develop *intrapreneurs* within your team

- Build a team that makes decisions fast, fails fast, and improves fast—a team that accomplishes more in 100 days than most teams do in a year

Let me show you how to achieve moonshot goals and become a brand that can't stop winning.

But before we do that, there are eight rules that leaders who innovate the Unicorn Team way use to play the game.

UNICORN TEAM RULES FOR SUCCESS

Rule #1: We make every decision based on our values.

Every Unicorn Team has a set of core values.

These values express why we exist, what we care about, and what we want to be known for.

We make every decision based on these values.

If an initiative doesn't align with our values, then we shouldn't be doing it at all.

Rule #2: We move fast, because we only work on the right hard things.

We make decisions quickly, test ideas quickly, gather data quickly, and pivot quickly.

We don't hustle—we flow. Because we rally around what really matters, quick turnarounds, sprint rounds, and "impossible" timelines don't intimidate us—they motivate us.

Doing the right hard things makes the effort we put in worthy of our time and energy.

Failing slowly kills culture and keeps the value we create from getting to the right people.

We embrace pressure to create diamonds together.

Rule #3: We don't try. We win.

As a Unicorn Team, we're obsessed with winning, because we know what we're working toward matters.

We meticulously track data to make sure we're on track with our goals. We course correct quickly and assertively when we're off the mark.

We'd like to win every time. However, we know the scoreboard doesn't tell the whole story. One loss doesn't necessarily mean we're on the wrong path.

Losing can help us choose the winning paths faster.

Rule #4: We win because we Visionize, Strategize, and Mobilize.

Visionize: We imagine a new and better future—where we need to go as a company or society—and come up with the big idea that will take us there.

Strategize: We map out the big strategic moves to get from here to there—including how to get our idea in front of the people who need it, get their attention, and create demand.

Mobilize: We break the big moves into small tasks and rock it out: complete the to-do list, finish the deliverables, close the loop, get it done.

Some Unicorns are strong Visionizers, some are powerful Strategizers, some are exceptional Mobilizers, and some can perform multiple roles.

Our team functions best when the Unicorns know and own their roles and doesn't function when we don't.

Rule #5: We share the responsibility to succeed.

Being part of a Unicorn Team doesn't include othering when things don't go well ("It was her idea to do this, not mine!") and centering when things do ("I made this happen. You're welcome!").

As a Unicorn Team, we share the disappointments and share the victories too.

Rule #6: We say what needs to be said, even when it's uncomfortable.

We address the elephant in the room.

We reward Unicorns who are willing to speak the unsaid.

We lean in to hard conversations with dignity and honesty.

We invite thoughtful discourse, embrace conflict, and seek to solve obstacles, threats, and confusion to achieve the meaningful outcomes we want.

Rule #7: We treat every Unicorn with respect.

Each Unicorn is critically important for the team's success.

Whether a Unicorn's job title is CEO, marketing director, administrative assistant, customer support rep, or consultant, this person performs a vital role on the team. We can't win without their contribution.

There are no overlords or underlings on a Unicorn Team. Every Unicorn is a leader, not a follower.

Rule #8: We honor our humanity.

We can't do our greatest work when we're depleted. Bringing great ideas to life requires Unicorn Energy.

We honor the fact that Unicorns are human beings, not machines. Unicorns have limits. Unicorns need fuel. Unicorns need sleep. Unicorns need time away from work to recharge.

We take care of ourselves like elite athletes, pouring into our mental and physical well-being so that we can come together, play big, and win.

PRIMER: THE UNICORN INNOVATION MODEL

	VSM Process	● VISIONIZE		▲ STRATEGIZE			■ MOBILIZE			
IDEATION NEW Launch brand-new initiatives	**Navigate** How we make decisions together and choose the right idea to pursue	Ideastorm		DOIT			BEIT			ITERATION BAU Improve existing initiatives
	Motivate How we lead and the energy we bring to the team	V Types		S Types			M Types			
		VV	VS	VM	SV	SS	SM	MV	MS	MM	
	Communicate How we get aligned, work on the right priorities together, and get things done at warp speed	Brandcast		Stratagem			Prototype			
	< ~ ~ ~ UNICORN ENERGY ~ ~ ~ >									

The Unicorn Innovation Model is the framework that you'll use throughout this book to:

- Identify the problem you want to solve (this could be a problem that you see in the world, in your industry, or inside the company you currently work for)

- Generate possible solutions, evaluate ideas, and choose the winning concept to pursue

- Determine which types of Unicorns you need on your team to bring this idea to life

- Communicate with your fellow Unicorns clearly so each person understands their role, what success means for the team, and how valuable their contribution is

- Become a winning team that brings extraordinary ideas into the world

As a brief primer, let's go through the components of the model and how they fit together, so that as you read on, you'll know how to use this book to bring your great ideas to life.

Are you a visual or auditory learner?

Do you prefer hearing new information explained aloud rather than reading text on a page?

I've got you covered.

Scan the code to see a short video where I take you through the Unicorn Innovation Model. Watch me explain what each section means and how it all connects together.

Ideation vs. Iteration

On the left side of the model, you'll notice a section called Ideation. On the right side, you'll see Iteration.

Ideation is all about brand-new initiatives, which we simply call *NEW*. These initiatives consist of products, services, features, workflows, and processes that don't exist yet. Think: "This is so exciting! We don't have anything like this yet." Or: "Nothing like this exists in the world yet! It's radically new! Revolutionary!"

Iteration is all about business as usual, which we simply call *BAU*. This category includes current products, services, features, workflows, and processes that have been implemented in the past but need an upgrade or rebrand. Think: "We already have this, but it hasn't been updated in a while and could be better." Or: "We need a new twist on this classic idea."

Once you launch a brand-new Ideation initiative and do it for a while, it eventually becomes an established Iteration initiative. This is good. The goal is to continually improve the original idea over and over again, staying ahead of what the market wants and what the future needs.

Whether your idea is NEW (a brand-new initiative) or BAU (an upgrade on something that already exists), you need a playbook to make the idea happen.

VSM PROCESS

There are three tracks to bring great ideas to life: Navigate, Motivate, and Communicate.

Track 1: Navigate

Navigate means "how we make decisions together and choose the right idea to pursue." First, we have to determine if the big idea is actually worth doing.

These are some of the questions we ask in this track: Is this a winning idea or mediocre? Is it truly *the* idea we want to pursue, or could there be a better alternative? Will it be worth the resources required to pull it off? What are the trade-offs if we proceed? Why will our dream user care about this idea, and how can we build demand for it?

We navigate questions like these and come to a decision using three tools: Ideastorm, DOIT Analysis, and BEIT Analysis, which give you the green light to proceed with bringing your idea to life.

Track 2: Motivate

Motivate means "how we lead and the energy we bring to the team." Once we've identified the great idea we want to pursue, we need to rally the right people around it: Unicorns working together to make it real.

Everyone is a Unicorn (or has the potential to become one, when placed in the right team environment). There are nine types of Unicorns. You are one of them.

These nine profiles are called Unicorn Leadership Types. Yes, if you're wondering, there's an assessment in the book that you (and your teammates) can take to discover your type.

Each Unicorn Leadership Type represents a particular energy that this person brings to the team. Visionizer Unicorns bring a visionary, forward-thinking, futuristic energy. Strategizers understand how to translate the big, lofty vision into a strategy that others can rally behind. Mobilizers know how to get deliverables done, on time, on budget, and their work is impeccable.

You don't want a team of people who all have the same Unicorn Leadership Type. You want a mix of types. You need different strengths, skills, and energies blending together to achieve more than any individual Unicorn could do alone.

Track 3: Communicate

Communicate means "how we get aligned, work on the right priorities together, and get things done at warp speed." Successful Unicorn Teams communicate with clarity and confidence. The three communication tools in this model—Brandcast, Stratagem, and Prototype—create an elegant and crisp flow of direction and completion so the team doesn't get lost in chaos.

The best part about the Communicate track is that when you apply it, your greatest dream will come true: your team will actually start to read your mind and know what you're thinking ahead of time!

UNICORN ENERGY

At the bottom of the model, you'll see a section called Unicorn Energy. This is the ultimate end goal.

Unicorn Energy is what happens when the Navigate, Motivate, and Communicate tracks are working together harmoniously. It's the flow state of winning.

You know you've attained Unicorn Energy when your team (which may include contractors, freelancers, mentors, and anyone who contributes to the success of the idea) genuinely enjoys working together and feels energized at the end of a work session. The team feels less riddled with unhealthy pressure, friction, and noise. Decisions get made quickly. Projects move forward fast. Bottlenecks evaporate. KPIs and other success metrics are met and then exceeded. Each Unicorn on the team levels up because they're so inspired by their teammates. People notice that your brand is one not just worth watching, but one they want to buy from and work for.

To bring great ideas to life, you don't necessarily need more time or money. What you need is Unicorn Energy and lots of it. With Unicorn Energy, a team can accomplish in 100 days what it takes others years to do. And Unicorn Energy happens only when you bring the right people together to work on the right idea with the right model.

If you're obsessed with models and frameworks, then I know you're salivating right now and can't wait to tear ahead.

It's time to put this model into action!

PART I

NAVIGATE TRACK

The Unicorn Innovation Model

VSM Process		● VISIONIZE			▲ STRATEGIZE			■ MOBILIZE		
	Navigate How we make decisions together and choose the right idea to pursue	Ideastorm			DOIT			BEIT		
IDEATION **NEW** Launch brand-new initiatives	**Motivate** How we lead and the energy we bring to the team	V Types			S Types			M Types		
		VV	VS	VM	SV	SS	SM	MV	MS	MM
	Communicate How we get aligned, work on the right priorities together, and get things done at warp speed	Brandcast			Stratagem			Prototype		
	‹ ~ ~ ~ UNICORN ENERGY ~ ~ ~ ›									

ITERATION **BAU** Improve existing initiatives

> "I have a great idea that could change the world / change my industry / change the company where I work / etc. At least, I think it might be a great idea. But I'm not entirely sure."
>
> "Is my idea actually . . . great? Or is it just okay?"
>
> "How can I make sure it's a winning concept before pouring time, energy, money, and other resources into it?"

You might have a ton of ideas tumbling around in your head.

If you have an entrepreneurial spirit, you may envision businesses you could build. Products you could launch into the marketplace. Exciting ways to improve the world.

If you work for a company, you might want to improve your department, upgrade the workplace systems, or revolutionize your industry, and you've got a whole notebook chock full of ideas.

But which ideas are actually worth pursuing?

Before you assemble your Unicorn Team, let's make sure you've got an idea that is actually worth doing. Because you can have an outrageously creative, talented, loyal, and hardworking team, but if you're working on the wrong idea, it's like trying to sail a sinking ship with a gaping hole in it. You won't get very far.

In Part I: Navigate, you'll learn how to evaluate ideas and pick a winner.

Navigate is the first track in the Unicorn Innovation Model, and it's all about how we make decisions together and choose the right idea to pursue.

CHAPTER 1

HOW TO DETERMINE IF YOUR IDEA IS WORTH PURSUING

"I need some help."[1]

That's what Alon Matas said to himself. Rather than feeling like his usual self, he dreaded going into work and wasn't looking forward to the future the way he used to. He felt like he was possibly dealing with clinical depression, though he wasn't completely sure.[2]

Matas wanted to see a therapist, but battling traffic on a drive across town, finding a coveted parking spot, doing a one-hour session at the provider's office, then rushing home afterward . . . well, it was hugely inconvenient. *It shouldn't be this difficult to get support*, he thought.

This dilemma sparked an idea: What if you could see a licensed therapist via video chat on your phone? Professional care, privately and confidentially, but without the hassle.

This "Eureka!" moment inspired Alon Matas to join forces with Danny Bragonier and co-found a mental health company called BetterHelp. Less than 10 years after opening its virtual doors, BetterHelp has become the world's largest online counseling platform, with 23,000 therapists, 2.5 million customers,[3] and a valuation over $1 billion.[4]

Matas knew he wasn't the only person struggling with his mental health, or struggling with all the logistical obstacles that make working with a therapist exhausting and inconvenient. In an interview with the Good Men Project, Matas observed, "Most people who need help are actually not getting it."[5] So he did something to change this.

Proving that it's possible to hit 10 figures *and* tend to those in need, BetterHelp has donated thousands of hours of free therapy (95,647 and counting) to survivors of war, people living below the poverty line, transgender and nonbinary people, and formerly incarcerated individuals.[6]

Big money. Big impact. It all starts with a big idea.

What is yours?

HOW TO FIND YOUR BILLION-DOLLAR IDEA

Every billion-dollar brand begins with a big idea—an idea that is so compelling, so exciting, so needed, people get obsessed with it. An idea with the potential to change the way we live. An idea that is not mediocre, not okay, not just good, but great.

Many books on brand futurism, business, and leadership say, "When you've got a really good idea, you just *know*," "You can feel it," and "Just trust your gut." I respectfully disagree.

Should you listen to your instincts? Definitely. But don't rely on instinct alone. That's a costly mistake. Instead, use a process to evaluate an idea and determine if it's worth your time.

In the Unicorn Innovation Model, this process is contained in the first track: Navigate. I'll show you how to navigate your ideas and ultimately answer the billion-dollar question:

"Is this idea worth doing?"

We'll use three tools to navigate this decision and come to a conclusion: Ideastorm (this tool is used in the Visionize step), DOIT Analysis (Strategize), and BEIT Analysis (Mobilize).

This chart gives a preview of what this decision-making process looks like and the main questions you and your team will consider at each step.

VSM Process	Visionize	Strategize	Mobilize
Questions	What is the new and better future we want to build? What is the big idea that will bring us into the future? How can we make this big idea even bigger?	Who will benefit from this idea, and where do these people hang out? How can we build demand for this idea? What would make our Dream User say yes or say no to this idea?	What is the cost (time, energy, money) to make this idea happen? What are the trade-offs? (If we do this, how will this impact the team / processes / offers we have in place?) What is a big win we could achieve in the first 100 days of pursuing this idea?
Tool to Determine If We Should Proceed	Ideastorm	DOIT Analysis	BEIT Analysis
Outcome	Confirm that this idea solves a specific problem. Not just any problem, but the problem we want to tackle as a team.	Confirm that our Dream User wants this idea, even if they don't know it yet because it doesn't exist yet.	Confirm that the rewards of pursuing this idea are bigger than the cost. And confirm that we have the capacity to move quickly.

DON'T GUESS—EVALUATE, DECIDE, AND TEST

I created the Unicorn Innovation Model while working for one of the world's leading telecom companies, a behemoth with an enterprise value of $340 billion.[7] It's how I helped my then employer launch a brand-new offer that's now called "streaming video." While I didn't use the terms *Visionize > Strategize > Mobilize* at the time, this is the model we used to clarify that, yes, streaming was the right next thing to build. It's also how we brought it to market faster than any competitors.

Let me show you how to do each step.

1) VISIONIZE

An idea that is not dangerous is unworthy
of being called an idea at all.
— OSCAR WILDE

This step is all about envisioning *where* we're going and the big idea that will take us to that new and better future. To generate visionary ideas, you'll do what I call an **Ideastorm**.

You need three things: (1) a time constraint, (2) a few Unicorns who are willing to play with you, and (3) a set of questions, which I'll provide in a moment.

Time Constraint

I recommend 30 to 60 minutes for your Ideastorm. Keep it snappy. Think: sprint. If 30 minutes isn't enough to reach a resolution, extend the timeline for 24 to 72 hours max. For instance, as the Ideastorm comes to an end, you can tell your fellow Unicorns, "Keep thinking about these questions. Write down your answers. Let's report back in 72 hours to share our findings." A quick timeline keeps the energy elevated and exciting, instead of letting it fizzle out.

Unicorns

Invite a small group of Unicorns to do an Ideastorm with you. These can be colleagues, friends, family members, mentors, coaches, freelancers, employees, or a combination. It doesn't matter if they're paid employees or not. What matters is, they're people who share your values, who will be frank and honest with you if they don't agree with a particular idea, who will speak up if they have a better idea, and who want you to win.

Questions

As a group, do an Ideastorm by discussing the following questions together.

Remember: you have a quick time constraint. Keep the conversation moving from person to person. For each question, you can set a timer to give each Unicorn a few minutes to share their thoughts. This will prevent anyone from hogging the mic and droning on for too long.

1. *Where do we want this business to be in the future?*

   Alternate wording: Where do we want society / the human race / the world to be?

2. *What is one idea that can take us to this new and better future?*

   This may be an idea that you already came up with, and you're wondering if it's a great idea or just good-ish. Propose your idea to the group. We will call this "idea A."

3. *What problem does this idea solve?*

   There is an infinite number of problems in our world, from enormous ones like poverty and racism to everyday annoyances like coffee that gets cold too quickly or spending all of your free time doing laundry instead of relaxing with your loved ones.

   Remember that when it comes to business, not every "problem" is solemn, sad, or emotionally heavy. For instance, "feeling bored and craving entertainment" is one type of problem, and balloons could be a solution—or cupcake delivery, or an educational app that teaches you how to do magic tricks. What's the issue, irritation, or situation that your idea alleviates?

4. *Is this the problem that we want to focus on?*

   Is this *the* problem that you and your team want to be known for solving? If not, why not? If yes, do we have evidence to confirm that millions of people grapple with this exact problem and crave a solution?

5. *What are some alternative ideas?*

   If we couldn't pursue idea A for some reason, what else could we do to reach the new and better future that we envision?

   Come up with alternative options: ideas B, C, D, E, F, etc.—as many ideas as you and your team can generate within the time constraint.

6. *Circling back to idea A: Is this idea big enough, or are we playing too small?*

   How could we make it even bigger? Think: moonshot, wild, audacious, outrageous, disruptive.

7. *Flip it around: If we wanted to create the problem (not solve it), what could we do? How could we make the problem bigger, worse, or more pervasive?*

   This question is purely a thought experiment. You're not actually hoping to create the problem or make it worse. However, by exploring how you *could* do this, you may identify an even better solution (idea Z!) that you hadn't considered before.

8. *Given everything we just discussed, is idea A still our favorite idea to pursue? Or has a new favorite emerged?*

Discuss these eight questions with your partner or team. The key to a productive Ideastorm is having creative license to list as many ideas as possible (quantity) paired with a healthy time constraint to help you go faster and get to the right problem (quality).

Rapid Ideation	Ideastorm	Problem Creation
→		←
Generate as many ideas as possible within the time constraint.		Look at the situation from the opposite perspective.
Consider Parkinson's Law: work expands to fill the time available for its completion.		Instead of asking, "How can we solve this problem?" ask, "How can we cause this problem?"
Rapid Ideation leverages this phenomenon to produce high-quality ideas without overthinking.		Problem Creation allows you to reverse engineer to find the best solution.

During this step, you have full permission to be silly, wild, outrageous, or controversial. Nobody is allowed to talk about "how" to make this idea happen, nor complain about why it's going to be difficult, unlikely, improbable, expensive, and so on. There is no "how" during this step in the process. Asking "How?" is like throwing a damp towel on the fire. It's an important question, but this is not the moment to wrestle with it.

As you do the Ideastorm with your team, use big, ambitious, expansive, visionary language like "Our mission is to . . . " "We want to create . . . " and "What if we could . . . ?"

As the Ideastorm continues, a favorite idea will likely emerge—an idea that gives everyone shivers of excitement, sparks emotion, and makes people feel obsessed with it.

During this step, the goal is to home in on the leading idea and confirm that it solves a specific problem. Not just any problem, but *the* problem you and your fellow Unicorns want to tackle as a team. Once you've done that, then your idea has "passed" the Visionize step. Then move on to step two: Strategize.

2) STRATEGIZE

> For there are no new ideas. There are only
> new ways of making them felt.
> — AUDRE LORDE

The Strategize step is about *what* we need to do to make people respond to our idea and say yes to adopting it, purchasing it, or doing it. As you Strategize, you're answering these questions:

1. Who are the people that this idea helps?

2. What are the places (online, offline, or both) where these people are already gathering, hanging out, spending time, or looking for solutions?

3. What can we do to build demand for this idea?

4. Is there a market for this idea? If yes, what evidence do we have to prove that this market exists?

For an idea to be great, not just good, it must have a market that wants it (even if it doesn't know about it yet), and the market must have places where it can access the idea.

To determine if an idea passes the strategic sniff test, you'll do what I call a **DOIT Analysis**.

D = Drivers

O = Obstacles

I = Identity

T = Triggers

This is not the SWOT analysis that organizations commonly use to assess the strengths, weaknesses, opportunities, and threats associated with an idea. The DOIT Analysis is different, because it determines if an idea is worth doing by putting you in the shoes of the actual person that the idea helps—the decision-maker who is ultimately going to purchase this idea or not. We call this decider our Dream User.

DOIT Analysis

DREAM USER	
Describe who the Dream User is, what problem they want solved, and where they hang out.	
Drivers	**Obstacles**
Why would the Dream User want this idea?	What would keep the Dream User from saying yes to this idea?
Identity	**Triggers**
What helps the Dream User to feel seen, heard, and understood, and to feel that they belong if they say yes to this idea?	What environmental and psychological factors influence the Dream User's purchasing decisions?

Bottom line: Does this idea have value to the Dream User? Will it make the Dream User's life significantly more beautiful, more joyful, more healthy, more successful, more "something"? If yes, your idea has "passed" the Strategize step. Then move on to step three: Mobilize.

3) MOBILIZE

A pile of rocks ceases to be a rock pile when somebody contemplates it with the idea of a cathedral in mind.
— ANTOINE DE SAINT-EXUPÉRY

In step three, Mobilize, the core question is: *How?* How do we bring this idea to life? What's it gonna take to pull this off? What will it cost in terms of time, energy, and money to get this idea to market?

To understand the cost, you'll need to do what I call a **BEIT Analysis.**

B = Budget

E = Energy

I = Integrations

T = Timing

BEIT Analysis

UNICORN TEAM	
Describe the people who will work on your idea and bring it into the world.	
This might include employees, freelancers, consultants, mentors, coaches, investors, friends, family, volunteers, interns, etc.	
Budget	**Energy**
What are the financial costs of implementing this idea? What is the financial upside of implementing this idea?	Do we have enough people / bandwidth to work on this idea and make it happen? What would we have to do to free up capacity to mobilize this idea?
Integrations	**Timing**
Let's think about our current processes, departments, and products. Which ones will be impacted if we proceed with this idea?	What's a big win we can achieve in the first 100 days of pursuing this idea? What are the milestones we need to hit, and by when, in order to create that big win?

Why 100 days? So that we can begin working on this idea, fail fast, improve fast, and stay motivated along the way. Nothing kills a team's momentum more than a ginormous timeline. A hundred days is long enough to secure a big win, but not so long that everyone fizzles out.

Look at your BEIT Analysis to determine: Does this idea still feel worth pursuing? Are the rewards bigger than the costs? If so, *proceed*!

YOUR GREEN-LIGHT CHECKLIST

To sum it up, your idea should:

☐ Lead to a better, brighter future.

☐ Address a problem—not just any problem, but *the* problem that you and your team want to tackle.

☐ Provide an exciting solution.

☐ Add value to the Dream User's life and be something they strongly desire.

☐ Have been evaluated to determine the cost in terms of money, energy, time, and impact on current processes, and

☐ Have rewards that are significantly bigger than its costs.

If your idea meets all of these requirements, you can move forward confidently. Green light! Go! You have a winner to work on the next 100 days.

However, you're not done yet . . .

As you and your team charge forward with this big idea, be on the lookout for clues that the idea is *very* close, *incredibly* close, yet still not quite exactly right. Pay attention to the signs. Be ready to pivot quickly, if needed. You may need to adjust your idea—and this is not a setback. It's how teams win.

FAIL FAST TO WIN BIG

Starbucks's former co-owner and CEO Howard Schultz envisioned Starbucks becoming a "third place."[8] *Third place* is a term that sociologist Ray Oldenburg coined.[9] If home is the "first place" and work is the "second place," each Starbucks location would be a third place—a place to socialize and connect, a place for coffee lovers to find respite, and a gathering place for students to study, parents to grab a much-needed spike of caffeine before picking up the kids, friends to meet up, or anyone seeking refreshment in the midst of their busy day.

When Schultz retired from day-to-day operations, the leadership team at Starbucks knew it needed a way to communicate what was next and what was new to its large-scale enterprise—30,000 stores worldwide and 330,000 partners serving 100 million customers a week. Schultz's energy was visionary, expansive, and infectious—spurring big ideas that made Starbucks the undisputed champion in its category. The company needed a way to keep the Schultz vibes rolling even after his retirement.

That's why in 2017, they created the Tryer Center, an innovation lab anchored in Schultz's famous principles, where the team could create new product prototypes, form new operational models, and test new equipment. An official press release published on the company's website describes the Tryer Center as "the Starbucks lab where anything is possible."[10]

At the Tryer Center, innovators were to work on a quick timeline. Ideas needed to be launched into the marketplace in 100 days or less, instead of going through the long-tail innovation that is so common in large companies. The approach was: keep it fun, keep it fast, and if something doesn't work out, let's pivot quickly before sinking any more resources into it.

When Rosalind "Roz" Brewer became COO and group president of Starbucks, she had a powerful opportunity—to be a voice for innovation and a role model for women everywhere, particularly women of color. As the first Black person and first woman to serve as Starbucks COO,[11] she understood the historic significance of this moment.

As Roz took her position, Starbucks had a moonshot goal: to become the number-one recognized brand in the world. Not the number-one coffee brand, mind you—the number-one brand. Of any industry. Period. To achieve this, its vision was to turn a humble commodity—coffee—into not just a drink, but an *experience*.

Roz Brewer had previously been a tea drinker, but after joining Starbucks, she rolled up her sleeves and learned how to meticulously craft the perfect pour-over coffee.[12] She wanted to understand the business on every level, and it was important to her to understand a typical day for baristas, not just for the suits in the C-suite.

Brewer gave the team at the Tryer Center an assignment: to develop a healthier beverage option that Starbucks consumers would love. She knew that many customers wanted lighter, less calorie-dense drink options. Not everyone wants a white-chocolate mocha or caramel macchiato topped with whipped cream every day. So, the folks at the Tryer Center developed good-for-you smoothies featuring frozen fruit and veggies.

The product was delicious. Taste testers agreed. Consumer feedback was overwhelmingly good. And the financials looked legit. All systems go. Launch! Starbucks introduced its new lineup of smoothies and began selling them in stores.

Shortly after the launch, Brewer visited one of the stores. With a wide smile, she asked the barista, "Hey, I'd love to have one of the new smoothies. Could you make one for me?" The barista quickly whipped out the ingredients, eager to impress. However, Brewer noticed something . . . odd. The barista seemed a bit defeated. Crestfallen, even.

Although the smoothie was nutritious and delicious, the process was long and laborious for the barista. Brewer took a sip and asked the barista what she *really* thought about the new smoothies.

The response? Yes, these drinks were tasty, but they were annoying to prepare and horrendous to clean up after. From the time the customer ordered to the time the smoothie was ready, customers got impatient. Baristas felt agitated. It left a bad taste in everyone's mouth (pun very much intended).

Brewer made a game-time decision. Even though the financials looked good, the product was tasty, and customers indicated that they wanted healthy options, Brewer decided to take the smoothies off the market. Effective immediately. A bold move, one that many leaders wouldn't be courageous enough to make. But Brewer understood that it's better to fail fast rather than fail slow. It was time to go back to the lab for another concept.

Under Brewer's leadership, the Tryer Center rolled out another idea: cold-brew iced coffee. And this time? They had a legendary hit. Cold brew became so popular that many stores' ice machines couldn't keep up with the demand. They had to upgrade to new equipment just to keep up with the relentless demand for that smooth, silky cold brew. Customers loved the delicious taste, big boost of caffeine, no sugar added, and low calories. Plus, it was super easy and quick for baristas, because all they needed to do was pour the premade chilled coffee over ice. Voila. Fast-forward a few years, and iced coffee drinks (including the ultrapopular cold brew) now compose 75 percent of Starbucks revenue.[13]

If Brewer and her team had remained stubbornly fixated on making the smoothies work, they would have missed an opportunity to roll out a new product that led to billions in sales.

In her video presentation for MasterClass.com, Brewer says, "You don't want to be able to just look around the corner to the next thing. It's the thing that's around the corner . . . from around the corner."[14]

Don't try to force the wrong idea to be the right one. Be willing to kill an idea that's not working and get back to innovating. When you're addressing the right problem and getting close to the right solution but not quite there yet, go back to step one and do another Ideastorm.

Your initial idea might be smoothies. But the truly great idea, the Unicorn idea, that one that changes your company forever, might be cold brew. Innovators understand that ideas need to be flexible, and a truly great idea can be adjacent to one that's just good.

WHAT IS INNOVATION?

Innovation is one of those buzzwords that gets tossed around . . . but most people don't actually know what it means. Or each person on the team has a different definition, and no one agrees.

Innovation means one of two things:

1. You're bringing a brand-new idea into the world (in the Unicorn Innovation Model, we call this Ideation).

Or:

2. You're upgrading an existing idea to make it better (we call this Iteration).

Either way, you're bringing a great idea to life.

You may have an innovative idea that pops into your head, but an idea alone is not innovation. Innovation requires execution—turning the idea into reality, actually getting the thing finished. Once you and your team bring the idea to life—it's real, it's done, it's out in the world, and it's impacting lives—that's innovation.

How the Unicorn Frappuccino Was Born

Another Starbucks leader, Luigi Bonini, joined the company in 2011 as senior vice president of innovation and product development. Bonini understood that innovation creates conversation and the ways to develop new products to get everyone talking.

Besides customer favorites like the Cloud Macchiato, Mango Dragonfruit Refreshers, Chestnut Praline Latte, Bistro Boxes, and sous vide Egg Bites (which foodie website Eater.com declared "disconcertingly good")[15]—all of which were ideated and tested in the Tryer Center innovation lab—there was one idea that literally broke the Internet and made people line up around the block just to get a taste.

The legendary Unicorn Frappuccino, the most viral drink in company history.

Starbucks released this creamy, glitter-topped, color-changing milkshake as a specialty edition item, as mystical and rare as its namesake, available only for a limited time—just five days.

The reviews? Mixed. Some loved it. Some thought it was excessively sweet and disgusting. But it was a controversial drink that got everyone buzzing. Social media influencers ate (or drank, drank, drank) it up. TikTok and Instagram influencers clamored to post photos of this undeniably photogenic drink, generating 180,000 photos in less than a week.[16] Nail technicians created Unicorn Frapp-inspired manicures, beauty influencers dyed their hair to match the drink's pastel color palette, and the entire world was drunk on Unicorn juice. Starbucks reported a huge uptick in sales of all beverages, not just Frappuccinos.

"People would introduce me at dinners or parties and say, 'You know the Unicorn Frappuccino? His team invented that,'" Bonini said.

Yup, a *Unicorn* Frappuccino.

I can't make this stuff up.

Here's what Starbucks did right, both with cold-brew iced coffee and the Unicorn Frappuccino—they gave their team a place to play, ideate, test new ideas, and launch fast (100 days or less), and in doing so, created a culture of innovation.

You may not have a billion-dollar budget like Starbucks (yet), but in your own way, on your own scale, you can create an Innovation Lab for yourself and your team. It could be a weekly Ideastorm date with a colleague, or giving your employees one day every month where they're allowed to leave their desks, explore the world outside of the office, get inspired, and generate fresh ideas.

What is your personal version of the Tryer Center?

YOU'VE GOT AN IDEA TO PURSUE. NOW WHAT?

You put your idea through the Navigate track. Congratulations! You now have an idea that's ready to move forward into the next phase of the Unicorn Innovation Model. This might be a Unicorn idea, or (just like Roz Brewer and the smoothie debacle) it might be Unicorn-adjacent, a necessary failure that brings you closer to the big win.

When you have a great idea that you're itching to bring into the world, the first question on your mind is usually, "Okay, how can I make this happen?"

What if I told you, that's the wrong question.

The right question is not "How?" but "Who?"

Who are the people I need on my team to pull this off? This is what we will explore next.

TOP TAKEAWAYS

- You may have lots of ideas that bounce into your head, but not every idea is worth pursuing.

- To determine if an idea is worth doing, take your idea through the first track in the Unicorn Innovation Model, which is called Navigate. Use the three tools: Ideastorm, DOIT Analysis, and BEIT Analysis.

- These steps help you evaluate the idea to determine: What is the problem that this idea solves? Is there a market for this idea? What will it cost to bring this idea to life? Do the rewards justify the price?

- By using this process, you'll weed out the mediocre ideas, the okay ideas, and the good ideas, and home in on the great ideas.

- Innovation requires flexibility and quick decision-making. If you pursue an idea and realize it's not working, pivot fast. Your best idea may be right around the corner from a failed concept.

- No matter what size you are right now, you can create your own Innovation Lab as part of the way you determine whether to bring your ideas to market or not. In fact, it's what will assure your ideas are not just okay, but great.

CHAPTER 2

WHY MOST GREAT IDEAS NEVER HAPPEN AND HOW TO FIX THIS

In the classic 1952 movie *Clash by Night*, the character Mae Doyle (played by Barbara Stanwyck) returns home to her family after spending a decade elsewhere. When asked what happened during her time away, Mae bitterly replies: "Big dreams, small results."[1]

We can all relate to this cynical outlook. We've all been discouraged by initiatives that start out with a burst of passion and then wither on the vine.

Why do most great ideas go nowhere?

Because most of us focus excessively (or exclusively) on *how* to make the idea happen. We forget to ask a far more important question: *Who?*

- Who can help me figure this out?
- Who do I need in my corner?
- Who will inspire me to do my greatest work?
- Who will push me to be my greatest self?
- Who can bring a new perspective to this project?
- Who has a particular set of skills that this initiative requires?

- Who do I need to bring onto my team first (or next)?

- Who are the Unicorns who can help me win?

In the previous chapter, you used three tools—Ideastorm, DOIT Analysis, and BEIT Analysis—to figure out which idea is worth pursuing.

You probably noticed that one of these steps felt natural for you ("I'm good at this!") while other steps felt less natural ("This is harder for me"). This is because all Unicorns have different strengths. Some Unicorns are what I call Visionizers, some are Strategizers, and some are Mobilizers. To create an ubersuccessful Unicorn Team, you need people who can perform each of these three roles.

THREE ROLES, NINE TYPES

There are three types of Visionizer Unicorns, three types of Strategizer Unicorns, and three types of Mobilizer Unicorns, for a total of nine types.

These nine personality profiles are called Unicorn Leadership Types.

What's your type? You'll find out in Chapter 6, which contains an assessment plus details about each type. But right now, I want to give you a quick overview of the nine Unicorn Leadership Types so you can start getting familiar with these terms:

- Visionizing Strategizer (VS)

- Visionizing Mobilizer (VM)

- Pure Visionizer (VV)

- Strategizing Visionizer (SV)

- Strategizing Mobilizer (SM)

- Pure Strategizer (SS)

- Mobilizing Visionizer (MV)

- Mobilizing Strategizer (MS)

- Pure Mobilizer (MM)

Your Unicorn Leadership Type indicates the role you are best suited to play on a team.

For instance, if you're a Visionizing Strategizer (VS), this means your top strength is Visionizer and your second strength is Strategizer. You are well suited to perform the Visionizer role on your team and could confidently do the Strategizer role too. However, you will likely struggle in a Mobilizer role, because that's not one of your strengths. It would be smart for you to bring Mobilizer Unicorns onto your team so they can perform the role that you're weakest at.

You don't want a homogenous team that is 100 percent Visionizers, or Strategizers, or Mobilizers. You need a blend of all three leadership energies to bring great ideas to life. To get big things done with astonishing speed, surround yourself with other Unicorn types.

WHAT IS A UNICORN? AND WHAT IS A UNICORN TEAM?

A Unicorn is someone who is extremely good at what they do, whether it's brain surgery, fundraising, engineering, accounting, cooking, customer service, or any other kind of work.

It's the person whose abilities feel magical, almost mystical. They deliver massive value. They exude excellence. They perform at an exceptionally high level, consistently, day after day.

You know someone is a Unicorn when colleagues say they are "a total rock star," "one in a million," "the best of the best," or "an unbelievable asset to the company." This type of person is always in demand. Everyone wants to hire them, keep them, and be them. You're one yourself and probably know other Unicorns too.

You may think, *Okay, so if I find a couple of Unicorns and have them work together, that's a Unicorn Team.* Yes; however, there's more to it than that. After working with hundreds of clients over the last 20 years—including 7-, 8-, 9-, and 10-figure brands—I've identified the main ingredients that you need to create your very own Unicorn Team.

Three Roles

A Unicorn Team must include people who can perform the Visionizer, Strategizer, and Mobilizer roles. If one (or more) of these roles is missing, the team does not function. Big ideas will fizzle out, projects will stall, and disappointment will abound.

Values Alignment

To be a Unicorn Team, each team member's personal values align (at least somewhat) with the company's values. It doesn't have to be a perfect match, but some overlap is required.

Owner Mindset

On a Unicorn Team, each person owns their role and understands exactly what they need to deliver to the team. Each team member behaves like a leader, not a follower; an owner, not a minion.

Meaningful Goal

Unicorn Teams love to play big. The team must have a big idea to pursue, a goal that is meaningful and worth getting excited about.

Swift Timeline

The Unicorn Team needs a quick timeline to make a specific phase of the great idea happen—100 days or less. Then the clock starts again on the next phase of what that great idea needs next.

PROCESS TO FOLLOW

It's not just about bringing the right people together. You also need a process to follow so that everyone understands "This is how we collaborate together and make big things happen." This process, as you may have guessed by now, is called the Unicorn Innovation Model. You can establish this process by understanding each person's strengths and making sure they know how they need to apply them.

To do that, let's look closer at what composes the first ingredient of your Unicorn Team: the three roles known as the Visionizer, Strategizer, and Mobilizer.

VISIONIZER

On a Unicorn Team, the Visionizer comes up with the big vision. The Visionizer says:

> "Let's develop a cure that eradicates cancer."

> "Our mission is to inspire 100 million people to quit smoking forever."

> "We can create a zero-waste diaper that's good for babies and good for the environment."

> "Humans will be living on Mars within the next 100 years. This is where society is headed."

> "What if every human being on earth stopped driving a car?"

> "What if we increased our revenue by 10x in the next 30 days?"

The Visionizer is focused on the future. They visualize the world (or the business) as it could and should be. The Visionizer envisions a tomorrow that is brighter and better than our present conditions. The word that best expresses Visionizer energy is *where*. As in, "This is *where* we need to go . . ."

On a Unicorn Team, the Visionizer's role is to come up with the big, wild, audacious vision. This vision isn't necessarily "Let's bring a new product to market," although it often is. The vision could be "Let's shift to a three-day workweek," "Let's inspire 100 new clients to sign with us," "Let's bring a million new subscribers onto our mailing list," or something else.

The Visionizer is usually charismatic and inspirational, with that star quality that makes people believe "Yes, we can do this."

Every Unicorn Team needs one (or more) people fulfilling the Visionizer role. Without Visionizer energy on the team, there's no direction for the business, no mission to believe in, no future worth fighting for. Work feels meaningless. The business becomes stagnant.

STRATEGIZER

The Visionizer has the grand vision, but Visionizers don't always know how to break it down into a plan that is practical, sensible, and doable. They see where we need to go, but not necessarily what's required to get there. They may have a phenomenal idea but may not understand how to make this idea appealing to consumers and a big hit in the marketplace.

Enter: the Strategizer.

This is the person who says: "Amazing vision! Okay, here's what we need to do to get from here to there . . ."

Strategizers figure out *what*, as in, what's the strategy to get there? What can we do to build demand for this idea and make people want it? What are the moves to win in the marketplace?

Visionizers sometimes (though not always) speak in wild, lofty language that most people just don't get. Imagine Steve Jobs back in 1970, saying, "One day telephones will be an extension of the human arm." Most people would think, *I have no idea what you are talking about, but you should probably get some psychiatric help.* Part of the Strategizer's role is to take the Visionizer's thrilling idea and translate the vision into a strategy that the rest of the team can understand.

Every Unicorn Team needs one (or more) people fulfilling the Strategizer role. Without Strategizer energy on the team, there's an innovative vision but no clear path to get there.

MOBILIZER

The Visionizer comes up with a vision that sends tingles of excitement down people's spines. The Strategizer figures out the playbook to make it happen. Next, we need Mobilizers to tackle strategic initiatives and get things done.

Mobilizers jump in to make the to-do list, the Gantt chart, the Excel spreadsheet. Mobilizers divide up the tasks and determine who's responsible for doing what. Mobilizers file the paperwork, design the logo, write the copy, set the table, book the flight, reply to the e-mail, and get the dang thing done.

Mobilizers love to close loops and tie up loose ends. *Done* is their favorite word. These are the people who say, "You need XYZ by 5 P.M.? Consider it done." "I'll handle that for you. I'm on it." "That thing you requested? It's already finished. It's in your in-box." "Okay, what's next? How can I help?"

Every Unicorn Team needs one (or more) people fulfilling the Mobilizer role. Without Mobilizer energy on the team, you'll notice a whole lot of projects getting started but not finished. Most businesses need a small number of Visionizers, a small number of Strategizers, and a *lot* of skilled Mobilizers.

ROLES, NOT PEOPLE. AND IT'S AN ENERGY THING.

Visionizers dream up *where* we're going and the big idea that will take us there.

Strategizers figure out *what* the big-picture strategy is to get there, including how to make this idea exciting to consumers and build obsessive demand for it.

Mobilizers are all about *how* to bring this idea to life—the practical action steps, the deliverables—and excel at getting things finished.

Every Unicorn Team needs Visionizer, Strategizer, and Mobilizer energy to achieve big things quickly. You may think, *Okay, got it. So this means I need a team of three people: one Visionizer, one Strategizer, and one Mobilizer. Boom. That's my Unicorn Team.*

Not quite. Visionizer, Strategizer, and Mobilizer are *roles* that need to be performed on the team, but a Unicorn Team can have 3, 5, 10, 20, or hundreds of people. Although it *is* possible to have a Unicorn Team with just two people, those two Unicorns must successfully fulfill all three roles. The number of people doesn't matter. What matters is that you have people who can own each role.

Let me show you how this can play out with a 10-person team and a 2-person team.

A 10-Person Team

Let's say you run a creative agency that does video production. You are the founder, and you have one full-time employee and eight part-time freelancers, for a total of 10 people.

Like many founders, you're a strong Visionizer. You have a big, ambitious dream of where this company can go. You're constantly coming up with wildly creative ideas that you can't wait to share with your team. On Thursday, you envision an innovative new camera lens that will change the whole industry and show colors the human eye has never seen before. On Friday, you're in the shower and have a flash of insight about a new filming device that would allow pregnant mothers to see their babies tumbling around inside the womb from anywhere, no doctor required, like an at-home ultrasound. By Saturday morning, you're already bored with your previous two ideas and want to partner with NASA to put a streaming webcam on Mars. Classic Visionizer energy.

Your full-time employee is a strong Strategizer. This person is brilliant at figuring out the playbook to make your genius ideas actually happen.

Your freelancers are Mobilizers who get specific tasks done. Record videos, edit content, adjust audio, deliver the finished product to the customer, and so on.

A Unicorn Team's success doesn't hinge on any individual person. Different people can pop into different roles as needed. For instance, when your full-time employee has a baby and goes on parental leave, one freelancer (who happens to be a strong Mobilizer and strong Strategizer too) temporarily steps into this Strategizer role and crushes it. Your team continues to function beautifully even when one Unicorn is absent.

A 2-Person Team

It's possible to have a Unicorn Team with just two people, such as two business partners who co-own the company 50/50, a founder plus an assistant, or two creative partners collaborating on a project.

For example, while writing this book, I set a very audacious goal. So audacious, I actually felt nervous and sweaty about it.

I wanted to get the manuscript finished in less than six months. Why? Because I wanted to get the book completed before my upcoming birthday so that I could commemorate this big milestone, fly to Italy with my friends and family to celebrate, and not be stressed about publishing deadlines.

My Unicorn Leadership Type is SV, which means that Strategizer is my top energetic strength, followed by Visionizer. However, I score pretty low in Mobilizer. So the *M* in VSM was the missing ingredient from my Unicorn Book Team.

My next move: I hired a writing partner and editor who is MS, which means that Mobilizer is her top energetic strength, and Strategizer is her secondary.

Between the two of us, we had the holy Trinity: VSM.

I knew: "With our powers combined, we're going to get this project done incredibly well and incredibly fast." And we did. In fact, we wrote the first half of the book in just five days—while laughing and having a delightful time! We felt energized rather than frantic and drained. My V energy inspired her to think bigger, and her M energy inspired me to focus, type, and actually finish chapters (not just start them).

In this example, we have two people performing three roles.

Visionize: I created the big vision for the book.

Strategize: My colleague and I collaborated to create the strategy to get the project completed quickly.

Mobilize: My colleague helped me buckle down and put words onto the page instead of just brainstorming and talking all day long; plus, she edited my work to turn the rough chapters into a more finished product.

Neither one of us working alone could possibly have created this book on the timeline I wanted. But with our Unicorn powers combined, we were able to turn my idea into a finished product.

Whether you identify as an entrepreneur (company founder), intrapreneur (employee working inside of an established company), or artistpreneur (a creative, a musician, or an entertainer), to play big and win, you need to rally the right people around your ideas. It doesn't matter if your idea is a protein bar, smartphone app, Broadway show, or any other type of company or brand. The same principles apply: you need to use the Visionize > Strategize > Mobilize formula to bring your idea to market quickly.

HOW *HADESTOWN* WENT FROM FOLK-MUSIC ALBUM TO BOX-OFFICE-SHATTERING SUCCESS

Anaïs Mitchell was driving in her car when she heard Greek gods singing in her head.[2] No, she wasn't having an auditory hallucination. She's a singer-songwriter from a small town in Vermont and was on the road heading to a gig.[3] As often happens for highly creative people, Anaïs was having one of those moments like you do when you're in the car or taking a hot shower and the muse knocks on the door of your mind.

As the melody swirled in Anaïs's mind, she immediately thought about the ancient Greek tragedy of Orpheus and Eurydice, the lovers who become ensnared by Hades and can't leave his underworld kingdom without paying a terrible price. The music poured through her like water. She felt as though she wasn't even writing it herself; she was merely the vessel, the channel, and something was flowing through her into the world.

Once Anaïs had enough material, she called together a few musician buddies (including Justin Vernon, the singer-songwriter best known for his band Bon Iver, and folk-rock legend Ani DiFranco) and recorded an ethereal, dreamy concept album that she called *Hadestown*.

Anaïs's Unicorn Leadership Type is what I would categorize as Mobilizing Visionizer (MV). A strong Mobilizer, she's a disciplined musician who can write original pieces, record, and deliver a finished product to market—in this case, an album with 20 songs. She also has a big dash of Visionizer. She's an artist, dreamer, muse, and romantic, the person who sees what the world could be and the brighter future we can move toward.

The *Hadestown* concept album dropped in 2010 and was critically acclaimed, although sales and streaming numbers were modest at best. It had a small cult following of fans who passion-ately loved it, but it never achieved mainstream success. Anaïs crammed her band into a converted VW bus and drove across the U.S., touring with limited funds and bringing the music to small venues. It was a small-scale, homespun project, and it could have easily remained an obscure album with a few thousand listeners. However, there was something undeniably magical about the mu-sic. It had the potential to become something bigger. But Anaïs couldn't do it alone. She needed a Unicorn Team.

Enter: Dale Franzen. Dale, a retired opera singer, was now run-ning the Broad Stage, a brand-new, $50 million performing arts center in Santa Monica, California.[4] Every week, Dale received stacks of albums from musicians, each hoping for the chance to get booked and perform at the Broad. Dale found most of these albums unimpressive and tossed them into the *no* pile. But when she played *Hadestown*, she was enraptured. This music was unlike anything she'd heard before, with poetic lyrics and melodies that haunted her.

Dale's Unicorn Leadership Type is Visionizing Strategizer (VS), meaning she's a major Visionizer with a good dose of Strategizer. This is a woman who sees the bigger vision before others do.

Dale arranged a meeting with Anaïs and told her, "This could be more than just an album. I see this becoming a Broadway mu-sical." Anaïs dreamed big, but Dale dreamed even bigger. And so, Dale took Anaïs under her wing. And without knowing exactly how it would happen or how long it would take, they began taking steps toward the Broadway lights.

Dale is a gifted artist in her own right, but her superpower is fundraising. She knows how to communicate a big idea in a way that gets people—extremely wealthy people—excited to be in-volved. Her fundraising philosophy is "I'm not begging people to donate, I'm providing an *opportunity* for people to be part of something bigger, something important, something that makes a lasting impact." She says, "A lot of rich people are bored and want to be part of something exciting." And what's more excit-ing than the chance to be part of the next big hit Broadway show? Dale got to work finding early investors to bring *Hadestown* to the next level. But Anaïs and Dale had a vacant role on their Unicorn Team—a Mobilizer.

Dale recruited Mara Isaacs[5] to join the Unicorn Team. Mara's Unicorn Leadership Type is what I have dubbed Mobilizing Strategizer (MS). While Anaïs and Dale talked loftily about the transformational power of love and how art can change the world, Mara, a major Mobilizer, created a project timeline, refined the budget, and did behind-the-scenes work to move the project forward.

Mara is a strong Strategizer too and had years of experience developing new plays and other theatrical productions. She understood the steps that needed to happen to move from big idea to finished product. Mara and Dale recruited more Unicorns to join the team, including more producers and investors, a director, stage manager, and marketing and PR specialists.

Broadway is a brutal industry. It's extremely difficult to open a show in one of New York City's 42 theaters in the Broadway district. Many aspire. Few succeed. It's even more difficult to stay in business. Out of all the shows that open on Broadway, only a few remain open for more than a season or two. One out of five shows breaks even financially.[6] While there are a few cash-cow shows like *Wicked* and *Cats* that consistently rake in the coins, these are the exception, not the rule.

As far as Broadway musicals go, *Hadestown* was an underdog. It was a quirky show with unconventional music that Broadway theatergoers do not usually expect. It had a title that many people weren't sure how to pronounce. What's more, it was the first musical in Broadway's history to have two lead women producers, a woman composer, and a woman director. On top of that, Anaïs, Dale, and Mara had never created a Broadway show before. This was a first for all of them.

After a few more years of fundraising, refining, and test performances at smaller venues and eventually the National Theatre in London, *Hadestown* opened on Broadway on April 17, 2019, and was an instant hit. The *New York Times* called it "gorgeous" and "hypnotic,"[7] tickets sold like hotcakes, and it became one of the most financially successful shows to hit Broadway since *Hamilton*.

In fact, *Hamilton*'s creator, Lin-Manuel Miranda, praised *Hadestown* on X (back then known as Twitter), posting to Anaïs, "Maestro, your baby's all grown up [. . .] WRACKED sobs in the audience. Bravo!"[8] He added that it's "the most goosebump-inducing thing I've seen this season." With that ringing endorsement, tickets continued to fly.

By November 2019, the show recouped its $11.5 million investment,[9] just a few short months after opening night (a speed unheard of in the musical theater industry). The show swept the Tony Awards, scooping up eight awards including Best Musical, making it the most awarded show that year. A Grammy Award for the Broadway cast recording soon followed. In the first five years since opening night, the Broadway production grossed over $180 million,[10] and that's not counting any revenue from the show's lucrative tours across North America, Europe, and Canada, as well as a South Korean production featuring a K-pop star in a leading role.

Beyond its financial success, *Hadestown* captured people's emotions. Fans showed up to performances dressed as their favorite characters, wearing red flowers pinned to their clothing—the same red flower that Orpheus hands to his lover Eurydice in the show. Teenagers drew anime-inspired *Hadestown* fan art and posted it on TikTok and Instagram. More than a musical, it was becoming a cultural phenomenon.

Hadestown is what many shows aspire to be but few become: a Unicorn musical, one with the potential to generate a billion dollars in the years to come between the numerous tours, licensing deals, and the movie adaptation that's in the works.

Anaïs didn't do it alone. Neither did Dale or Mara. But when these three Unicorns combined their powers, they achieved the right balance of Visionizer, Strategizer, and Mobilizer energy, the holy trinity that's required to bring great ideas to life and create a brand that is wildly successful.

Hadestown's financial success has encouraged Broadway to take female producers, writers, and directors more seriously, and the show has led to greater diversity and gender equity in the largely male-dominated industry. When a project not only enchants audiences but also disrupts the status quo and makes the world better than it was before, that's a true Unicorn project.

WHAT IS A BRAND?

Brand, much like *innovation*, is one of those words that's thrown around constantly in business conversations, but many don't really understand what it means. It can be anything from a Broadway show to a soft-drink company to a cruise ship to a person.

Here's a simple definition: a brand is what you're known for.

It's your reputation and what people expect from you, your offer, or your company.

For example, when you crack open an ice-cold bottle of Coca-Cola, you know you'll be greeted with a sweet and refreshing taste. You may have nostalgic memories about sipping Coca-Cola with your friends on weekends and holding the cool bottle up to your sweaty forehead after playing hard in the sun. You may recall those iconic Christmas commercials where Coca-Cola convinced you that polar bears are gentle, fluffy giants who want to share a beverage with you and not the largest and most dangerous predators on land. Words like *sweet*, *refreshing*, *bubbly*, *friends*, *family*, *happiness*, and *connection* sum up the Coca-Cola brand.

There are three main types of brands.

PERSONAL BRAND

What do you want to be known for as an individual? This is your Personal Brand.

For example, E. L. James (author of the *Fifty Shades of Grey* trilogy, later adapted into a movie franchise that has generated more than $1.3 billion[11]) is an author who's known for writing novels that are sexy, graphic, controversial, and NSFW. If she made a dramatic pivot and released a nonfiction book about the history of Croatia, people would understandably be confused, because it would be extremely off-brand.

When it comes to your work, what do you want to be known for?

Let's say you're a freelancer and want to be known as the rock star web designer who's so good, you have a 12-month waitlist of clients dying to work with you.

Or you lead a department at your organization. You want to be known as the supervisor who always gets the job done early and under budget.

The skills you bring to the table, the energy you exude, the way people feel around you, the type of leader you are—all of this represents your Personal Brand.

OFFER BRAND

An offer is a product, service, or experience that's available in the marketplace for people to purchase. An Offer Brand is what this particular company or person is known for creating and delivering.

For example, Disney Cruise Line launched a new ship called the *Disney Treasure* and invited Disneyphiles to book a seven-day trip through the Caribbean. This particular offer is described as a place where "the spirit of adventure meets the daring tales of classic Disney films." Words like *imaginative*, *exciting*, and *adventurous* sum up what this Offer Brand is all about. You'll see those qualities expressed in every detail of the Offer Brand, from the website to the purchase confirmation e-mail to the decor of the ship and the customer service on board.

What is the main offer you sell, or plan to sell? What do you want this offer to be known for? How do you want people to describe this offer when they're talking among their friends? This is your Offer Brand.

COMPANY BRAND

Every company, whether it employs two people or thousands, is known for something. Whatever your company is known for, that's your Company Brand.

Consider a company like Google. If you had to describe what it's like to work at Google, what would you say? Probably, "It's highly competitive and hard to get hired there." "They only want the best of the best, the top talent in the world." "It's an innovative and exciting place to work." However, "The work hours will be long and strenuous. Work-life balance probably isn't very good." Words like *great*, *industry leader*, *innovative*, *competitive*, and *rigorous* sum up what Google is all about. This is the Company Brand.

Who establishes the Company Brand? The founder . . . along with everyone else on the team. Every Unicorn contributes in some way to the Company Brand, whether they greet people at the front desk, type P&L reports, or make billion-dollar decisions in the C-suite. Your Company Brand is a big part of what determines if the world's most talented Unicorns want to come work for you or not.

WHAT IS A UNICORN BRAND?

A Unicorn Brand is any brand that is remarkably successful. Think: best of the best, crème de la crème, *top tier of excellence, award-winning, iconic, beloved.* These brands may reach the billion-dollar mark, become household names (though not every founder has the desire to scale to that level), and set the standard that other brands try to meet.

Personal Brands, Offer Brands, and Company Brands can all become Unicorn Brands by assembling Unicorn Teams.

HOW TO CREATE YOUR FIRST (OR NEXT) UNICORN TEAM

By now, you're likely wondering, *How can I build my very own Unicorn Team? Where are my Unicorns hiding? How do I find them?*

The quick answer is: you may already know them.

Meet Sarah Paikai, one of the most valuable Unicorns I've ever worked with. She's my right-hand woman, my second brain, the guava jam to my crunchy peanut butter. The first Unicorn I brought onto my team when I left the corporate world, though not the last.

The first time I met Sarah, I was leading a six-week program for aspiring small business owners on Oahu, the Hawaiian island where I grew up. I come from a rural sugarcane town on the North Shore, where my mom and Filipina grandma raised me—a far cry from the bougie Napa Valley vineyard that I now call home.

This particular program cost zero dollars to participate in. It was a freebie for local residents, funded in part by a grant from the state government and a nonprofit that focused on skills development in rural areas. Teaching this program was my way of giving back to the community that shaped me into who I am.

Sarah never went to college. She held a high school diploma, had four children under the age of seven (the number of diapers she went through in a week: staggering), was a stay-at-home mom, and had rarely left the island.

She was not an aspiring entrepreneur, but her husband, Landen, was. Landen (a strong Visionizer) was a dreamer with grand visions of a graphic design company and getting his artwork printed on T-shirts. He saw the vision but had no idea how to get there. What's more, he dreamed of getting elected to serve in the state government so that he could impact policies and laws—all the systems impacting the people of Hawaii, particularly native Hawaiians like himself. Like many Visionizer Unicorns, Landen had a lot of big ideas. His ideas were so inspiring, though sometimes disorganized and impractical.

"He's got his head in the clouds!" Sarah lamented to me. But she loved him and wanted to help make his dreams a reality.

Week after week, I noticed an interesting pattern. While many of the program participants showed up to class late, flaked out, made excuses, or struggled to finish their assignments on time, Landen's homework was done, impeccably, every time.

"Landen, you're a rock star!" I told him, and (respectful husband that he is!) he corrected me, saying, "It's all because of Sarah. She keeps me focused and makes sure I get things done."

Ding, ding, ding! Unicorn chimes sounded in my head. Clearly, Landen (Visionizer that he is) was blessed to have Sarah (a powerhouse Mobilizer) helping him bring tasks across the finish line.

As the free program ended, out of 20 participants, only 4 showed up for graduation day. Everyone else had dropped out along the way. The finishers were Sarah and Landen, plus another husband-and-wife duo. (That couple ended up building a cleaning business, and—following my advice—they focused on securing lucrative government contracts rather than doing cleaning for individual homes. Their business is now much bigger than mine is.)

One year into creating my own business, I was at a big decision point. Should I play small and continue being a one-woman show, offering one-on-one consulting and doing the occasional speaking gig? Or did I want to play bigger, build a team, and create a business with the potential to scale to eight figures and beyond?

I decided to go bigger, but (Strategizer that I am!) I wanted to move forward in a methodical way. Step one: hire a part-time assistant.

I posted a message on Facebook and explained that I wanted to hire someone 10 hours a week to help me record videos and post content online.

"I'll do it!" Sarah Paikai messaged me. I remembered Sarah vividly from my program and was honestly shocked that she'd be interested.

"Are you sure? You'll probably be bored in two weeks and want to quit . . . also, do you have any experience doing videography?"

"No, but I can figure it out. Let's just try it," she suggested, and thus our experiment began.

To kick off our first trial week, I told Sarah my vision of the future. I wanted to create more visibility for my work as a brand and business strategist, become the top provider in my field, and train other people in my methodology. On top of that, I wanted to serve as an inspiration to other leaders who looked like me, an Asian American woman (for which mainstream role models felt hard to see or find). I envisioned getting a book deal with a major publisher so that my children and descendants could see their family name in print. To reach these lofty goals, I needed to create a stronger presence online. It was time to stop hiding behind my desk and put myself out there in a more public way.

Sarah listened to my grand plan and immediately got my entire Ideastorm organized.

"We should take a stroll through this park," she told me. "I'll ask you a list of questions, you answer, I'll film you while you're talking, and then I'll edit to get the best clips so we can post them online." Hello, Mobilizer energy to the max! I felt so relieved and energized. She's the M to my V and S! The missing piece of my business puzzle.

Sarah didn't remain a part-time assistant for long. She was hungry to grow, and continually asked for greater responsibility. Within just four years of working together, she was promoted to COO of my company, the author of a number-one Amazon best-selling book (yes, she beat me to the bookshelf!), and now owns a bigger house than I do. She has traveled around the world (a business trip with me to Austin, Texas, was her first big trip as an adult outside of the islands) and is the ultimate second-in-command. By forming a Unicorn Team and working together, we've both leveled up tremendously. Win-win.

Many people wouldn't take a chance on a mom of four with no college degree or relevant work experience, but my attitude was "I know a Unicorn when I see one." Sarah had the get-it-done energy that I sorely needed and was willing to learn the skills that she didn't possess. I was willing to bet on her, because I could sense "This is a woman who gets sh*t done." Skills can be acquired, but natural strengths are either there or not.

Sarah's been with my company for over 10 years, a timeframe that is practically unheard of nowadays. (In the U.S., employees typically stick with a company for about four years, on average.[12]) After working together for such a long time, we've reached that level where I can open my mouth and begin to say, "I think we should . . ." and then she finishes my sentence. It makes working together feel like magic. Yes, I pay her a competitive salary, but it is important to me that she also feels valued, appreciated, and respected at work. I'm a Unicorn. She is too, and she knows it. She knows that her contributions are just as critical as mine.

Since Sarah came on board, my business has grown from seven figures to multiple eight, but our growth is more than just monetary. We have served more clients, rolled out new programs and products, codified our processes, and built new systems. And that book deal I dreamed about? Well, you're holding the result in your hands.

EXERCISE

The Accidental Unicorn Team

It's possible to create a Unicorn Team "by accident" without realizing you're doing it.

Think about something exciting that you achieved in the past. This could be a professional accomplishment (you wooed a major investor, delivered an incredible presentation, finished a big project ahead of schedule) or personal achievement (you produced a successful fundraiser for your kid's school, ran a 10K race, renovated your home).

To achieve this feat, did you have a Unicorn Team supporting you?

Who was on your team?

Who performed the Visionizer, Strategizer, and Mobilizer roles?

Consider all the people who helped make this happen, including (but not limited to) people you paid, such as employees or contractors.

You may have created an accidental Unicorn Team in the past. But going forward, it won't be an accident. From now on, you know that you need strong Visionizer, Strategizer, and Mobilizer energy to round out your team, and you have the process to build this type of team intentionally and achieve the greatest success.

"WHERE IS MY SARAH?"

Ambitious people (particularly my Visionizer clients) always want to know "Where can I find my Sarah?"

I reply, "Your Sarah is looking for you just as much as you're looking for her." And I remind them, "Your next Unicorn might arrive in a package you didn't expect."

She may not be a Stanford graduate (or even a high school graduate). They may not have any prior experience in business, marketing, sales, or whatever skill you think you need most. He may not apply for a job that you posted online, and instead, you might meet in a completely different way—at a class, on a flight, at an event. The Unicorn who radically changes your company, project, or entire life might be trotting on a treadmill next to you at the gym.

Just like Bruce.

MEET BRUCE, THE UNICORN IN THE GYM SHORTS

"Raise your hand if you've been part of a million-dollar exit," the facilitator asked, eyeing the room expectantly. Numerous people shot their hands in the air, including mine.

I was attending a business mastermind in Miami—a room filled with leaders gathering to swap war stories, exchange ideas, and help each other solve their most daunting business dilemmas.

"Okay, now raise your hand if you've done a ten-million-dollar exit," the facilitator continued. Several hands shot up.

"A hundred million." Fewer hands in the air this time.

"A billion." One lone hand popped into the air—attached to a remarkably burly arm. We all craned our necks to see who it was.

It was a man that I can only describe (and I say this with respect and admiration) as a big, velvet teddy bear. His name, I was about to find out, was Bruce Cardenas. Who exactly was this Billion-Dollar Bruce, this Unicorn among Unicorns? Later that day, I pulled him aside to find out the story.

Serve, Protect, and Support

Bruce is a protector. He served in the U.S. Marines, worked as a police officer, then went freelance and became a celebrity bodyguard. Grounded and humble, this salt-of-the-earth guy from New Jersey didn't enjoy the spotlight but was more than happy to stand on the sidelines and defend those who did. By his own admission, he never wanted to be the CEO of anything. He was always happiest playing a supporting role.[13]

One day at the gym, Bruce noticed a woman nibbling a home-made snack wrapped in tinfoil.

"What's that you got there?" he asked, with genuine curiosity. "Looks good."

She introduced herself as Shannan Penna and explained that she made protein bars in her kitchen at home. Fun flavors like mint chocolate, cookie dough, and pineapple upside-down cake. Tasty, made with clean, simple ingredients, and packed with 25 grams of protein.

Shannan had an intriguing story.[14] Her mom was an excellent cook and her dad was a professional bodybuilder—one of the only men ever to beat Arnold Schwarzenegger in a competition. Shannan followed in their footsteps and began her career in the health and fitness industry.

A certified trainer, she wanted high-protein snacks, but most of the bars at the grocery store weren't up to her standards (this was back in 2010,[15] when the options were limited and tasted like cardboard). So she started making her own. She often sent her husband, Ron, into work with a stash of homemade bars. Soon, Ron's colleagues and friends were pleading for more. Even folks with zero interest in nutrition wanted more, simply because they tasted so good.

"That's when I knew, maybe we're onto something," Shannan continued.

Bruce took a bite and agreed. "These are really good."

His mental wheels began turning. Bruce's A-list celebrity clients were disciplined gym-goers who worked hard to maintain their physiques. They had wildly busy schedules and needed consistent energy all day long for high-stakes meetings, press junkets, photoshoots, performances, and gala events. These celebs packed a year's worth of action into a 24-hour period. Stopping for a leisurely meal was sometimes tough.

"Hey, could I have a couple bars to share with my clients?" Bruce asked. He suspected they'd love them.

Shannan said, "Sure," and brought several bars lovingly packaged in Reynolds Wrap the next time she came to the gym.

Soon Bruce was handing Shannan and Ron's protein bars to Hollywood's elite. Mario Lopez went wild over them during a golf tournament. Jessica Simpson carried a stash in her purse. Khloé Kardashian (known for her intense, twice-a-day workouts and her own dramatic weight-loss journey) was obsessed.

Bruce's top strength is Mobilizer, followed by Visionizer in second place. I call this type a Mobilizing Visionizer (MV). He's a practical guy who gets things done, but he also has the ability to see the bigger picture even before others do. He saw what this brand could become and wanted to move things in the right direction.

However, there's nothing cunning or Machiavellian about Bruce. He never thought, *I'm going to convince these celebs to endorse the brand and in doing so, build a billion-dollar empire so I can cash out and become extremely rich.* In his mind, giving bars to celebs was just plain old common sense. His job was to serve and protect his clients and to keep them safe, happy, and healthy. Bringing snacks was just a nice thing to do. If certain people loved the bars and talked about them, well, all the better. That meant more people could discover these snacks and achieve their fitness goals.

Bruce became Shannan and Ron's unofficial (and, for a time, unpaid) brand ambassador. For two years, he toted bars around for his clients, and even convinced a few to become investors. As dollars poured in, Shannan and Ron took their operation from side hustle to a legitimate business. Bruce was their Fairy Godfather, the Mobilizer putting in the legwork to bring their big Vision into reality.

Eventually, Bruce was showing up to work for Shannan and Ron four or five days a week, and being a protein bar spokesperson was becoming his full-time job. Shannan and Ron told him, "You can't keep working for free! Please, you have to let us pay you!" and Bruce shrugged it off. But they insisted and wouldn't take no for an answer. Soon, Bruce was an official employee of Quest Nutrition (chief communications officer) and owned equity in the company too.

After three years, the nutrition company's revenue surpassed $42 million. One year after that, *Inc.* named Quest the world's second-fastest-growing company, with products in 70 countries and over 40,000 distribution outlets. Just 10 years after its inception, Shannan and Ron decided to sell Quest to Simply Good Foods for a cool one billion dollars.[16]

Shannan, Ron, and Bruce (along with other people who joined their Unicorn Team along the way, such as husband-and-wife power couple Tom and Lisa Bilyeu) are still close friends and business collaborators to this day.

When I asked Bruce, "What made you want to partner with Quest in the first place?" he replied, "I like helping. It feels good to be part of something bigger."

HOW TO SPOT UNICORNS IN THE WILD

How do you spot Unicorns in the wild? There are clues. It's not so much about what's on their resume or LinkedIn page. It's more about the energy they bring into a room and the way they impact those around them.

When you're spending time with a Visionizer, you can't help but think bigger, dream wilder, and feel like anything is possible. When someone describes an idea and most people in the room think, *Is she serious? He's joking, right? Well,* that *sounds pretty unrealistic*, chances are, the person speaking is a Visionizer. Visionizers live their lives a step or 2 (or 20) ahead of the rest of society. Future-focused, they're the people doing yoga and ice plunges, stirring reishi mushrooms into their coffee, or championing new, progressive causes before these movements hit the mainstream. Start-up incubators and programs for emerging entrepreneurs are often filled with V types. (Though other types of Unicorns can be company founders too.)

When you're talking to a Strategizer, the fog lifts and the path becomes clear. You can see how to travel from here to a future destination. You may notice a Strategizer sitting quietly during a meeting—observing, listening, thinking—and then this person comes forward with a genius strategic plan that blows everyone away. Strategizers are often drawn to careers in branding, marketing, and sales, because they naturally understand how to build demand for an offer and make people want whatever "it" is, even if nothing like it has ever existed before. You may spot a Strategizer creating models and frameworks much like the Unicorn Innovation Model, because they can see in their head how all the pieces need to come together to make things happen and want a way to explain their strategy to others. Look at the founder of a billion-dollar brand, and often their second-in-command is a strong Strategizer.

You'll know a Mobilizer in the wild, because when you hang with them, stuff gets organized and work gets finished. When you're co-working with a Mobilizer, you wrap up the day and think, *I can't believe how much I just got done.* Their natural ability to close loops is contagious. When you ask them to do something, you can truly "consider it done." These are M types.

In many companies, Mobilizers get relegated to lower-level and lower-paid positions, or they're not viewed as leaders on the same level as the V- and S-type Unicorns, which is a mistake. Mobilizers are not underlings. Many Mobilizers are highly skilled specialists. Because they love to do things with excellence, to completion, and with repetition, these are the people who put in their 10,000 hours to gain mastery of their craft. The seasoned coder, the killer copywriter, the customer service agent who can soothe a furious client and turn them into a lifelong fan—when you spot masterful specialists like these, you're likely looking at a Mobilizer. Treat this person with the respect they deserve so they'll want to bring their finely honed skills to your Unicorn Team.

ENROLL YOUR UNICORNS (EVEN IF YOU CAN'T PAY THEM . . . YET)

If you don't have the financial resources to hire your next Unicorn, good news: you don't have to. Instead of thinking, *I need to hire*, think, *I need to enroll, recruit,* or *inspire.*

Just like Shannan and Bruce's fateful meeting at the gym, your next Unicorn might be a friend, family member, colleague, gym buddy, even a complete stranger who's intrigued about something you're doing and wants to get involved—with pay or without.

Remember, too, that there are numerous ways to compensate someone for their contributions. Providing a salary is one option. You can also provide equity in the company, pay someone on a commission basis, barter, or give perks that are worth even more (to them) than money. In Chapter 10, you'll learn more about Creative Compensation, which is all about identifying what really matters to each Unicorn on your team and how to offer compensation that matches their values, which may (or may not) mean more money.

To be perfectly clear, I am 100 percent here for paying your team members a generous salary, because nobody can pay their mortgage with banana bread or bartered goods. However, depending on the phase of business you're in, be open to all possible compensation options. Lack of funding does not need to stop you from building your first Unicorn Team. There are plenty of people, like Bruce Cardenas, who want to get involved with an exciting idea even if there's no paycheck on day one.

EXERCISE

Who Do You Need in Your Life?

Think about something you want to accomplish either personally (renovate your home, plan a wedding, save a certain amount for your child's college tuition fund) or professionally (bring a new product to market, launch a big idea that changes your city or community).

Make a list of who can help you do this.

Write down your dream team, even if they seem improbable or financially out of reach.

Do you want the entire *Queer Eye* team, the Fab Five, to give your home a makeover?

Do you want Kris Jenner to be your manager?

Do you need a full-time personal assistant that you think you can't afford to hire yet?

Map out who your Dream Unicorns would be.

The purpose of this exercise is to envision the specific types of Unicorns that you need to rally around your idea to make it real.

You don't have to literally convince Kris Jenner to manage your brand, but you can go find your own personal Jenner, a Unicorn who embodies Jenner-esque powers and skills.

Give yourself space to imagine the *who*. Figure out the *how* later.

~~WHAT~~ WHO AM I MISSING?

To close out this chapter, let me bring you one final story . . . about a Unicorn who was committed to win bigger: Rachel Rodgers, an attorney turned entrepreneur.

Rodgers founded her company as a solo operation (just her, a laptop, and a dream) and hustled hard to grow it from $0 to a couple million in annual revenue. In the early years, Rodgers's company was a law practice catering to small business owners. She supported her clients with trademarks, copyrights, patents, and other intellectual property matters. Fairly quickly, though, Rodgers realized that her main passion wasn't law. It was money. Specifically, she loved teaching small business owners how to leverage their intellectual property to generate exponentially more revenue and scale from six figures to seven.

As a Black woman and mother of four, she often reminded her clients, "Money doesn't solve every problem, but it sure does solve a lot of them." She rebranded her company with this new vision in mind. Formerly the Rodgers Collective, it became Hello Seven as a way to let her future clients know this was the place to help them make seven figures. She had no investors and maxed out her credit cards, but she launched a new website, rolled out new offers, and bet on herself to win. And win she did.

Quickly, Rodgers recognized that she couldn't reach her audacious goals alone and began building a small team of brilliant people. But after hitting a couple million in revenue (a proud accomplishment for sure), the company hit a plateau. While most clients were thrilled with their services, revenue wasn't growing in a sustainable way. Something was "off," and Rodgers wanted to solve it.

Rodgers—classic Visionizer, charismatic, with that X factor that leads to appearances on *Good Morning America* and millions of podcast downloads—had tons of ambitious ideas to grow the business. She envisioned hitting at least $10 million annually (and eventually $100 million), building a nonprofit in addition to the main business, and changing millions of lives. But each time she presented a new, visionary idea to her team, the people on her team seemed on board to do it, but the actions they were taking continued to create plateaued results, or they just couldn't get it all the way done at the level of confidence they desired. Many times, Rodgers had to jump in to push things over the finish line, and it was causing burnout all around.

Like many small businesses with rapid growth potential, they had a lot of initiatives to get done and not a lot of time to do them. Rodgers was determined to find a better way to achieve her vision of making Hello Seven the top wealth coaching and education company for entrepreneurs in her industry.

A new idea to scale their revenue past the plateau came to Rodgers's mind: What if we created an innovative live conference that brought our core audience together? A live conference isn't a small feat and requires lots of strategy, planning, and logistics. She knew it would be a stretch but trusted her intuition and intellect—it was something that could change the game by bringing people together in one place and growing her platform and the company's revenue at the same time. One problem: it required them to solve their capacity issue. She knew that it was the right move, though, and like other Visionizers who are committed to win, she sought professional insight (something she encourages her own clients to do every day).

Rodgers came to me with this predicament. "What am I missing?" she wanted to know.

I invited her to switch the word *what* to *who*.

Rodgers is a Visionizer. Many folks on her team were Mobilizers. In fact, she had an army of Mobilizers ready and willing to get things done; yet, as a team, they kept struggling to reach their goals at the level they all knew was possible. The missing link? A Strategizer Unicorn who could take Rodgers's visionary ideas and translate each one into a strategy that the team could rally around. Rodgers had been acting as the main Strategizer because marketing, sales, and branding required her energy to move the money needle, but she didn't have the bandwidth to commit to the role completely.

But that's not all. She also needed a trusted Strategizer who would occasionally tell her, "No, we're not doing that, and here's why . . ." or, "This is a beautiful idea; however, the team is already maxed out. No new strategic initiatives until Q4." A great Strategizer knows when to say no, or "Not yet." And they are willing to have that conversation when others won't.

After assessing her big goals and the current team who could boldly achieve them, we were looking for *who* Hello Seven really needed next, using the tenets of the Unicorn Innovation Model. Soon after, Rodgers promoted her longtime staffer (Brittany Martin, a top-notch jane-of-all-trades who had the trust of the team and had demonstrated a remarkable ability to translate Rodgers's vision into well-executed ideas online and offline) to a clear leadership position and allowed her to fully own this new Strategizer role. Together, within the following year and along with the other Unicorns on the team, their momentum took the company from their previous seven-figure ceiling to an impressive eight figures in revenue. What's more, they accomplished this feat in 2020 during the pandemic, at a time when many businesses were merely hoping to stay open and few were aiming for growth. Most of all, they now have a model to use whenever the next "who" is needed as they continue to shoot for the moon.

And that visionary idea—the live conference for entrepreneurs that Rodgers ideated? That became ROI: The Millionaire

Summit, a three-day event that has become a highly attended, highly rated gathering place for the hundred of attendees that Hello Seven serves. Something the Hello Seven Unicorn Team is really proud to produce and, best of all, produces high value to their company and their clients.

If you take away nothing else from this book, remember this: every Unicorn Team needs people who can perform the Visionizer, Strategizer, and Mobilizer roles. The team can be any size, but these three roles must be filled. When you find the right "who" to own each role, suddenly, you're galloping toward your goals instead of being stuck in the mud.

YOUR UNICORNS ARE SEARCHING FOR YOU

No matter what type of Unicorn you are, other Unicorns are out there . . . and they're looking for you just as much as you're looking for them.

If you're a strong Visionizer, you're searching for people who can translate your grand vision into a grounded plan and make it happen.

If you're a strong Strategizer, you're seeking a big idea that excites you, something worth fighting for, a project that's worthy of your sharp, strategic mind.

If you're a strong Mobilizer, you're seeking the joy that comes from knowing you're helping to accomplish something bigger than yourself.

No Unicorn is "better" or "more valuable" than another. There's no hierarchy with V at the top, S in the middle, and M on the bottom rung. All Unicorns contribute to the team's success, and each Unicorn needs one another.

Now that you've gotten that "who" is the answer to making big ideas happen, let's dig more deeply under what motivates the Unicorns on the team to win.

TOP TAKEAWAYS

- Lots of people have great ideas. Tragically, most of these ideas never happen.

- Why? Because most people (1) try to do it alone, or (2) try to build a team but don't really know how to do it, and therefore the team ends up being disappointing.

- For a legit Unicorn Team, you must have people who can perform the Visionizer, Strategizer, and Mobilizer roles, and the team must have values alignment, an owner mindset, a meaningful goal, a swift timeline to make it happen, and a repeatable process to follow.

- You can build your first (or next) Unicorn Team today. Start by finding just one Unicorn and enrolling them to join forces with you.

- You don't necessarily need to hire new employees right this second. It's possible to assemble your Unicorn Team by bringing together freelancers, mentors, consultants, investors, family, friends, and other people who can help you win.

- Your goal is to create a well-rounded team that has a blend of Visionizer, Strategizer, and Mobilizer energy. Whatever you (or your team) currently lacks, these are the types of Unicorns you need to go find and recruit.

- Your Unicorns are seeking you just as much as you're looking for them.

PART II

MOTIVATE TRACK

The Unicorn Innovation Model

<table>
<tr><td rowspan="6">IDEATION
NEW
Launch brand-new initiatives</td><td>VSM Process</td><td colspan="3">● VISIONIZE</td><td colspan="3">▲ STRATEGIZE</td><td colspan="3">■ MOBILIZE</td><td rowspan="6">ITERATION
BAU
Improve existing initiatives</td></tr>
<tr><td>Navigate
How we make decisions together and choose the right idea to pursue</td><td colspan="3">Ideastorm</td><td colspan="3">DOIT</td><td colspan="3">BEIT</td></tr>
<tr><td rowspan="2">Motivate
How we lead and the energy we bring to the team</td><td colspan="3">V Types</td><td colspan="3">S Types</td><td colspan="3">M Types</td></tr>
<tr><td>VV</td><td>VS</td><td>VM</td><td>SV</td><td>SS</td><td>SM</td><td>MV</td><td>MS</td><td>MM</td></tr>
<tr><td>Communicate
How we get aligned, work on the right priorities together, and get things done at warp speed</td><td colspan="3">Brandcast</td><td colspan="3">Stratagem</td><td colspan="3">Prototype</td></tr>
<tr><td colspan="10">< ~ ~ ~ UNICORN ENERGY ~ ~ ~ ></td></tr>
</table>

> "Okay, I vetted my idea, and I'm confident that it's a winner."
>
> "I recognize that I can't do this alone. I need a Unicorn Team.
>
> "Which types of Unicorns do I need on my team, and why?"
>
> "What are my team members privately thinking and feeling . . . and how can I understand their psychology better?"
>
> "As a team, how can we keep each other motivated and achieve big things quickly?"

In Part II, we'll do a deeper dive into the three roles that every Unicorn Team must include: Visionizer, Strategizer, and Mobilizer.

You got a quick crash course in Part I, but now we're going into all the nuances and nitty-gritty details.

What do Visionizers fear more than anything?

What drives Strategizers bananas?

Why do so many Mobilizers feel unappreciated?

I want you to understand the other Unicorns on your team—their psychology, what drives them, what irritates them, and how to put each Unicorn in the ideal role so they can work their magic.

There are three types of Visionizers, three types of Strategizers, and three types of Mobilizers, for a total of nine Unicorn Leadership Types.

I've provided a comprehensive diagnostic to find out your type, called the Unicorn Leadership Type Assessment (ULTA®). Once you know your Unicorn Leadership Type, you'll understand your strengths, weaknesses, the ideal role for you to play on the team, and which kinds of Unicorns you need to recruit.

Part II focuses on the second track in the Unicorn Innovation Model. It's all about how we lead, the energy we bring to the team, and how we keep each other motivated to win.

Motivate means to stimulate, drive, or move someone to do something. A Unicorn Team is a self-motivating force. When the right people come together around the right idea, each person invigorates their fellow Unicorns, spurring their teammates to be their best selves and do their best work.

When a team includes a combination of all three leadership energies—Visionizer, Strategizer, and Mobilizer—people feel naturally motivated. That's when you hear team members say, "I can't believe how much we've accomplished!" "The time just flew by!" "I feel so energized when we're working together." "I've never been part of a team like this before."

Get ready to meet the future members of your Unicorn Team.

The people who will bring your great idea to life.

The people who will take your brand from good to great to iconic.

The people who will help you win bigger than you could ever manage to do on your own.

CHAPTER 3

THE VISIONIZER

Inspirational—Futuristic—Innovative

The Unicorn Innovation Model

	VSM Process	● VISIONIZE		▲ STRATEGIZE			■ MOBILIZE			
	Navigate How we make decisions together and choose the right idea to pursue	Ideastorm		DOIT			BEIT			
IDEATION **NEW** Launch brand-new initiatives	**Motivate** How we lead and the energy we bring to the team	V Types		S Types			M Types			**ITERATION** **BAU** Improve existing initiatives
		VV	VS	VM	SV	SS	SM	MV	MS	MM
	Communicate How we get aligned, work on the right priorities together, and get things done at warp speed	Brandcast		Stratagem			Prototype			
	‹ ~ ~ ~ UNICORN ENERGY ~ ~ ~ ›									

Visionizers are the people we most associate with the word *Unicorn*. They are bold, risk taking, charismatic, and magnetic. Many times, they are competitive AF. *Impact* is a word they're obsessed with.

It doesn't matter if they display as introverts or extroverts; they have that It Factor—an energy that makes people want to listen, follow, and jump on their bandwagon.

Visionizer Unicorns are legends who bring the great, next-level ideas into the industry and mainstream. Many Visionizers have founded companies whose brands you trust with your whole lives. The car you drive. The apps you use. The airlines you fly.

We deem Visionizers brave and courageous and willing to do anything to bring their big ideas to life. They have a willpower and chutzpah that make them the 3 percent that society worships and admires.

But Visionizers have a problem—they often suck at leadership. We celebrate them like we cheer on the lead singer of a band, but they can never keep the band together and happy. They don't form systems. They don't understand how long things take. They don't always know how to motivate people. Often, they make unrealistic demands of their team, which is how companies can fall apart. But Visionizers deserve credit and empathy. Even if they've been branded as superheroes, they're actually humans with super ideas. These ideas are the ones that make us gasp with awe, offer solutions we've prayed for, and delight us daily. Their intensity and obsession with their ideas are what have improved our quality of life.

Here are a few well-known Visionizers that you may recognize, along with the key Strategizers and Mobilizers who turned their exciting visions into reality. Do you see similarities in yourself to any of these Visionizers?

Business Leaders	Celebrities	Fictional Characters
V—Tony Robbins, founder of Tony Robbins International	V—Oprah Winfrey, founder of OWN and talk show host	V—Tony Stark, chairman of Stark Industries and Iron Man
S—Dean Graziosi, co-founder of Mastermind.com M—Certified "Results Coaches"	S—Sheri Salata, former co-president of OWN M—Tina Perry, current president of OWN	S—Pepper Potts, CEO of Stark Industries M—J.A.R.V.I.S., Iron Man's Artificial Intelligence system
V—Kendra Scott, founder of Kendra Scott Jewelry	V—Jay-Z, founder of ROC Nation and former CEO of Def Jam Records	V—Miranda Priestly, editor-in-chief of *Runway* magazine
S—Tom Nolan, current CEO M—Lon Weingart, former Starbucks expansion leader	S—Desiree Perez, CEO of Roc Nation M—Alicia Keys and Rihanna, ROC Nation artists	S—Nigel, top advisor to Miranda M—Andy Sachs, first assistant to Miranda
V—Mark Zuckerberg, founder of Meta	V—Martha Stewart, founder of Martha Stewart Omnimedia	V—The Oracle, The Matrix series
S—Kevin Systrom, co-founder of Instagram M—Sheryl Sandberg, former COO of Meta	S—Kevin Sharkey, EVP, executive director of design for Martha Stewart brand M—30+ staff at Cantitoe Corners	S—Morpheus, captain and leader of the Matrix revolution in Zion M—Neo / Trinity, heroes of Zion and hackers in the Matrix

NEW IDEAS . . . AND OLD IDEAS, REIMAGINED

In some cases, Visionizers come up with completely new, radical, innovative ideas that never existed before. Think: the birth control pill; a rocket to Mars; or delicious beef grown in a lab, not from a cow. Other times, Visionizer, reimagine old ideas by dusting off the cobwebs, coming up with a vastly better solution, and creating technology that puts the power of choice in people's hands. This makes the problem they solve get fast adoption.

Brian Chesky, Nathan Blecharczyk, and Joe Gebbia reimagined short-term rentals and disrupted the hotel industry with their idea originally called Airbed & Breakfast, now known as Airbnb.

Jen Rubio and Stephanie Korey reimagined the travel experience with the Away luggage brand. Who knew there was room for more suitcase choices when Samsonite dominated the marketplace?

Dollar Shave Club founders Michael Dubin and Mark Levine, as well as Billie founder Georgina Cooley, reimagined shaving body hair without the inconvenience and bloated pricing in the traditional razor market, disrupting blue-chip stocks like mega-brand Gillette.

THE BILLION-DOLLAR QUESTION: "WHAT IF?"

DoorDash, the largest food delivery company in the United States, is a perfect example of a Unicorn Team taking a simple idea all the way to billion-dollar status.

Tony Xu, Stanley Tang, Andy Fang, and Evan Moore, four college students at Stanford, wanted to develop an app to help small business owners. They rolled out an initial concept that received a lukewarm reaction. Next, they circled back to their users to collect feedback on how to make the app more useful.

Chloe, a pastry maven who ran a macaron shop in Palo Alto,[1] a small city in the San Francisco Bay Area near their college campus, explained how she had to drive around town, battling traffic to hand-deliver each order by herself. "I have no drivers to fulfill [these orders], and I'm the one doing all of it," she told them.

The four founders were intrigued. This might be the billion-dollar problem that they could solve. Then they interviewed 200 business owners to find out their biggest pain point. Time and time again, they heard the same thing: *delivery*.

Business owners vented to them and said things like "Customers always ask if we do delivery. We wish we could offer that service, but it doesn't make sense for us financially." "We can't afford to hire a delivery driver right now. It's too costly." "I don't have time to do delivery runs by myself, because I'm busy doing literally everything else at the shop."

Most merchants didn't do delivery because it wasn't cost effective and therefore not a good use of their time, energy, or money. But *what if* small businesses could get their products delivered to any customer, anywhere in the region, at no cost to the business? Without needing to hire additional employees?

This exciting "What if?" question inspired the founders to tweak their app to focus on one thing: delivery services. They had a personal connection to this project too. As busy college students, getting food delivered to campus would be life-changing! At the time, only one restaurant in their small town offered delivery. But what if *every* restaurant could?

Within a few hours, they had a working prototype.[2] The next day, they had their first order. At the beginning, Xu, Tang, Fang, and Moore were the delivery drivers by night and continued as college students by day. Within five months of starting, they changed the business name to DoorDash and hired more drivers—and they needed more Mobilizers to join the team. At first, DoorDash focused solely on delivering food to students on the Stanford campus, but it quickly expanded to families and office workers in the area. Soon the founders wooed investors and raised $2.4 million in funding.

Ten years after delivering its first order, DoorDash is a $51 billion company and the 361st most valuable company in the world. And it all started with one Visionizer question: "What if?"

IMPACT, NOT FAME

You know DoorDash. But you've probably never heard Tony Xu, Stanley Tang, Andy Fang, and Evan Moore's names before unless you happen to be obsessed with the tech start-up space.

Most Visionizers in the world aren't household names or on the cover of *Forbes*, and they don't really care about being famous-first anyway. They care more about impacting lives, autonomy, and the liberation that comes with creating their own economies and empires. Some Visionizers are celebrities who serve as the face of the brand, but many are not. Visionizers can be founders of companies, but they can also be heads of departments, newly appointed CEOs, honorary chairpersons, or people championing new projects.

Whether their personal brands are known in the mainstream or not, they are definitely known inside of the companies they lead. Getting into an elevator with one of them can be an intimidating moment, because you know they created the hallowed halls you get to walk in.

THE VISIONIZER ROLE IN THE UNICORN TEAM

People look to Visionizers to find out what the future holds. "Where are we going? Show me." In the Unicorn Innovation Model, the Visionizer:

- Owns the future pacing of the brand.

- Communicates the vision of where the brand is headed and protects the vision like their life depends on it.

- Develops and nurtures relationships (including with key mentors, investors, and allies).

- Models the culture and ethos of what the brand stands for.

- Partners with and attracts the right Strategizers and Mobilizers to grow the business.

High-Fluency Zones

Every Unicorn has high-fluency zones and high-friction zones.

Your goal is to design your workday so that you're operating in a high-fluency, low-friction zone the majority of the time.

In a high-fluency zone, you're doing the things you're exceptionally good at. And you're collaborating with other Unicorns who can do the things that you suck at—the things that drain your energy and stall progress.

When each Unicorn on the team is in a high-fluency, low-friction state, the team works together harmoniously, fluidly, and elegantly, and achieves massive goals in record-breaking time.

These are the high-fluency zones for people who score high in Visionizer on the Unicorn Leadership Type Assessment:

- *Big Picture*—You can see all the dots in the field of opportunity, where the next big thing is going, and the meta-impact to all. You see an ecosystem, not just a dot.

- *Big Ideas*—You are passionate advocates of the BHAG ("big, hairy, audacious goal," a term that Jim Collins and Jerry Porras coined in their book *Built to Last*) and concoct many ideas on how to achieve what are seemingly intimidating goals.

- *Big Moves*—You create moonshot goals and zag when people zig, sometimes without notice or planning. You are a quick starter and fast mover.

- *Big Solutions*—You invent "the next big thing" that solves problems that plague everyday people, often in a surprisingly simple way. When confronted with roadblocks, you use your immense creativity to find another way through.

High-Friction Zones

Visionizers—like all Unicorns—have weak zones. There are certain things that Visionizer Unicorns are terrible at and common issues they get embroiled in. If you're a Visionizer, these are your high-friction zones. Visionizers are likely to:

- *Be Starters, Not Finishers*—You often struggle to fully finish what you start, often because you believe it's no longer relevant or worth your time, even if others are still working toward it.

- *Be Confusing Communicators*—You often speak in lofty concepts instead of clear, practical steps. You have a Unicorn dialect that no one (aside from yourself) fully understands.

- *Move On Too Quickly*—You get bored easily, want to abandon projects in motion, and prefer to move on to something shiny and new. Pivoting doesn't scare you, but you don't always consider the trade-offs and consequences that arise when you abruptly change the plan. Another Achilles' heel of the Visionizer? Impatience. "What's taking so long?" is a frequent question on your mind, paired with an exasperated sigh. "Just make it happen!" Many Visionizers get frustrated that their ideas don't come to life as fast as their mind creates them.

- *Get Frustrated When Others Can't Read Their Minds*—You assume people "get it" and feel disappointed when people can't read your mind or understand the impact you care so deeply about.

- *Seem Intimidating or Attract Yes-People*—You often mesmerize people with your X factor, charisma, and visionary ideas. As a result (and usually by accident), your teammates sometimes behave like fans rather than peers. Team members receive instructions and say, "Yes! On it!"—eager to do your bidding rather than probing, pushing back, or saying "I disagree, and here's why."

Visionizers need to double down on their high-fluency zones (do more of this) and delegate their high-friction zones to other Unicorns (do less of this and/or be mindful when your high-friction zone is showing up and derailing a project).

THE THREE COMMITMENTS OF A VISIONIZER

To be the greatest Visionizer you can be, there are three commitments you need to make. A commitment is your personal leadership pledge. It's what you commit to being and doing for yourself and for your team.

Commitment #1: Emotional Awareness

It's all about you.

- Understand that emotional regulation is required to make your vision real. If you are frequently frustrated, impatient, and stressed out, you'll struggle to find Unicorns who want to be on your team. Nobody wants to collaborate with a ticking time bomb.

- Make emotions your superpower instead of your kryptonite by processing them with qualified persons and tools (coach, therapist, mentor)—not your staff.

- Model vulnerability and authenticity by communicating your motivations and intentions in alignment with the core values of the company.

- Know that delegating can be hard. Accept this as the "right type of hard" and become the leader your team needs so that you can move more easily into your bigger vision.

- Take a breath before you make a decision. Take a beat before you speak. Visionizers can be intense. You can afford to pause more than your brain wants you to believe.

Commitment #2: Relational Awareness

It's not all about you.

- Understand that you are not the only Unicorn in the forest. Invite others to keep winning with you.

- Create an identity and personal brand within the company that is approachable and values driven. Walk your talk and live the ethos of your vision.

- Communicate through your core values when you're disappointed with a person or outcome. Say, "The way this project turned out didn't express our value of excellence," or, "One of our core values is generosity, and this decision doesn't reflect that."

- Realize that personal performance is directly linked to company performance, and incentivize that link for everyone who is helping to make the vision real.

- Don't apologize for being fully in your high fluency, and support others to be in their high fluency too. Own your passion for what you're good at and reward the other Unicorns to do the same.

Commitment #3: Logical Awareness

It is about results. Don't let anyone tell you otherwise.

- Remember that you are building a company, not a hobby or temporary passion project. Your vision is changing lives.

- Commit to being a leader, not a manager.

- Trust the plan and the data before you make big swings.

- Fire yourself from being the one who has to meticulously organize everything. That's not your high-fluency zone. There are better-qualified Unicorns to do that.

- Know that your intuition and instincts provide a form of data too. You are highly fluent in using your inner GPS system powerfully.

VISIONIZER FLASH ASSESSMENT

Are you a Visionizer Unicorn?

Take the quick quiz below to see how high you score when it comes to the Visionizer role.

> To take the full Unicorn Leadership Type Assessment (ULTA) and get a more detailed picture of your Unicorn Leadership Type, head to **https://UnicornTeamBook.com/ULTA**.

For each statement below, rank yourself on a scale of 1 to 5:

1 Not me at all	2 Rarely me	3 Sometimes me	4 Mostly me	5 Me all the time

1. The future motivates me much more than the data of the present or past.

2. I'm an idea machine. I never run out of them. And I love it.

3. People tend to follow me blindly.

4. My highest frustration comes from people not getting what I'm putting out.

5. Process matters to me, but only if it doesn't interrupt the flow of what makes my idea work.

6. I use both intellect and intuition equally as guides to bring my ideas to life.

7. I love solving problems.

8. I get very irritated when people push back and say, "Your idea isn't realistic," or "We don't have the resources to do that right now."

9. I'm highly passionate about new things and very bored by what's already been implemented.

10. I geek out at learning, researching, and discovering what's possible.

11. Open loops don't bother me.

12. I understand that my ideas are important way past my lifetime.

13. I have little patience for small talk.

14. I proudly advocate for our core values and vision.

15. I feel most creative when I'm ideating and dreaming.

16. Microdetails make my head hurt.

17. I see potential in people way past what they think of themselves.

18. I'm highly competitive and like to win.

19. I speak in a dialect that people tell me hasn't been spoken yet.

20. Those who "get it" are the only people I really like being around.

Results and Key:

Low V 20–49	Mid V 50–79	High V 80–100

Whether you scored high or low in the Visionizer scale, you now understand how Visionizers tick and what motivates a leader with this energy the most. Whether you're thinking about your own work or collaborating with another Visionizer, you'll understand the way Visionizers think and how to help enable a high-fluency, low-friction flow.

WHAT'S NEXT?

When a Visionizer Unicorn starts a company, they often become the head of sales, the closer, the moneymaker who brings revenue in the door. For a while, this works. Visionizers are naturally charismatic, which means people want to buy whatever they're selling. However, at a certain point in the company's development, the Visionizer needs to stop being the strategic planner of sales and marketing and hand the Unicorn reins to someone else—otherwise, they're restricting the company's growth. But it can be very hard to let go of this role. After all, most Visionizers start off hustling their ideas and wares to build their company—and they arguably continue to be the best salespeople on the team. Visionizers are also the original payroll payer, the problem-solver, the butcher, the baker, the candlestick maker, the janitor, and CEO. Making money, cash flow, profit—all these things matter, and you are convinced you can't just delegate any of them to someone else.

But the good news is: you *can*.

I'm about to introduce you to the person you've been longing for, the secret stuff of legends, the rainmaker you've been looking for.

With this Unicorn on the team, you can bring your great ideas to life with astonishing speed and keep your revenue right where you want it (and take it beyond). Finally, you can have the vision translator, the architect, the partner you so desperately need.

Get ready to meet the Strategizer.

TOP TAKEAWAYS

- The Visionizer role on the Unicorn Team is all about what's new and what's next, where we're going, and the future we can build together.

- People who are strong Visionizers tend to get bored easily, especially when it comes to business-as-usual activities. They want to move on to something new.

- Visionizers are not always detail oriented and are not always great at follow-through and bringing projects over the finish line.

- Visionizers are incredible at thinking big, inspiring, motivating, and evoking emotion. People naturally want to follow Visionizers to the moon, stars, and beyond.

- If you're a strong Visionizer, you need to surround yourself with Strategizer and Mobilizer Unicorns, because they'll bring different energies and strengths that you lack. Round out your team with Strategizer and Mobilizer types to make your big ideas a reality.

CHAPTER 4

THE STRATEGIZER

Alchemizing—Translating—Initiating

The Unicorn Innovation Model

VSM Process		● VISIONIZE	▲ STRATEGIZE	■ MOBILIZE	
IDEATION **NEW** Launch brand-new initiatives	**Navigate** How we make decisions together and choose the right idea to pursue	Ideastorm	DOIT	BEIT	**ITERATION** **BAU** Improve existing initiatives
	Motivate How we lead and the energy we bring to the team	V Types	S Types.	M Types	
		VV / VS / VM	SV / SS / SM	MV / MS / MM	
	Communicate How we get aligned, work on the right priorities together, and get things done at warp speed	Brandcast	Stratagem	Prototype	
		< ~ ~ ~ UNICORN ENERGY ~ ~ ~ >			

Behind every Visionizer with wild, outlandish ideas that will change the world is a Strategizer who sees how to take those ideas and actually make them a reality.

While the Visionizer Unicorn sees *where* we're going, Strategizers see *what* and *why*—what plays we need to make as a team and why this goal matters in the first place.

Visionizers often (though not always) end up being famous. Visionizer personalities have that charisma, star quality, and super-human X factor that compels people to listen and follow wherever their vision may lead. Visionizer types can have quiet magnetism, like Martha Stewart, or a big, bold, larger-than-life personality, like Tony Robbins.

The Strategizer role is usually filled by someone who doesn't crave the spotlight (think: "secret weapon") and who is content working behind the scenes—creating the winning strategy that takes the team all the way to the top. The Strategizer doesn't necessarily want to be the face of the brand, but perhaps more so than anyone on the Unicorn Team, they want to play big and win.

When you step into a boardroom where people are making 10-figure deals, you'll likely see the Visionizer at the helm of the table, flanked by their Strategizer to the right.

I tell my clients that a Strategizer can be the trickiest and most elusive Unicorn to hire. An excellent, seasoned Strategizer isn't easy to find.

Here are examples of people who acted as a Strategizer in some capacity. When you see their name, notice which brands they worked on and with, and it will give you an idea of the very real impact they had.

Do you see similarities in yourself to any of these Strategizers? If you do, you're probably one of those "best-kept secret" types of people.

Business Leaders	Celebrities	Fictional Characters
V—Tony Robbins, founder of Tony Robbins International	V—Oprah Winfrey, founder of OWN and talk show host	V—Tony Stark, chairman of Stark Industries and Iron Man
S—Dean Graziosi, co-founder of Mastermind.com	S—Sheri Salata, former co-president of OWN	S—Pepper Potts, CEO of Stark Industries
M—Certified "Results Coaches"	M—Tina Perry, current president of OWN	M—J.A.R.V.I.S., Iron Man's Artificial Intelligence system
V—Kendra Scott, founder of Kendra Scott Jewelry	V—Jay-Z, founder of ROC Nation and former CEO of Def Jam Records	V—Miranda Priestly, editor-in-chief of *Runway* magazine
S—Tom Nolan, current CEO	S—Desiree Perez, CEO of Roc Nation	S—Nigel, top advisor to Miranda
M—Lon Weingart, former Starbucks expansion leader	M—Alicia Keys and Rihanna, ROC Nation artists	M—Andy Sachs, first assistant to Miranda
V—Mark Zuckerberg, founder of Meta	V—Martha Stewart, founder of Martha Stewart Omnimedia	V—The Oracle, The Matrix series
S—Kevin Systrom, co-founder of Instagram	S—Kevin Sharkey, EVP, executive director of design for Martha Stewart brand	S—Morpheus, captain and leader of the Matrix revolution in Zion
M—Sheryl Sandberg, former COO of Meta	M—30+ staff at Cantitoe Corners	M—Neo / Trinity, heroes of Zion and hackers in the Matrix

BEHIND-THE-SCENES, BUT NOT SECOND FIDDLE

Don't get it twisted: being a Strategizer personality (like me) doesn't necessarily mean you're forever going to be second-in-command or the secret weapon. Many Strategizers become founders and start their own companies, nonprofits, and world-changing projects too.

Any type of Unicorn (Visionizer, Strategizer, or Mobilizer) can become an entrepreneur and phenomenal leader if they want to. For example, I spent the early portion of my career leaning heavily in to my Strategizer gifts. But midcareer, I realized that I wanted to put on my Visionizer hat and create a bigger, more ambitious concept for my company. While I still use my Strategizer superpowers on a daily basis, I'm now in my Visionizer era and tend to play that role on my team most often.

VISION TO EXECUTION

A Strategizer translates vision into execution through planning and communication. The Strategizer Unicorn is the glue that holds the strategy, marketing, and sales together to form a formidable brand. Many brand and marketing agencies are led by (and filled with) Strategizer Unicorns who excel in providing services like copywriting, advertising, public relations and media, and go-to-market planning. They are the strategic planners, the product managers, the creative messengers, the rainmakers, the deal doulas, the brand strategists, the Visionizer's trusted confidant, and the person the Mobilizers look to so they can understand the winning game plan. Many times they have titles like chief marketing officer, head of product, brand manager, or head of business development.

The Strategizer role is one of the hardest to fill because of the limitations of budget and availability of qualified Strategizers in the marketplace. (However, there are ways to bring a Strategizer onto your team even if you can't afford to pay them a hefty salary—yet. More on this when I share Kendra Scott's incredible story with you in Chapter 13, and in Chapter 10 when we discuss team performance and creative compensation.)

The good news is that regardless of your current budget, you can develop Strategizer thinking in your organization.

A recent example of this came up in my own world. A successful *New York Times* best-selling cookbook author hit me up in my DMs on Instagram, asking if I could help with taking her personal brand and restaurant companies to the next level of her vision.

I'm a major foodie, so I was especially interested and delighted to connect with her. I already owned her cookbook, and one of her recipes made me look like a rock star at my house during a dinner party.

After getting to know each other on a quick video call to feel out if my company could really help her, I invited her to come to our offices to do a Stratagem Session with me and my team.

"Stratagem? What's that, exactly?" she asked.

"It's where a Visionizer, like you, expresses your vision. You tell me where you see your work going and describe the future that you envision. And then a Strategizer, like me, listens and picks up all the gems that you're dropping. Then we take your gems and translate them into a strategy and plan that you can mobilize quickly," I replied.

"That's a thing? I've always wanted to do something like this." She went on to explain, "I'm good at developing innovative recipes that everyday people can make. The people on my team are restaurant workers who know how to make really good food."

She was the Visionizer. Most of her team members were Mobilizers. The missing link? A Strategizer who could translate the vision into a strategy that the Mobilizers could understand and implement.

She continued, "I'm tired of thinking about how to position and market and sell more. We hired a social media team, an SEO specialist, and a PR agency, and we do local marketing where our restaurants are, but I feel like everything is disjointed and I'm not even sure if what we're spending is getting the return we expect. I have a great marketing manager and an executive assistant helping me with this, but I feel like we're throwing a lot of spaghetti at the wall." Restaurant pun intended.

"I have a vision of what I want to create in my mind, but when I try to communicate to my team what that is, it's like they're hearing that weird *wah-wah-wah-wah* sound that Charlie Brown hears when he's listening to an adult. I think I'm explaining myself clearly, but the words are not landing, and it's so frustrating."

A classic Visionizer dilemma. Remember, Visionizer Unicorns bring world-changing ideas but often struggle with communicating them clearly in language that non-V earthlings can understand. That's where Strategizers come in.

I nodded. "You're not alone. You have a vision, your team wants to execute your vision, but you need a role that's in the middle—creating a strategy and connecting the dots. Once you have a Strategizer on your Unicorn Team, then you can stop trying to fill a role that's not your strengths, and you can play more in your happy place—creating masterpieces in the kitchen and writing your next book."

I could feel her mix of excitement and skepticism, and a couple weeks later, we got in a room and got to work.

By the end of the Stratagem Session, we created her:

- *Unique Brand Message*—The strategic brand bible her team would use to direct all strategic marketing and selling activities.

- *One-Page Strategic Plan*—The quarterly goals that supported her vision and the company's mission.

- *Sustainable Scale Dashboard*—The Unicorn Team tool kit that her team would use to track performance in a clear and objective way, including who on the Unicorn Team owned what action item.

Want to access bonus templates to create your own Unique Brand Message, One-Page Strategic Plan, and Sustainable Scale Dashboard?

Download templates for these materials at:

https://UnicornTeamBook.com/Bonus

Halfway through our Stratagem Session, the author made an observation. "I've been racking my brain all day, asking myself, *Who do you remind me of?* And I realized, you're the Benny Medina to my JLo!"

Never heard of Medina? Many people haven't. But let me tell you about Benny. He's the Strategizer Unicorn who has managed Visionizer talent like Mariah Carey, Tyra Banks, and Jennifer Lopez. Medina is a record executive, dealmaker, and godfather to JLo's children—the A-list manager who sees the potential of a celebrity brand and what needs to happen to get there. Being compared to Medina was a highlight of my career, because he's one of the king Strategizers of the world. Years later, I'm still glowing from that compliment.

STRATEGY VS. PLAN

Strategizers lend their strategic brilliance to the Unicorn Team. But is a strategy the same thing as a plan? Not exactly.

In a *Harvard Business Review* piece on defining what "strategy" means, Roger Martin, a co-author of *Playing to Win: How Strategy Really Works*, outlines the distinction between strategy and a plan.[1] He says that a strategy is based on a hypothesis that you think will make you win, while a plan is how you intend to use the resources you've currently got.

STRATEGY	PLAN
Think: Here's how we're going to win.	**Think:** Here's how we're going to use our resources (money, time, equipment, supplies, and people) to bring the strategy to life.
"These are the big plays we need to make to win, and here's why I believe this will work." *"Here's how we will build massive demand for this offer and make people care about it, think about it, talk about it . . ."*	*"We can spend X dollars on hiring a publicist, we can delegate Y to these five people, we have enough time to finish Z by Friday."*

A plan is comforting, but a strategy pushes the company or team out of their comfort zone, because a strategy is not guaranteed to work and usually needs to be tweaked along the way.

The takeaway here? Strategizers try things based on data, market trends, their excellent instincts, and knowing where the winning games should be played. Strategizers base their risk tolerance on knowing nothing will be perfect but that they can still aim for the highest win possible.

Like Visionizers, Strategizers are not necessarily the most organized people, but they do need order and structure to feel free inside of their creative and strategic flow. Some even have a project management background and can communicate in a way that will influence people to buy into the game plan at hand.

Let's take a glimpse into how an effective Strategizer thinks.

The scenario: You need to outsource services for a project. You want to hire an agency that does paid advertising, because your current team doesn't have the bandwidth or expertise to do this. You interview an agency that you're considering.

When you're interviewing the agency to determine if they're a fit, the rep from the agency asks you:

A. What's your budget for paid ads?

Or:

B. What are the specific outcomes (leads, sales, brand awareness) you want to achieve with paid ads?

If the agency asks question B, it means they're thinking like a Strategizer. Once they hear the end result that you want, they can develop a strategy to travel from here to there. If they ask question A, they're thinking more like a Mobilizer. Is it important to understand your budget? Sure. But this shouldn't be the first question in the conversation. What matters most of all (and what Strategizers understand) is the result you want to achieve in the end.

WHAT WOULD HAVE TO BE TRUE?

The most important question a Strategizer asks is: "What would have to be true?"

(Shout out again to Roger Martin, who coined this excellent question.)

As in, what would have to be true for that goal to be achieved, for that theory to be proven, or for that result to happen?

Ask this question more, and you'll make more money, get promoted, be asked to lead very cool projects, and become next in line for a very big gig . . .

WWHTBT?

I'm calling this the official tagline of Strategizers everywhere. I think we should get T-shirts made for this so we never forget how important it is to ask.

IT'S ALL ABOUT THE OUTCOME

Strategizers are obsessed with results, whereas Visionizers are obsessed with ideas. Many Visionizers fall in love with their ideas and honestly do not care that much about key performance indicators like revenue. They don't want to be the person who is driving these outcomes. This is not their happy place or flow state.

Strategizers, on the other hand, love driving results and feel devastated when their team is not achieving them. If you have a colleague who practically has "results, results, results" tattooed on their forehead, this person might be a Strategizer Unicorn.

HIGH-FLUENCY ZONES

Strategizers typically excel at:

- *Super Connection*—You identify who, what, and how the dots connect and are able to communicate this to the team. You know what matters and what doesn't and focus on the collective goals that need to be met to make the vision and mission happen. You never lose sight of the long game even when focusing on short-term wins.

- *Super Sniffing*—You are hyperaware of what's happening in the zeitgeist and what could impact the strategy at hand. You can "smell the money" and have a knack for picking the winning concept. You may not always come up with the billion-dollar idea yourself, but you know it when you see it.

- *Super Collaboration*—You have the respect of stakeholders in the pursuit of the strategic goals by knowing how to make each team member understand their impact on the outcome, as well as what makes them tick. You know the brand lives and thrives by the culture of its people and their ability to execute the strategy.

- *Super Decision-Making*—You understand that data and intuition are both important when making decisions, and you're comfortable deciding what to do next if asked. You understand that at the end of the day, your job is to understand human behavior and why people choose things. You are fluid and flexible but always focused on the end game.

HIGH-FRICTION ZONES

High-friction zones are areas where Strategizer types can get into trouble and become irritated, frustrated, or want to throw up their hands and leave the team.

When a Strategizer Unicorn is operating from a high-friction zone, it stalls progress and makes it extremely difficult for the team to move forward and win.

Strategizers are typically known to:

- *Be Excessively Intense and Direct*—Mainly because they're passionate about results. They pride themselves on "knowing all the things," and so their eagerness to get a result can sometimes be off-putting. When someone straight-up says, "This is not good enough, not anywhere close," that's the shadow side of Strategizer energy.

- *Be Triggered When the Vision Changes*—Visionizers are notorious for throwing curveballs ("Last week, my vision was X, but now it's Y!") and Strategizers can become especially irritated with these shenanigans. The Strategizer thinks, *I've laid out a winning strategy, stop messing with it, just let me win!*

- *Get Annoyed When Other Unicorns Aren't Following the Plan*—Strategy is the act of creating a game plan that puts us in the best position to win. When the game plan isn't being followed, Strategizers get antsy. (On my darker days, I've noticed myself blurting out things like "Just do what I tell you to do!" That's Strategizer Shadow Side, right there.)

- *Have a 0 Percent Tolerance for Wasting Time*—Wasting time is intolerable for a Strategizer. When fellow team members get stuck in "analysis paralysis" (excessive research, endless talking, overthinking) and aren't moving forward, Strategizers can become apoplectic. They love leverage and understand where the real shortcuts are and where they're not. They want to win—and win fast.

- *Overcomplicate the Strategy*—Strategizers live, breathe, eat, and sleep strategy. Nothing makes them happier than figuring out the master strategy to move from point A to point B. However, this can sometimes result in a strategy that is too long, too detailed, and with too many moving parts, a process that causes more harm than good. Strategizers need to be reminded, "Keep it simple."

THE THREE COMMITMENTS OF A STRATEGIZER

Commitment #1: Emotional Awareness

It's all about you.

- Being the "best-kept secret" isn't a curse. It's most important that the right people know you, respect you, and are in awe of how you navigate what you do best.

- Be aware of when your frustration can come off as cocky or arrogant. Your confidence is natural because your skills and instincts are honed. There's no need to flex or posture.

- Trust your gut and experience more and share it openly with other Unicorns.

- Be a long-game thinker. Don't let blips in the plan cause you to make hasty decisions for false short-term gains.

- Ask better questions of yourself and others.

Commitment #2: Relational Awareness

It's not all about you.

- Storytelling is one of your superpowers. Use it to get others committed and involved.

- Not all people have the ability to hold both abstract and linear thoughts like you do. Be patient and clear.

- Describe what's happening in the world—what's in the zeitgeist, what's in the news, what's on everyone's minds—and how this affects the strategy, because other Unicorns may not sense these cultural shifts the way you do.

- Show your team what's in it for them.

- Invite collaborative ideas to be a part of the winning strategy.

Commitment #3: Logical Awareness

It is about results. Don't let anyone tell you otherwise.

- Ask the magic question often: WWHTBT. What would have to be true?

- Strategies are not plans, and plans are not necessarily strategic. Know the difference and lead accordingly.

- You attract better specialists when the strategy is sound.

- People buy brands, not ideas.

- Translation isn't the same for everyone. Communicate and then ask fellow Unicorns to echo back what they've heard. Check in to make sure you're being understood.

STRATEGIZER FLASH ASSESSMENT

Are you a Strategizer Unicorn? Take the quick quiz below to see how high you score when it comes to the Strategizer role.

> To take the full Unicorn Leadership Type Assessment (ULTA) and get a more detailed picture of your Unicorn Leadership Type, head to **https://UnicornTeamBook.com/ULTA.**

For each statement below, rank yourself on a scale of 1 to 5:

1 Not me at all	2 Rarely me	3 Sometimes me	4 Mostly me	5 Me all the time

1. I am very comfortable testing theories that could improve our results.

2. I don't wait to be told what to do.

3. I respond and anticipate unexpected changes better than most.

4. I love taking big ideas and figuring out how to make them a reality.

5. The long-term results are just as important as short-term wins.

6. I am all about results, results, results.

7. I can speak the language and interface with every level inside of an organization.

8. I believe that decisions should be made based on data, intuition, and common sense.

9. I thrive when I am given creative license to solve things.

10. I need to learn something new about the industry every day.

11. If something needs to be said so that we win, I will say it, even if it ruffles feathers.

12. Because people learn differently, different options will always be needed.

13. I believe there should be no division between departments when it comes to executing a strategy.

14. I'm comfortable making presentations.

15. I naturally get people aligned around a goal and an idea.

16. Messaging is a core strength of mine.

17. I'm interested in world news, pop culture, politics, and the competition—anything that customers consume, I need to know too.

18. I can be in my values and hear other perspectives that aren't the same as mine without getting triggered or influenced significantly.

19. I truly love marketing and sales.

20. I am a confident decision-maker.

Results and Key:

Low S 20–49	Mid S 50–79	High S 80–100

Whether you scored high or low on the Strategizer scale, you now understand how Strategizers tick and what motivates a leader with this energy the most. Whether you're thinking about your own work or collaborating with another Strategizer, you now understand the way Strategizers think and how to help enable a high-fluency, low-friction flow.

Remember earlier, when my client enthusiastically said that I was the Benny Medina to her JLo?

I didn't finish the story.

My client ended her proclamation by saying, "You know what? I've never met someone who is both Benny *and* Jenny!"

(Being compared to two of my favorite Unicorns of all time, Benny and Jenny, was music to my ears!)

In me, she saw both Strategizer and Visionizer. This makes sense, since my Unicorn Leadership Type is Strategic Visionizer (SV), which means Strategizer is my top strength, followed by Visionizer. You have a unique Unicorn Leadership Type, too, which we'll uncover in Chapter 6.

WHAT'S NEXT?

Strategizers believe that implementation without strategy is a waste of time.

But in the words of Oprah Winfrey, do you want to know "what they know for sure"?

Strategy without implementation is an even *bigger* waste of time.

That's why their favorite people to partner with to make the magic come alive have a role that is overgeneralized, underrealized, and in most circles (and books) isn't thought to be held by traditional leaders in an organization.

This is dangerous folly and dinosauric thinking in a world where an 18-year-old can make millions on YouTube without ever entering the traditional workforce. A person with fast implementation skills has more career options than ever before, and if you're not careful, you'll be a nonoption for them.

In the Unicorn Innovation Model, these folks are the heartbeat of the *how*.

The precision mechanics that allow our ideas to fly.

The people who delight and thrive in the things that make Visionizers and Strategizers squirm with discomfort.

Without them, nothing gets done.

Meet the people who make the vision and the strategy real: the Mobilizers.

TOP TAKEAWAYS

- The Strategizer role on the Unicorn Team is all about taking the big vision and crafting a strategy that's going to work.

- These are the masterminds and the rainmakers who see the next hundred moves when most people see only the next two.

- Strong Strategizers excel in marketing, branding, and sales and understand how to translate a big idea into an offer that consumers will be obsessed with.

- Strategizers are often the most difficult Unicorns to find and recruit. They are the most rare, especially seasoned Strategizers who can bring years of experience to the table. But they are out there.

- If you're a strong Strategizer, you need to partner with a Visionizer who will provide a big idea that's worthy of your skills and awaken the genius strategizing ideas inside of you. You also need to surround yourself with Mobilizers who can implement your strategy and make sh*t happen.

CHAPTER 5

THE MOBILIZER

Executing—Measuring—Integrating

The Unicorn Innovation Model

	VSM Process	● VISIONIZE			▲ STRATEGIZE			■ MOBILIZE			
IDEATION **NEW** Launch brand-new initiatives	**Navigate** How we make decisions together and choose the right idea to pursue	Ideastorm			DOIT			BEIT			**ITERATION** **BAU** Improve existing initiatives
	Motivate How we lead and the energy we bring to the team	V Types			S Types			M Types			
		VV	VS	VM	SV	SS	SM	MV	MS	MM	
	Communicate How we get aligned, work on the right priorities together, and get things done at warp speed	Brandcast			Stratagem			Prototype			
		< ~ ~ ~ UNICORN ENERGY ~ ~ ~ >									

Mobilizers are the most unseen (and often underestimated) rock stars of the Unicorn Team. But let's be clear: they're just as critical to the team's success as the Visionizer and Strategizer Unicorns who tend to get more of the praise and glory. The word *mobilize* means to prepare for action, to organize for a purpose, and to bring resources into use in order to achieve a particular goal, and this is what Mobilizers do better than anyone.

Mobilizers take the vision and strategy and put it into motion. These are the Unicorns who write the speech, design the code, build the website, cook the meal, deliver the order, follow up with the lead, close the sale, tie up loose ends, and complete the checklist—and usually manage the other specialists who are working toward the big goal.

Done is their favorite word.

Your team may have spectacular ideas and a genius strategy to get to the future you want, but without Mobilizer Unicorns, nothing happens.

Here are some examples of people who thrive as Mobilizers.

Business Leaders	Celebrities	Fictional Characters
V—Tony Robbins, founder of Tony Robbins International S—Dean Graziosi, co-founder of Mastermind.com M—Certified "Results Coaches"	V—Oprah Winfrey, founder of OWN and talk show host S—Sheri Salata, former co-president of OWN M—Tina Perry, current president of OWN	V—Tony Stark, chairman of Stark Industries and Iron Man S—Pepper Potts, CEO of Stark Industries M—J.A.R.V.I.S., Iron Man's Artificial Intelligence system
V—Kendra Scott, founder of Kendra Scott Jewelry S—Tom Nolan, current CEO M—Lon Weingart, former Starbucks expansion leader	V—Jay-Z, founder of ROC Nation and former CEO of Def Jam Records S—Desiree Perez, CEO of Roc Nation M—Alicia Keys and Rihanna, ROC Nation artists	V—Miranda Priestly, editor-in-chief of *Runway* magazine S—Nigel, top advisor to Miranda M—Andy Sachs, first assistant to Miranda
V—Mark Zuckerberg, founder of Meta S—Kevin Systrom, co-founder of Instagram M—Sheryl Sandberg, former COO of Meta	V—Martha Stewart, founder of Martha Stewart Omnimedia S—Kevin Sharkey, EVP, executive director of design for Martha Stewart brand M—30+ staff at Cantitoe Corners	V—The Oracle, The Matrix series S—Morpheus, captain and leader of the Matrix revolution in Zion M—Neo / Trinity, heroes of Zion and hackers in the Matrix

VISIONIZERS CAN SUPPORT, MOBILIZERS CAN LEAD

On many teams, you see the following dynamic play out: a charismatic Visionizer is the founder and CEO of the business. Their right-hand person is a strong Strategizer who translates the CEO's ideas into language that others can comprehend. And then working below those two leaders, there's an army of Mobilizers who roll up their sleeves and get all the small, menial, or lower-paid work done. In many companies, Mobilizers are the interns, the assistants, the people who do the "grunt work" that's required to bring an idea to life.

While this hierarchical dynamic is common (Visionizer at the top, Strategizer in the middle, Mobilizer on the bottom rung), that doesn't mean it's the right way to build a winning team. This top-down dynamic leads to burnout and frustration, and it's why you frequently have talented Mobilizers quitting and seeking work elsewhere. Why would anyone want to stay when they feel disrespected or if their contribution is treated as trivial?

In the Unicorn Innovation Model, each type of Unicorn (Visionizer, Strategizer, and Mobilizer) is equally vital for the team's success. Each type brings valuable skills to the table. Each type is a leader in a different way—responsible for leading the team forward toward the outcome.

Visionizers lead by bringing the big idea. Strategizers lead by creating the strategy to travel into the desired future. Mobilizers lead by integrating and implementing—these Unicorns have an uncanny ability to deliver, follow through, and close loops. All three of these leadership roles are crucial, none is "better" or "more important" than another, and if one role is missing, the team doesn't function.

Let me underscore this point: if you have a knack for the Mobilizer role, this doesn't mean you're meant to be a lowly underling, fading into the background while the Visionizers found companies and make millions. Not at all. Mobilizers can be founders of megasuccessful brands too.

Take Martha Stewart: the Queen of Domestic Bliss, the Empress of the Kitchen. She's a woman who is very strong in the

Mobilizer role—she loves to tend to her garden, collect eggs from her chickens, cook exquisite meals, and create a beautiful home—and she's extremely good at these tasks. "Getting things done" is her high-fluency zone. However, at a certain point in her career, she stepped into her Visionizer era, turning her specialized skills into the multimillion-dollar brand Martha Stewart Living Omnimedia, which sold to Sequential Brands Group for $350 million in 2015.[1]

Regardless of whether you're a Visionizer, Strategizer, or Mobilizer Unicorn, you can launch your own company (if you want to), lead, and inspire. Just because you excel in the Mobilizer role doesn't mean you never have visionary ideas. It just means that when you have a great idea, you need to surround yourself with Visionizer and Strategizer Unicorns who have the high-fluency zones that you lack.

SPECIALISTS, NOT MINIONS

Mobilizer Unicorns are often thought of as "minions," scurrying behind the scenes and doing the CEO's bidding. Let's disrupt this concept right now and give Mobilizers the respect they deserve. Mobilizers are not underlings; they are highly skilled *specialists*.

Mobilizer is a specific role in leadership where organization, preparation, systemization, and execution are all part of the equation. They own the spectrum of making sh*t happen. They manage the side of the coin where the actual money is accepted and redistributed. They assess what resources are needed to achieve a big goal and keep the people accountable to them. They are the project managers, executive managers, administrative assistants, help desk, accountants, lawyers, subject matter experts, line workers, and engineers. They protect the back end of the company and are the first folks your customers interface with. They finish the jobs they are given.

Visionizers and Strategizers are told endlessly that they need to be more "productive." What a high-friction waste of time! The only truly productive people on a team are the Mobilizers. Let's give them credit for being the best at that.

In a company, Mobilizers own the operations, finance, support, and governance areas. Their titles include chief operations officer, human resources manager, PMO director, comptroller, director of customer service, and general counsel. Oftentimes these roles are outsourced through technology systems, virtual admin support, and customer service help desks.

GROUNDED AND PRACTICAL

Mobilizers live in a grounded and tangible, practical world. They perform best when they have a goal, an assignment, and a checklist to ensure the job is done. They love spreadsheets and tables, formulas, and deductive reasoning. They speak through their finished work.

Many Mobilizers don't have a desire to be in the spotlight, because fame and attention aren't their strongest motivators. But they do want respect, recognition, and appreciation. Their ability to support and serve are the necessary ingredients to making visionary dreams and strategic goals a reality. They don't live in the exclamation point (those are for Visionizers) or the comma (those are for Strategizers). Instead, their favorite punctuation is the period. Meaning: Done. Complete. Fin. *Period.*

They create, build, code, engineer, develop, and protect the brand's assets—past, present, and future. They are masters of manufacturing, financial specialists, Inbox Zero advocates, and list makers, and they're geeky about all things organized, especially systems that help them understand Visionizers and Strategizers. Focus is their superpower. They have a magical way of doing things in record time, with quality results.

HIGH-FLUENCY ZONES

People who score high on the Mobilizer scale typically excel at:

- *Mega-Action*—You are a master of taking strategy and turning it into clear, actionable steps and tasks. When things are decided and predicted in advance, you are the Olympic gold medalist on your team. Crossing the finish line is your aim every day.

- *Closing Loops*—You abhor an open loop and will always prioritize action over everything. Closing loops is your happy place. Highly responsive, you prefer to do things now rather than in the future, just so it can be checked off. "Talk less, do more" is your mantra. "Consider it done" is your personal slogan. Accomplishment is your dopamine rush.

- *Order and Structure*—You like to navigate all things in an orderly way. Rules, laws, standards, and organization give you comfort and are the key to your success. As a natural list maker and planner, you value structure and schedules. You're the best qualified to structure Visionizers' and Strategizers' time (which they desperately need).

- *Precision Details*—You aren't just fast, you're fastidious. Meticulousness and quality are built in to the way you think and do, and you don't get overwhelmed with microdetails or long lists. Your ability to see things through is critically important, because the machine doesn't work without the individual parts working efficiently and effectively. In this way, you are an extremely precise decision-maker. You feel a high responsibility for things to work, and work well. As far as you are concerned, things need to be made as they "ought to" and "should" be.

- *Repetition and Consistency*—You can easily see the exact patterns and identify categories that make things get done right. This pattern recognition helps you collapse repetitive tasks into repeatable ones that can be replicated by other people and technology. This also helps you deliver things on brand, on budget, and on time.

HIGH-FRICTION ZONES

Mobilizers are known to:

- *Fear Being Wrong*—In your mind, if you're wrong, things break and bad things happen. Your strength in structure and systems can also have a rigid effect. When you perceive that you've done something wrong, you spend more time thinking about ways to defend it rather than fix it—even though you're the most qualified fixer ever. You are always keeping a mental checklist. When you cross something off your list, you consider it complete and not open to reconsideration.

- *Be Passive-Aggressive*—When under extreme pressure, you can exhibit behavior that resists the plan without being able to express your ideas clearly to Visionizers and Strategizers. This can look like resentment and opposition to demands that you don't feel apply to you, or a hands-off approach so you're not blamed (remember, your greatest fear is being wrong!). Your passive-aggressive tone in response to something you don't believe in can escalate tensions instead of defuse them. Your intent is almost always one of fairness and results, though, so be mindful that it's more of a trigger, not necessarily an intrinsic trait.

- *Be Disconcerted during the Messy Middle*—You want to know "What do I need to accomplish today?" If the answer is "We're not sure yet," it can be your personal hell. You don't like ambiguous, in-between situations. Going through a messy middle, or transitioning to something new that isn't fully clear yet, can feel distressing to you.

- *Struggle with Pivoting*—When you are right in the middle of a project and joyfully getting things done, and then a Strategizer announces, "Hey, team! Pivot! New strategy," this is when you internally groan, "Noooo." A lack of order, structure, and ability to see things through to the end make you frustrated and stressed, but once you get the contingency plan in action, all will be well again.

- *Be Risk Averse*—When rules need to be adjusted, you can get prickly because you perceive this as risky. You err on the side of lower risk and see that as an insurance investment compared to the more risk-tolerant, fast-growth traits of the Visionizers and Strategizers. Like the saying goes, "no risk, no reward." Your risk intolerance can hold the company back.

All of the things that make a Mobilizer operate at a high level are important to a Unicorn Team's success. Their perspective, very different from those of the Visionizer and Strategizer roles, balances the velocity and upward momentum that can either break the company or make it sustainable, successful, and legendary.

THE PROTOTYPING PROCESS

In my experience and research working with teams that leverage Mobilizers' role most effectively, the game-changing activity that 10x's their productivity (one of their favorite words) is a process that I call Prototyping.

If you want a Mobilizer to think like a Strategizer and empathize with a Visionizer, then you have to give them the power to show you their work and make it feel like it was a great use of their time.

I developed the Prototyping Process when I was running go-to-market launches of new initiatives as head of business-to-business markets at one of the top technology companies in the world. We saw major organizational change; culture-shifting stuff that was disrupting the status quo meant lots of resistance, feigned ignorance, and roadblocks were everywhere. I was brought in to work with the most aggressive moonshot initiatives, the ones where wrangling the people and communicating the mission was imperative. No one at the company wanted this job, but as a Strategizer, it was natural for me.

Back then, I was known as the "Olivia Pope" of the company, a reference to the hit TV show *Scandal*. Kerry Washington plays Olivia Pope, the main character; she's the "fixer" who gets called in when there's a crisis in Washington, D.C., that nobody knows how to solve. She helps Fitzgerald Grant (played by Tony Goldwyn) win his presidential campaign, keeping his public image pure as the driven snow and managing the many dramas that threaten his success. Her character is loosely based on Judy Smith, the attorney and crisis manager who served as George H. W. Bush's deputy press secretary.

When I came on board with this company, they were running the standard playbook. The Visionizers—the C- and board-level folks—said, "This is where we need to go next, so let's just get it done." They had optimism, excitement, and sweeping and grandiose proclamations of how "this" would be the next big thing and were very proud of how innovative they were being.

Strategizers like me helped shape these proclamations into models, forecasts, positioning statements, test markets, and marketing campaigns. I created the internal communication plan to make it all happen. I pieced the main details together and assembled the puzzle so that the rest of the company understood where we were going.

And the Mobilizers? They were side-eyeing all of it, mentally counting the number of wrenches that were being thrown into their daily work machines and calculating how much that would cost them. Not happy, but sure pretending to be. Still committed to getting it done but feeling the discomfort of knowing the extra load on them. Silently thinking, *Sure, they think that's going to work, but if they only knew what I really know . . .*

This picture isn't new if you've managed a project or two. I realized that if I wanted to actually fix it, I had to change the way Mobilizers were being treated and invite them to collaborate in a different way. This realization became the seed of what is now the Unicorn Innovation Model.

Instead of saying, "Here's the plan, now go execute it," I took a different approach. I'd sit down with a Mobilizer, read the strategy to them, and ask them to come up with their own interpretation of what they thought this initiative was achieving.

I'd say, "We want to achieve XYZ. This is the current strategy to do it. Here's the part where you come in. Come up with a plan. Outline the steps you're going to do, but before you get started, show me what you propose"—giving them a one- to three-day timeline to come up with something.

Instead of simply being told what to do, the Mobilizer now had an opportunity to create their own to-do list based on their interpretation of the vision and strategy. They'd show me their prototype ("Here's what I intend to do. What do you think about this concept?"). I'd clarify what needed to be updated to be better aligned with the vision and strategy. Together, we'd approve the prototype. Then I'd let the Mobilizer get to work.

By creating a prototype, Mobilizers felt ownership, felt seen and heard, and felt better about why we were changing everything they were used to doing. It helped to soothe the high-friction areas that would usually plague them. And by getting their prototypes approved, they overcame their worry about being wrong. Win-win-win.

By doing this approach, we created more strategic Mobilizers and more mindful Strategizers, and that's what building a Unicorn Team is all about.

The term *Prototyping* that I use now came from the main Mobilizer on my team, Sarah Paikai—who not only uses it to onboard all our staff, contractors, and freelancers, but also as a Unicorn Team Certified Advisor for other companies that we serve.

Want to try Prototyping with your team?

Turn to Chapter 9 for specific instructions and examples of how this works.

Prototyping Scenario

Here's a fun example, especially for those of you who have to pay taxes (yes, I said "fun" and "taxes" in the same sentence).

The scenario: It's tax season. Company and individual taxes need to get done. Common-sense outcome? Minimize your tax liability as much as (reasonably and legally) possible. Pay less to the government and keep more in your own pocket. That's the goal.

Which type of Mobilizer do you want on your team? Someone who says:

A. "Here are the standard rules and guidelines we must use to calculate your taxes owed. The due date is mm/dd/yyyy. We made $XYZ income last year, so get ready for a big payment. Make sure to have that money ready tomorrow."

Or:

B. "These are the standards. However, I have a list of questions for you. Let's go through these questions, because it's likely that you're entitled to more write-offs and credits than we originally thought. There are some ways we can be creative that are legal, yet unconventional. I've put a list of those together for you/the company, and let's maximize what's possible. Then I'll complete the paperwork and update all the systems to reflect this."

If you chose A, you've probably been taught that the letter of the law is the ultimate authority on matters like taxes, accounting, and legal determinations. Whatever the rule book says, you follow it, no questions and no exceptions. This is how some Mobilizers operate.

I invite you to consider Option B as what the company or your client actually wants you to do. They don't want you to simply "follow the rules"; they want you to interpret the rules and then come up with your own plan to achieve the desired result. They want you to push back and say, "There's a better way to do this. Let me show you." "I see what you're asking; however, I have a proposition for you." "Let me propose a different/better plan to get this done."

Traditional Mobilizers will follow exactly what's in the tax law and statutes. They will take the most conservative view, leaning on protection versus growth. They believe their role is to protect at all costs.

Unicorn Team Mobilizers will search for loopholes, subjective interpretations, trade-offs, and risks, and then finish the job. They recognize that being creative and curious will protect the brand more than Option A allows. (In cases that involve a strict checklist, like airline safety guidelines or a chemical recipe that requires precise formulations, of course, there is less room for interpretation.) The key takeaway here is to remember that when first asking if we could look at this another way, sometimes the answer is actually no. The shift here is about being open to asking the question at all.

Speaking from experience as someone who worked over a decade in the traditional corporate world as an executive and founded my own company almost 20 years ago, Option B Mobilizers are the leaders we're looking for. When you embody that way of thinking, doing, and leading, your value will be respected, honored, and wanted, and it will make your company more successful.

Don't be an Option A Mobilizer. Embody Option B.

THE THREE COMMITMENTS OF A MOBILIZER

Commitment #1: Emotional Awareness

It's all about you.

- Your fear of being wrong is keeping you from leading and doing what you love most.

- Notice when resentment is building up. Instead of focusing on what you're resenting, ask yourself what you're resisting and address that.

- You're a finisher. Never apologize for that.
- Structure creates freedom, and you're a great model for that.
- You're not at the bottom of the pyramid. Your influence and impact are very palpable.

Commitment #2: Relational Awareness

It's not all about you.

- Visionizers think a lot differently than you. Forgive them for it.
- Strategizers are looking to partner with you. Let them know you exist.
- Your team of mini Mobilizers are looking to you to bless their vision and strategy so they can feel accomplished.
- Collaboration is the best way to get things done right.
- You're more strategic than you give yourself credit for.

Commitment #3: Logical Awareness

It is about results. Don't let anyone tell you otherwise.

- Getting things done is still the most important thing.
- Measurements and metrics are gold.
- Systems solve the most wasteful activity.
- You own the brand experience. The customer service, the website design, the way clients feel when they arrive at the event—none of this would exist without your get-it-done energy.
- The best way to automate, implement systems like artificial intelligence, and outsource the right work is for you to own those requirements.

MOBILIZER FLASH ASSESSMENT

Are you a Mobilizer Unicorn? Take the quick quiz below to see how high you score when it comes to the Mobilizer role.

> To take the full Unicorn Leadership Type Assessment (ULTA) and get a more detailed picture of your Unicorn Leadership Type, head to **https://UnicornTeamBook.com/ULTA.**

For each statement below, rank yourself on a scale of 1 to 5:

1 Not me at all	2 Rarely me	3 Sometimes me	4 Mostly me	5 Me all the time

1. Finishing what I have to get done daily is a must.
2. The rules are there to help us get more done.
3. I hear problems and immediately start creating a checklist of how to solve them.
4. If I don't have the context, I struggle with what actually needs to get done.
5. Mess and disorganization trigger me.
6. People who value Inbox Zero are my kind of people.
7. Doing is more important than thinking or talking.
8. Data and metrics are the most reliable indicator of whether things are going well or not.
9. I get excited when I am given a list of things to do and a timeline to get it done.
10. Strategy is helpful but not necessary for me to finish what I need to do.
11. I don't care about being right, but I do care if what I'm doing is wrong.

12. If I had to choose, I would say that profit is more important than cash flow.

13. What I work on is an integral part of brand experience.

14. When faced with a pivot, I already have a backup plan prepared.

15. Details delight and impress me.

16. A checklist *is* a plan.

17. Done is better than perfect.

18. I am practical in my approach to problem-solving.

19. When I hear visionary people, I instinctively can see how to categorize their thoughts into implementation steps.

20. I thrive best in a culture of doers.

Results and Key:

Low M 20–49	Mid M 50–79	High M 80–100

Whether you scored high or low on the Mobilizer scale, you now understand how Mobilizers tick and what motivates a leader with this energy the most. Whether you're thinking about your own work or collaborating with another Mobilizer, you now understand the way Mobilizers think and how to help enable a high-fluency, low-friction flow.

MAIN LESSONS FOR MOBILIZERS

What do Mobilizer Unicorns need to know?

Don't just follow the orders handed to you—*interpret and prototype*. Consider the vision and strategy. Consider the desired future and end result that you want. Then interpret the vision and strategy to come up with your own action plan. Present this plan (your "prototype") to your team to check in and say, "Here's my interpretation. Did I get this right?" Confirm that your plan aligns. Then rock it out and get sh*t done.

Remember that your team *wants* you to push back and say, "I think there's a better way to get this done." "I hear what you're asking, but I would actually recommend a different approach, and here's why." Don't just tick things off a checklist. Propose ideas.

Focus on the spirit of the law, not the letter of the law. With every rule book, think about the intention behind the words. Be flexible, not literal.

Own your Mobilizer powers. We can win only if we have leaders like you on the team.

EVERY UNICORN CONTAINS MULTITUDES

Every Unicorn naturally gravitates toward a Visionizer, Strategizer, or Mobilizer role. But just because one of these roles is your happy place doesn't mean you're permanently exempt from the other roles.

There will be times in your career when, either by necessity or choice, you need to perform other roles—and you can. Putting on a different hat may feel like an uncomfortable stretch, but you can do it, and you'll bring your own magic to that role.

For example, there may be a moment when everyone on the Unicorn Team needs to tap into their Visionizer energy:
"Let's all put on our Visionizer hats for a moment and generate some new ideas . . ."

Or a situation where everyone needs to step into the Strategizer role:
"The current strategy isn't working, and we need to pivot. Let's take the next hour to talk through it and strategize together."

Or a time when every team member needs to unleash their inner Mobilizer:
"The deadline is tomorrow. All hands on deck—we need everyone on the team tying up loose ends and getting things done!"

You contain all the Unicorn ingredients—Visionizer, Strategizer, and Mobilizer—and can tap into each of these qualities whenever you need or want to. You want to play in your high-fluency zone the majority of the time, but you'll occasionally play in other zones too. Every Unicorn contains multitudes.

TOP TAKEAWAYS

- The Mobilizer role on the Unicorn Team is all about getting things accomplished. Nothing makes a Mobilizer happier than a job well done—with an emphasis on *done.*

- These are the makers, the implementers, the boots on the ground, and the people who break the strategy into actionable steps and get each task finished.

- While some may consider Mobilizers to be underlings whose job is to do the Visionizer or Strategizer's bidding, this is not accurate (and, frankly, offensive). A better term for Mobilizer would be *specialist*. These are Unicorns who have mastered a particular craft, whether it's cooking, coding, or customer service.

- Mobilizers have a knack for understanding what it *really* takes to make an idea happen—the cost in terms of time, energy, and money, and the trade-offs and the risks. While some Visionizers have a fantasy, head-in-the-clouds attitude, Mobilizers are grounded in reality.

- If you're a strong Mobilizer, surround yourself with Visionizer types who inspire you to play bigger and Strategizers who understand how to build insatiable demand for whatever "thing" you love to make.

You just got a peek into the minds of Visionizer, Strategizer, and Mobilizer Unicorns.

There are three variations of each for a total of nine Unicorn Leadership Types.

All nine types are powerful in different ways. All nine are invaluable assets to a team. All nine can lead, astonish, and inspire. And all have the ability to found a successful company (if they choose to) or join a team that someone else started (a great option too).

Are you ready to discover your full Unicorn Leadership Type? Next up is the full assessment to enable you to bring all the unique Unicorn energies together for success.

CHAPTER 6

ASSESSMENT: DISCOVER YOUR UNICORN LEADERSHIP TYPE

We all love a personality test, from knowing what type of Disney princess or *Star Wars* character we are to diagnostics like DiSC, StrengthsFinder, Myers-Briggs, Kolbe, and the Enneagram. Companies of all sizes use these assessments to determine individual personalities, strengths, motivators, and possibilities.

Introducing: the one assessment you haven't done yet.

It's the one that reveals which type of Unicorn you are and which types of Unicorns you need to surround yourself with to bring great ideas to life with speed and success.

WHICH TYPE OF UNICORN ARE YOU?

Your Unicorn Leadership Type is the "Da Vinci code" that reveals your top strengths, high-fluency zones, high-friction zones, the type of energy you bring to a team, and what kind of leadership you excel at.

Once you know your type, then you'll understand the role you need to own on your team and the roles you should *not* own and instead need to hand off to another Unicorn who is better skilled for that position.

Do what you excel at, not what you suck at; let other Unicorns do the same, and do this together. This simple yet powerful concept makes the difference between winning together or failing to launch.

In the previous three chapters, you did a flash assessment on the main roles of Visionizer, Strategizer, and Mobilizer. Now you have the opportunity to take that to a deeper, more integrated, and more powerful level when you learn the full scope of where your Unicorn Energy is best suited, actual examples of scenarios you will face, and how to apply and use your unique Unicorn lens to bring winning ideas to the world with others who rally around them.

There are nine Unicorn Leadership Types, and we've taken the questions (and more) from the flash assessments in Chapters 3 through 5 into an innovative and integrated diagnostic called the Unicorn Leadership Type Assessment (ULTA). It produces an individualized, custom report for you so that you can take what you've read in this book to the next level in a practical way based on 20-plus years of research on what makes brands win and innovate.

Take the full Unicorn Leadership Type Assessment (ULTA) online.
Your custom, unique report will be e-mailed to you.
https://UnicornTeamBook.com/ULTA

THE NINE UNICORN LEADERSHIP TYPES

There are nine Unicorn Leadership Types, which take into account the highest and most optimal energies you possess as an influential leader wanting to bring innovative, next-level ideas to the world.

Each type is equally powerful, albeit in different ways.

Visionizing Strategizer (VS) **The Legend**	Strategizing Visionizer (SV) **The Mastermind**	Mobilizing Visionizer (MV) **The Creator**
Visionizing Mobilizer (VM) **The Innovator**	Strategizing Mobilizer (SM) **The Chief**	Mobilizing Strategizer (MS) **The Guide**
Pure Visionizer (VV) **The Guru**	Pure Strategizer (SS) **The Sage**	Pure Mobilizer (MM) **The Specialist**

TWO LETTERS = YOUR TOP STRENGTHS

Your Unicorn Leadership Type has two letters. The first letter indicates your primary strength; the second is your secondary strength. Your primary strength infuses energy into your secondary strength, which motivates you to bring your best effort to big work.

For example, if you are a Visionizing Mobilizer (VM), this means:

You scored highest in the V type.

You bring visionary energy into the room. You dazzle people with your big ideas. When people are around you, they can't help but think futuristically and see bigger possibilities.

You scored second highest in the M type.

You have a natural ability to buckle down and get things done—perhaps you have a background in project management, or you're highly skilled in a specialized craft like writing, design, or architecture, and you have a remarkable ability to close loops and bring deliverables over the finish line.

What it also means is that your highest score (in this case, Visionizer) influences your second score (in this case, Mobilizer) very deeply. You're not motivated to bring a new idea to life with-

*out it proving to really cure a huge, present problem that you
have had the vision to fix and that no one has successfully done
already, at least by your standards. You like making things, but
won't love it unless it's practical and is what no one else is doing
well. This is what makes the "making" worth it for you.*

*The nickname for a VM is "the Innovator," and that's ap-
ropos, because this leader is someone who takes a wild, dreamy
idea and turns it into something that's approachable and desir-
able at the same time.*

One of my favorite examples of the Innovator is the CEO and
co-founder of the Canva app, Melanie Perkins. When she was a
part-time tutor for fellow graphic design specialists in college, she
saw the burden of needing advanced technical skills in proprietary
graphic software as a huge friction point for both freelancers and
the people that hired them. Her idea was to make a design platform
where no technical experience was required—to democratize design from logos to printed material to websites at the individual
level. By the time she was 32 years old, Perkins had taken Canva
into an elite, billion-dollar-valued company that happens to also
be one of the highest-valued woman-founded and -led start-ups
ever, from California to China. Canva's headquarters are in tiny
Perth, Australia—which shows that innovations like hers can be
founded from anywhere in the world.[1]

Regardless of what your unique Unicorn Leadership Type is,
you knowing what energizes you and makes you tick during both
high times and low times is the most important thing, since it also
allows you to surround yourself with an optimal mix of other Unicorn Types to achieve your big goals.

SURROUND YOURSELF WITH DIFFERENT TYPES

When building a team, look for people who have Unicorn Leadership Types that are different from yours, because these people
have strengths that you lack. You want a diverse team, not a
homogenous one.

For example, if you're a Visionizing Mobilizer (VM) and founder of a company, you might want to hire a Mobilizing Strategizer (MS) as your assistant. This person has a strong dose of Mobilizer energy (which means they will get things done with a high standard of excellence), plus the Strategizer energy that you don't have (and that your company needs). Over time, this MS Unicorn could graduate from assistant to director of marketing and sales, a position where they can flex their Strategizer strengths even more.

A successful Unicorn Team has a blend of different Unicorn Leadership Types.

When you're considering joining a team as an employee, contractor, freelancer, or consultant, first, investigate to figure out which types are currently missing and if there's a gap you can fill.

For instance, let's say you're speaking to a potential client. Based on what they tell you, you get the sense that this person is a Pure Mobilizer (MM) who loves to get things done, but they're stuck in the administrative weeds, doing busywork, and not seeing the bigger picture. They're so focused on completing their daily checklist that they're missing big opportunities that are right in front of them. You, a Visionizing Strategizer (VS), could show this client how to 10x their vision and play bigger.

Pay attention during conversations with potential employers, clients, partners, or investors. How do they describe their strengths and gifts (high-fluency zones)? What irritates them to no end (high-friction zones)? What type of Unicorn do you suspect they might be?

Ask them to take the Unicorn Leadership Type Assessment (ULTA) and have their team do it too. The results will reveal what type of energy is already present on the team, what's missing, and if there's a gap you could fill.

Let's meet each one of the nine types.

VISIONIZING STRATEGIZER (VS): THE LEGEND

If you're a Visionizing Strategizer, you're a futuristic thinker *and* you see the path to get to the future state you envision.

VS Unicorns are passionate about what they believe in, have a clear view of what needs to happen to travel into their desired future, know the market they want to win in, and excel in product sales and marketing. As a Visionizing Strategizer, you almost can't *help* but influence the world in a significant way.

VS types come up with big ideas that radically change their company, community, or society. Their ideas lead to massive, groundbreaking change—not itty-bitty, incremental change that makes things one percent better than before. The wheel, the light bulb, the printing press, the Internet. The concept of democracy, feminism, or human rights. The scientific method. The theory of evolution. When a VS Unicorn generates a big idea (and rallies the right team around it), the world as we know it will never be the same.

But here's what you lack: mobilization. You're incredible at starting. Finishing? Not so much. You may have a million open tabs on your Internet browser or a half-written book manuscript that could be the next legendary bestseller, and I'm willing to bet you have tons of open loops in your head. That's why you need Mobilizers on your team to execute your strategy with the excellence that you expect. You have high standards (some might even say unrealistically high) and need strong Mobilizers who can rise to the occasion.

One example of the Visionizing Strategizer type: Steve Jobs. He couldn't create a brand like Apple all by himself, and that's why he enrolled programmer Steve Wozniak, a Pure Mobilizer, to create the first beta product called the Apple-1. Legend has it that Jobs sold his Volkswagen bus and Wozniak sold his HP-65 calculator to finance the first Apple-1 home computer. To grow the Apple empire to its fullest potential, Jobs knew he needed to get the best Mobilizers to build upon this first idea.

Jobs believed with his entire being that people wanted more power at their fingertips through personal computing. And he believed with his entire being that people wanted to be closer to the people they cared about, which is why he envisioned the iPhone. He changed the music industry with the iPod and iTunes. As Jobs exemplifies, VS energy is disruptive and thrilling. It doesn't make things a little bit better. It changes the whole game. What a VS creates becomes legend.

VISIONIZING MOBILIZER (VM): THE INNOVATOR

This Unicorn Type is a dreamer first and doer second. They are a big-picture thinker who cares about the little details. The futurist who can see a brighter tomorrow, with a practical, grounded approach to making things happen.

If you're a Visionizing Mobilizer, you naturally inspire people to believe in a new, better, and reimagined future. You understand how to tap into people's imaginations, fantasies, and desires, and your greatest gift is creating an iconic brand no one can ignore, like Melanie Perkins is doing with the Canva app.

Walt Disney exemplifies the Visionizing Mobilizer. He started out as an animator, which, until his death, was his true passion and love. But he had bigger dreams that he couldn't ignore. Tired of being on the brink of bankruptcy trying to produce cartoons in his cramped design studio, he imagined a place where people's love of cartoons and characters could come to life. That became, of course, what we all know as Disneyland and the Disney brand, recently valued at $49.5 billion.[2] Every person who works at Disney is called a "cast member," and the engineers who design their parks, pictures, and everything in between are "Imagineers." At Disney, nobody is merely an employee. Everyone plays a bigger role in this universe of magic and joy. Very on-brand for the Innovator (VM).

"If you can dream it, you can do it," Walt Disney is most famously attributed as saying. I can't think of a better way to summarize the Visionizing Mobilizer's philosophy on life and work.

If you're a Visionizing Mobilizer, you may—like Walt Disney—start out your career in a Mobilizer capacity, honing your professional skills and becoming the best at whatever you do, whether it is drawing, writing, coding, baking, or accounting. But then, at a certain point in your journey, you shift gears and step into your Visionizer era. You lean more heavily into your V and envision a bigger impact you want to make on society. This is how a VM Unicorn's career trajectory often (though not always) plays out.

Who do you need on your team? A strong Strategizer. This person could be an SV, SM, or SS Unicorn Leadership Type—anyone who brings Strategizer energy to the table. This is the person who will map out the strategy to bring your idea to life. If you're a company founder, this Strategizer will likely become your right-hand Unicorn and second-in-command. For example, Walt Disney's right-hand Unicorn and top Strategizer was Marty Sklar.[3] If you're a Walt, who is your Marty? Rather than asking, "How can I bring my vision to life?" ask, "Who is the Strategizer who can help me bring this idea to the world?"

PURE VISIONIZER (VV): THE GURU

If your Unicorn Leadership Type is Pure Visionizer, you understand deep human desires—the desire to be loved, to be appreciated, to have security, to belong—in a way that most people don't. You have a natural talent for gathering people together around a shared vision. A healthy VV Unicorn is a maverick, a revolutionary, a rebel *with* a cause. An unhealthy or emotionally dysregulated VV might end up as a cult leader and the lead character in a Netflix documentary that goes viral for reasons they never imagined.

VV Unicorns excel at communicating what they believe with authority and get others to buy into their philosophy by being consistent and persistent in those beliefs. VVs see the long game. They are the purists of the futurists. They speak in a brand language that feels exciting and sometimes foreign. This is the type of Unicorn who might coin a new term or concept that nobody "gets" at first, but later becomes embedded in our collective vocabularies. If you're VV, you're extremely values driven and evoke a power guided by something larger than yourself. Some find you mesmerizing; others say you're intimidating. The Guru is a respected leader indeed, especially for people who seek answers outside themselves frequently.

Pure Visionizers have the most success getting people to follow them compared to the other Unicorn Leadership Types. VVs are charismatic and speak with great conviction, leading other people to believe they have all the answers. But they don't. They need help from other Unicorns on the team just as much as anybody else.

VVs typically don't shy away from the spotlight. They want their ideas to be heard and make themselves available to be found. They want to partner with Strategizer and Mobilizer Unicorns because they need to be surrounded with the energies, strengths, and skills that they sorely lack.

Sir Richard Branson is a Pure Visionizer Unicorn. As the extroverted founder of the Virgin Group, he lives by his highest value—fun—full out. You can feel the fun in all of his business ventures. When you fly on a Virgin Atlantic airplane, you're ushered on board with groovy purple lighting and music that makes you feel like you're heading to an after-party in Ibiza. Life-sucking beige and depressing pretzels? Nowhere to be found.

Branson started Virgin Records as a small mail-order record retailer and built a multibillion-dollar empire (Branson's net worth is estimated to be around $2.6 billion[4]) by adopting a revolutionary approach to business: putting opportunity in the people's hands by having them fully contribute using their Unicorn skills, instead of him dictating what those should be. Branson understands that when his employees' needs are met on a human level, his businesses will soar. He attracts Unicorns who bring his participative style of leadership into each business that's born from his original idea. He is undeterred by failure—in fact, he believes failure is the foundation of success—and his legions of admirers follow wherever he leads. They believe that if he believes it, they can believe it too.

Virgin is one of the world's most irresistible brands, and it has licensed its valuable brand equity into diverse sectors from travel to telecommunications, health to banking, and music to leisure. While all Visionizer Unicorns think big, Pure V Unicorns think on a galactic level. Not just world domination—we're talking about multiple solar systems.

STRATEGIZING VISIONIZER (SV): THE MASTERMIND

The Strategizing Visionizer, or the Mastermind, sees all the plays that need to happen to win the game before anyone else does.

If you ever watched *The Queen's Gambit*, you might remember how chess prodigy Beth Harmon (played by Anya Taylor-Joy) visualizes chess pieces moving on the ceiling, seeing each move that is required to crush her opponent. Even if it's going to require more than 50 moves to get there, she sees the path to the endgame. If her opponent does something unexpected and the game shifts in a new direction, that's not an issue for Harmon, because she sees all the countermoves she can make to reach her desired outcome: she understands that strategies have to be fluid and sometimes a dramatic pivot is required. What's more, she has a vision: to become the first woman to defeat all her male opponents at the World Chess Championship. *Checkmate.*

That right there? That's a Strategizing Visionizer in their highest form of energetic expression and leadership.

SV types excel in brand, marketing, and sales positions and are extremely good at building desire for a product or service and creating demand for new ideas. Naturally gifted at seeing where the market is going, they know how to create intrigue, hunger, and thirst for whatever they're selling.

SV Unicorns know how to create a tipping point that completely focuses attention on the brands they create or manage. They enjoy negotiation, understand the deal points, and are looking for not just the short-term win (although they do love the short-term win) but understand how to trade off what matters for long-term dominance. They are always on the lookout for Mobilizer types to take their strategies and execute all the details.

Kris Jenner, Rich Paul, and Benny Medina are SV Unicorn Types. Jenner has been the mastermind behind the Kardashian/Jenner empires; Paul is the founder of Klutch Sports, where he is the sports agent for LeBron James and navigates all of his deals and opportunities; and Medina has managed the careers of Jennifer Lopez, Mariah Carey, and Usher.

Another SV Unicorn? Taylor Swift, genius songwriter and extremely strategic thinker. She even has a song titled "Mastermind," where she explains the intricate machinations that go into getting exactly what she desires and how she engineers situations that on the surface seem like fate, luck, or serendipity. There's a reason why Swift is one of the world's top-10 highest-paid entertainers,[5] with a net worth that has surpassed $1.1 billion.[6] She has fully embraced her SV superpowers and doesn't shy away from using them.

The Strategizing Visionizer type isn't just reserved for entertainment or sports. This Unicorn is typically a go-to-market ideas expert. A mastermind who knows how to reach the masses. This is the Unicorn Type that I fall into, as someone who brings new brands to market as a profession.

STRATEGIZING MOBILIZER (SM): THE CHIEF

If you're a Strategizing Mobilizer, you see what needs to be done to reach the desired destination, and you understand how to build systems to get things done quickly, efficiently, and consistently. The SM Unicorn Leadership Type excels at managing people, processes, and technologies. You take what (to others) may seem like a chaotic juggling act and streamline it into a clear and focused plan of action.

SM Unicorns look at past data, find patterns, and create a strategy for success that's based on facts, not feelings. SMs delight in establishing standards and principles to help their team win. Think: brand voice guidelines, communication standards, standard operating procedures, best practices, five-year plan. Whichever team member practically salivates over these documents is, more than likely, a Strategizing Mobilizer.

SM Unicorns rally the right people through their ability to critically think, act, and do—and make it clear that each person must fully own their role on the team. Pure Mobilizer Unicorns (the strongest Mobilizers in the stables) love to work for Strategic Mobilizers, because they get clear direction. Pure Vs love to work with Strategic Mobilizers too, because they know the SM leader can be trusted to think ten steps ahead, not just one or two.

Ray Dalio is a Strategizing Mobilizer. As the founder of Bridge-water Associates, he built the largest hedge fund in the world. It all started in his two-bedroom apartment over 40 years ago, and from these humble beginnings he became one of the wealthiest people in the world. Dalio's net worth: $15 billion.[7]

Dalio's strategy: make his company a meritocracy, which Merriam-Webster defines as "a system, organization, or society in which people are chosen and moved into positions of success, power, and influence on the basis of their demonstrated abilities and merit."

At Bridgewater Associates, Dalio made sure each team member understood the outcomes they were being tasked to achieve with crystal clarity in a crystal-clear manner. He laid out standards of excellence. Those who met or exceeded these standards got rewarded. Those who fell short did not. And he was mindful to place people into roles where they could excel, noting in his *New York Times* best-selling book *Principles*, "The greatest gift you can give someone is the power to be successful."

Three of my favorite principles from Dalio's book, which is packed with other gems I reference quite frequently:

> "It's more important to do big things well than to do the small things perfectly."

> "To be effective you must not let your need to be right be more important than your need to find out what's true."

> "Create a culture in which it is okay to make mistakes and unacceptable not to learn from them."[8]

If you're a Strategizing Mobilizer, take a cue from Chief Dalio. Make sure that your fellow Unicorns understand what success looks like, and how they can achieve it individually and together.

PURE STRATEGIZER (SS): THE SAGE

If you're a Pure Strategizer, you are the resident psychologist of the Unicorn Team. You understand how people behave and what motivates them, and you excel in creating the strategies and triggers that evoke action and change.

Strategy is widely used in various contexts, but this definition by UCLA professor emeritus Richard Rumelt, author of *Good Strategy Bad Strategy*, is one that really supports how the SS type leads: "Strategy is how you overcome the obstacles that stand between where you are and what you want to achieve."[9] Ultimately, the SS type is the ultimate problem-solver, very interested in the root cause and how to fix it for good.

An SS Unicorn is an opportunist, a student of humans, and has no qualms with being contrarian, because what they really want is a better outcome. They love to figure things out and be listened to, because they have the purest instincts of the leadership types. Like all Pure types, these Unicorns are usually legends of the industries they work in, like advertising, technology, manufacturing, and politics. Because they care deeply about working on the right hard things, they will preach and teach until they're blue in the face about why a road map will work, or how you will fall off a cliff if you don't change course. This type is high in the it's-a-good-idea-to-listen-to-me department.

David Ogilvy was a Pure Strategizer Unicorn. Ogilvy is known as the "Father of Advertising." In 1962, *Time* magazine called David Ogilvy "the most sought-after wizard in today's advertising industry."[10] What's remarkable about Ogilvy's strategic prowess is that no matter how much time and technology has passed and progressed, his frameworks for brand campaigns are still relevant and used today.

Artificial intelligence models his strategies to create modern marketing messages—ones that support Ogilvy's belief that good marketing is the science of communicating the right context to the right person without it feeling like they were marketed to at all. He's an absolute strategic god in most professional circles, the ultimate sage they seek in how to influence others. Something I'm sure he would have liked to have known very much, because as an SS type, he was trusted to know the truth because he was obsessed with what peoples' truths really are.

MOBILIZING VISIONIZER (MV): THE CREATOR

The Mobilizing Visionizer is a Unicorn with a specific skill—a craft, talent, or art—usually one they've honed through 10,000 hours of practice. If you're an MV Unicorn, you make things that people want, whether it's exquisite jewelry, gourmet meals, time-saving apps, or sought-after professional services. You're a doer first, dreamer second, and you've got a knack for delivering your "thing" to the marketplace in a manner that's exciting, new, and fresh.

Martha Stewart is an MV Unicorn. She was one of the original influencers way before social media existed and didn't start her career as a home and lifestyle expert until she was 50 years old. Prior to that, she was a stockbroker on Wall Street and, in her spare time, enjoyed making recipes from scratch, DIY home improvements, and entertaining guests in her Connecticut home. She honed her skills for decades, gradually building her empire by publishing her recipes and appearing on television to share home tips and lifestyle advice. Gradually she developed a full-fledged media company and became a billionaire.

Mobilizing Visionizers aren't Pure M. They also have visionary energy and big, ambitious ideas. Never content with playing small, they hunger for more—more impact, more visibility, and in Stewart's case, more money (a fact that got her into a wee bit of legal trouble, leading to a five-month stint in a minimum-security prison,[11] where she used her time to reconnect with hobbies such as ceramics and crocheting). But while they have visionary ideas, make no mistake, they're Mobilizers first. This type of Unicorn loves to get tasks done with the highest level of excellence.

That's why, even though she's got a 10-figure net worth, Stewart still loves to roll up her sleeves and dig in the dirt with her teammates. For many years, even after becoming a billionaire, every morning she woke up early to meet her team at her 152-acre Cantitoe Corners estate with specific instructions and checklists of what the property needed.[12] Then she'd go into New York City to meet with her production and new-product teams to discuss what they were launching next and what improvements they had to make. She's a leader with a clear, exacting vision of what she wants.

If you're a Mobilizing Visionizer, you need to be on the look-out for Strategizer Unicorns who can round out your team and bring the strategic magic that you lack. An SV, SM, or SS Unicorn would be a particularly good addition to your team.

Your danger zone: unrealistically high standards. You take enormous pride in your work, you're masterful at whatever you do, and you need to remember that other Unicorns on your team may not be able to "do the thing" as expertly or as beautifully as you do—at least, not right away. For instance, say you're a Michelin-star-winning chef and you're distressed because nobody on your team can sear the Wagyu beef the way that only *you* can. You think you're the only one who cares enough, the only one who can handle the job that needs to be done. This is not necessarily true. Surround yourself with baby Unicorns who want you to mentor them—some might be Unicorns with strong Mobilizer strengths, like you—who are eager to grow. You can teach your methods to others and duplicate yourself, which will allow you to scale your vision and reach millions, not just dozens. Your natural creation energy will attract the others you need.

MOBILIZING STRATEGIZER (MS): THE GUIDE

The Mobilizing Strategizer's superpower is taking complex data, science, and frameworks and laying out the information in an approachable way that everyone can understand. They are respected as model supervisors, people who can be trusted to "check the work," and get tremendous fulfillment from mentoring, teaching, and guiding. "Here, let me show you how it works . . ." is their personal slogan.

The Mobilizing Strategizer is the professor of the Unicorn Innovation Model. The class (aka team of fellows) gets a front-row seat to not just how, but why their piece of the work makes the big idea happen. If you're an MS Unicorn, you're the internal thought leader whom people trust for accurate interpretations and guidance. Because you understand how the machine actually works, your energy emits "I get it, and I get you." The MS Unicorn might seem a little too strict and rule abiding for some of the team, but everyone appreciates that they know the playbook by heart when it's go time or when a problem erupts.

Emma Watson, known for playing Hermione Granger in the *Harry Potter* movies, is an example of an MS Unicorn. Smart, bookish, and studious, this graduate of Brown and Oxford is an activist who fights for gender equality and for every girl's right to get an education, and was named a UN Goodwill Ambassador.[13] In addition to championing the rights of women and girls, she's an outspoken environmentalist and led a panel on climate change with Greta Thunberg.[14] More than a typical Hollywood starlet, she's an activist, humanitarian, and intellectual leader. And let's be honest: without Hermione, Harry and Ron would have been in big trouble too many times to count. Shows how perfect the casting of Watson was in her breakout role, fully as her MS Unicorn type.

The MS Unicorn is the person with specialized skills that have been honed through tremendous effort. They have what seems like Ph.D.-level knowledge in their area of expertise, but aren't narrow-minded. They see the bigger picture of how the world works and protect the players involved. Visionizers should seek out MS types when data matters a lot to getting funded, gaining clients, and seeking accreditation or approval from a governing body.

PURE MOBILIZER (MM): THE SPECIALIST

The Pure Mobilizer's power skill is closing loops faster than a speeding bullet. They are the subject matter experts, coders, administrative assistants, accountants, and analysts. They are the cooks on the line who work for the Michelin-star chef whose name is on the front door of the restaurant. But don't mistake the Pure Mobilizer Unicorn for being insignificant. When a Pure Mobilizer Unicorn is in a leadership position and has a specific goal to hit, you can consider the job done.

Pure M Unicorns operate on accomplishment energy. They love to cross the finish line, and they're impeccably thorough.

There are no sloppy loose ends with a Pure M. An unfinished checklist is their personal hell.

They are masters of their craft, usually a sole craft in relation to the bigger picture. This type is high in the let-me-do-what-I'm-good-at department.

MMs aren't usually the person you see on the cover of *Forbes*. They like to keep things simple and organized, and that's how they win. But we all know a Pure M and how valuable they are. They will put in the reps, show up for practice, play full out in the game, and also relish winning big. Others in the company gush, "I'd love to have her on my team." They're known to be "clutch" in winning situations. If you want to bring that idea to life, go find the clutch players.

Toni Kukoč is an MM Unicorn. You may not know his name, but you'll recognize other people on his team—Michael Jordan, Scottie Pippen, Dennis Rodman, Horace Grant, and Steve Kerr. Real basketball fans know Toni as the "Croatian Sensation," a European prodigy who was a talent way before his time. He is also one of the most legendary NBA Sixth Man of the Year players of all time and the third-leading scorer in the Chicago Bulls' 1990s glory years and their famous three-peat world championships.[15] His contributions got him inducted into the Basketball Hall of Fame in 2021. As you can see, his statistics back up his excellence, and being the most famous person isn't what mattered most. He has the same rings as his more famous colleagues. When you want to rally a team to make world-changing ideas (and championships) happen, we all need specialists like Toni.

If you're an MM Unicorn, the best move you can make is to surround yourself with Visionizer Unicorns (VS, VM, or VV) and Strategizer Unicorns (SV, SM, and SS) who will bring the strengths and skills that you lack.

HOW TO USE YOUR UNICORN
LEADERSHIP TYPE RESULTS

When you get your results, review your high-fluency zones and your high-friction zones. What do you excel at? What do you suck at? What causes friction in your workday—frustration, tension, or a lethargic feeling?

You have strengths as well as gaps, and these gaps indicate which types of Unicorns you need to bring onto your team to get the big work done. Leaders solve for the gap, not for what's already working.

As you evaluate your current team, you might see that you have a lot of strengths in the Strategizer area, but there aren't enough strong Mobilizers. This explains why you have excellent plans that are highly likely to work but are struggling to gain traction. You need to find Mobilizers who can tackle individual tasks and get it done.

If you already have a team, have them take the assessment too. It will illuminate their strengths and gaps so you can see how they work with your type and with each other. Remember, this is useful for anyone who helps you, including fractional staff, consultants, freelancers—even family and friends if they're helping you bring your ideas to life.

WHO DO YOU NEED?

Let's play with a few examples to demonstrate who you need, depending on your Unicorn Leadership Type.

In these hypothetical examples, we're assuming that you are the idea creator. Meaning, you're the one who has a great idea and wants to get it out there. These examples show who you need to enroll onto your team. However, these examples work in reverse too. If you are in a supporting role and you're looking for a big idea to be a part of, these examples will help you see where you fit in and how to be the greatest asset to the team that you want to join.

Example: Bringing a new SaaS app to market

Your Unicorn Leadership Type is Visionizing Mobilizer (VM). This means your top strength is Visionizer followed by Mobilizer.

So, who do you need on your team to bring a new software as a service (SaaS) app to market? You need a Strategizer Unicorn (they might be an SV, SM, or SS type) who understands how to build massive demand for this new app and make millions of people want it.

Bring a Strategizer onto your team to develop a go-to-market plan for the SaaS product. You'll also want to rally Mobilizers with specialized skills that you don't have (coding, customer service, copywriting, etc.) to bring this idea to life.

Walt Disney was an ubersuccessful VM Unicorn.

What would Walt do to win in the first 100 days?

Example: Creating a new physical product

Your Unicorn Leadership Type is Pure Mobilizer (MM). You have an idea for a new product. It's a hat with silk on the interior lining that smooths frizzy hair while you wear it. Put on the hat, and when you pop it off, your hair is shiny and soft! You created an initial version of this product, and your friends love it. You could see this company going bigger, but you're not sure how to get there.

You're a powerful Mobilizer but wobbly in the Visionizer and Strategizer areas. You need a strong Visionizer (this person could be a VS, VM, or VV Unicorn) who pushes you to think bigger than you have ever dared and to see future possibilities that you never even remotely considered—probably a mentor or coach who has achieved similar things in your industry. And you need someone to express this vision in language that other people can understand and map out the big plays to make it all happen—a Strategizer's area of strength. Find a colleague with the SV, SM, or SS leadership type.

Because you're an ultrastrong Mobilizer, you're most likely obsessed with product design. Making, doing, getting projects done, that's your happy place. It's easy for you to hyperfocus on the craft that you love so much. Left to your own devices, you may get stubbornly fixated on the details and on perfecting the product. Your challenge is to stay connected to the bigger picture, and you need Visionizer and Strategizer Unicorns on your team to do that.

Basketball legend Toni Kukoč is an MM Unicorn.

What would Toni do to win in the first 100 days?

Example: Starting a new service-based business

Your Unicorn Leadership Type is Strategizing Visionizer (SV). You want to start a new business as a wellness coach. You can envision offering one-on-one coaching sessions as well as group programs and retreats.

As an SV, you have strong Strategizer abilities and know how to turn a vision into reality. You also understand how to build demand for an offer. Your main gap is mobilizing. Getting things finished is not your strong suit.

But remember: it's not your job to *do* every task; it's your job to *find* the right people to do it. Find a Mobilizer Unicorn (they might be MV, MS, or MM) to help you get organized, get moving, and get projects over the finish line. Their energy is exactly what you need to shift from dreaming to doing.

Kris Jenner is an example of an SV Unicorn.

What would Kris do to win in the first 100 days?

Example: Developing a fresh advertising campaign for an existing product

Your Unicorn Leadership Type is Pure Visionizer (VV). You lead the marketing department at a beloved breakfast cereal company. You've been asked to come up with a new advertising campaign for an existing cereal that's been around for decades. The company wants to breathe new life into this dusty, old cereal and get everyone talking about it.

Because you're a VV, you have genius ideas to make this ad campaign *epic*. I'm talking "'Think Different' Macintosh advertisement in 1984" level of epic. However, there are gaps you need to address. First, you need Strategizer energy on your team. Look for an SM or MS type who can organize your big, ethereal ideas into an actual campaign. You also need Mobilizers (MV, MS, or

MM) who can turn the strategy into a checklist and get each action item done. Remember, as a Pure V Unicorn, your job isn't to implement and execute (you're terrible at this, and we need your idea, so own it!). Your job is to communicate your vision to your fellow Unicorns and get them excited to be part of something big.

Richard Branson is a Pure V Unicorn.

What would Richard do to win in the first 100 days?

TOP TAKEAWAYS

- There are nine Unicorn Leadership Types, and you're one of them.

- Your Unicorn Leadership Type indicates the role that you're best suited to play on your team and where your energy will produce your best work. This is where your gifts will be utilized best and where you'll shine.

- When you get to perform the role that you're best suited for, you will crush it. You'll click into your high-fluency zone and produce the best work you've ever done.

- When every member of the team gets to operate from their high-fluency zone, the team is unstoppable.

- You did the ULTA and discovered your unique Unicorn Leadership Type. Take a look at your personalized report. What are the gaps you can address by bringing other Unicorns onto your team?

SEND OUT THE UNICORN SIGNAL AND LET THEM KNOW YOU'RE LOOKING FOR THEM TOO

Now that you know your ULT-imate role on a Unicorn Team, share it with the world.

Post your Unicorn Leadership Type on social media and tag #UnicornTeam when you do.

Show your colleagues what kind of Unicorn you are. Invite them to do the ULTA too, and compare results.

WHAT'S NEXT

Now that you've learned all about Unicorn Leadership Types and are hyped up about it, it's time to embody and activate them and to solve the biggest obstacles that get in the way of your big ideas coming to life in the way you envisioned.

Misunderstandings and misinterpretations are the enemies of a Unicorn Team's flow state. The good news is, we're fixing that in the next track: Communicate.

PART III

COMMUNICATE TRACK

The Unicorn Innovation Model

	VSM Process	● VISIONIZE			▲ STRATEGIZE			■ MOBILIZE			
IDEATION **NEW** Launch brand-new initiatives	**Navigate** How we make decisions together and choose the right idea to pursue	Ideastorm			DOIT			BEIT			**ITERATION** **BAU** Improve existing initiatives
	Motivate How we lead and the energy we bring to the team	V Types			S Types			M Types			
		VV	VS	VM	SV	SS	SM	MV	MS	MM	
	Communicate How we get aligned, work on the right priorities together, and get things done at warp speed	Brandcast			Stratagem			Prototype			
		< ~ ~ ~ UNICORN ENERGY ~ ~ ~ >									

> "I've rallied the right people around my idea. I've got my Unicorn Team!"
>
> "What is the best process to work together as a team? I want us to work together harmoniously and turn great ideas into reality. But . . . how?"
>
> "Human beings are complex, team dynamics can be tricky, many teams get stuck and fail to reach their potential. I don't want that to happen to us."
>
> "How do we communicate effectively, work together successfully, and get maximum results?"

In Part I: Navigate, you learned how to evaluate an idea to determine if it's worth pursuing.

In Part II: Motivate, you learned about the Visionizer, Strategizer, and Mobilizer roles and the nine Unicorn Leadership Types. You did the Unicorn Leadership Type Assessment (ULTA) to find out your type and which Unicorns you need to recruit to fill in the gaps for the strengths that you lack.

But once you've got your people, how should you actually *work* together? What's the secret to collaborating smoothly, staying focused on the right priorities, and getting big things done together without driving each other up the wall? How can you ensure that whatever needs to get done actually gets done . . . and gets done right?

Welcome to Part III: Communicate.

Here you'll learn how to work with your Unicorn Team successfully. These three magical tools will seal the Unicorn Team's fate in getting your next big idea to the world with speed and success:

The Brandcast—How the Visionizer communicates their big idea to the team, using values and stories to incite emotion and get people rallying around the cause.

The Stratagem Session—How the Strategizer works with the team to determine which strategic initiatives to do right now, which to postpone until later, and which are a hard pass.

The Prototyping Process—How the Mobilizer interprets the vision and strategy to produce a quick rough draft and shows their work to confirm "Is this what you mean?"

I've also added an additional tool that helps you check in regularly with members of your Unicorn Team:

The Performance Pulse—How managers (and other leaders) can do a monthly performance check-in to help each Unicorn to see if they're on track. The Performance Pulse also shows how their contributions are leading to meaningful outcomes, and how their individual values align with the company values.

Armed with these communication tools, your team will shift from being jumbled, chaotic, and underwhelming to being *excellent*. The team will become so aligned and well tuned, it'll be like watching elite athletes at the Super Bowl in overtime or the legendary Blue Angels (an elite U.S. Navy air squadron) flying in a perfect diamond formation at 400 miles an hour.

Here are the tools you need to communicate clearly and get big things done, the Unicorn Way.

CHAPTER 7

THE BRANDCAST

Visionizers are all about innovation, disruption, revolution, and seeing the future before others do.

On a Unicorn Team, the person performing the Visionizer role (which might be you, or not, depending on your Unicorn Leadership Type) comes up with the big idea for the brand.

It's the person who says, "Human beings can live on Mars," "I envision a future in which diabetes no longer exists," "We can compose music that cures depression," "No more graveyards. Instead, your ancestors bloom as flowers and grow into trees, bringing clean air to communities." Visionizers become famous for bringing the future to the now.

However, Visionizers often struggle to explain their big ideas clearly. When they try to explain their vision to others, they often ramble, use esoteric or ambiguous language, and struggle to find the right words—after all, how do you describe something that literally doesn't exist yet? Or something so big, bold, and audacious that most people don't believe it's even possible?

When speaking to colleagues, Visionizers are often met with raised eyebrows and confused expressions. The team wants to understand, but the words just aren't clicking.

Fortunately, there's a tool to help Visionizers communicate their vision to Strategizers and Mobilizers clearly, enabling the team to integrate, deploy, and bring the idea to market with velocity. I call this tool the Brandcast.

The Unicorn Innovation Model

VSM Process	● VISIONIZE			▲ STRATEGIZE			■ MOBILIZE			
Navigate How we make decisions together and choose the right idea to pursue	Ideastorm			DOIT			BEIT			
Motivate How we lead and the energy we bring to the team	V Types			S Types			M Types			
	VV	VS	VM	SV	SS	SM	MV	MS	MM	
Communicate How we get aligned, work on the right priorities together, and get things done at warp speed	Brandcast			Stratagem			Prototype			
< ~ ~ ~ UNICORN ENERGY ~ ~ ~ >										

IDEATION NEW Launch brand-new initiatives

ITERATION BAU Improve existing initiatives

A GUIDE TO BRANDCASTING

Brands shape culture, and Visionizers understand this so deeply that their passion and futuristic commentary gets people excited to be part of something bigger. In the Unicorn Innovation Model, Brandcasting is the Visionizer's number-one communication tool. If you're playing the Visionizer role on your team, learn this tool like the back of your hand and use it often.

The Brandcast is the Visionizer's broadcasting message to all stakeholders, internal and external. It's the broadcast that paints a vivid picture of the big idea—*why* we're doing this, *who* we're help-ing, and *what* the future is going to look like. It's important to note that the Brandcast does not communicate *how* we're going to get there. Figuring out how comes later, in the part of the process that the Strategizer and Mobilizer Unicorns on the team own.

Most people have heard the claim from author Simon Sinek in his viral TED talk "How Great Leaders Inspire Action":

"People don't buy what you do; people buy why you do it."[1]

Sinek isn't just talking about the customers who make buying decisions. He's also talking about your own team "buying into" where you're going so that people want what your brand is building, even when faced with pressure, friction, and noise. Brandcasting creates a culture of inspired action.

BRANDCAST COMPONENTS

A Brandcast includes three components, which are:

Values	Stories	Outcomes

1) Values

You have a big idea that you want to bring into the world. It will require tremendous energy, effort, and creativity to make it happen. Understandably, your team wants to know "Why are we doing this?"

As the Visionizer, you must communicate *why*, which means communicating the core values of your brand culture.

Values are what great companies base their decisions on. Values are a commitment to *being* something, not just doing various tasks. Values aren't nouns; they are verbs. They are behaviors, not thoughts.

Defining your core values the Unicorn Team way allows you to get to the root of why this idea matters at all.

To find out what your brand's core values are, you need to get inside of the Visionizer's brain. And yes, it starts with the actual person with the idea in the first place. If you don't start there, then you'll create a Brandcast that doesn't have a strong foundation.

Values start with the founder, and they are evolved by the Vision-izers that follow.

When you see the term *core values*, you may think about a string of inspiring words like *generosity, trustworthiness, compassion,* or *excellence.* Are these values? Sure. However, values are more than one-word qualities that you want to embody as a team. That's why I propose a different approach to uncovering core values. It's an equation that looks like this:

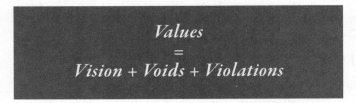

$$Values$$
$$=$$
$$Vision + Voids + Violations$$

Core Values Determination

VISION	VOIDS	VIOLATIONS
Future	Present	Past
"I imagine a future with X, Y, and Z." "The world will look like this, and this is how we will look like with it." "What doesn't exist yet, we will create. What is an outlier now will be mainstream in the future."	"The current state of affairs is failing us." "If we just solved this problem, we'd live in a more optimal world." "We've been missing this for too long, and we can no longer tolerate not having it."	"Doing what we've always done is no longer an option." "It's been done wrong all along." "We are healing traumas and eliminating bad actors."

These motivations ground the *why* into a rallying set of values that the people you want to help make that idea happen believe in. When a Visionizer takes the time to reflect on the future, present, and past, the truest form of purpose possible develops.

Too many times Vision is relegated only to the future state, and this loses people after the initial zing of excitement. When you can articulate the voids and violations that also make up the brand values of your company, the other Unicorns can see where their own values align with the Visionizer's. And at the end of the day, sharing your values clearly will convey why your brand brings people from the old normal to the new normal—making people want to be a part of it.

Now that you have determined (or redetermined) your brand values, they need to be placed inside a vehicle that will get people moving. And by moving, I don't just mean action. I mean being *moved*. Getting people all up in their feelings. Emotions produce chemicals in our bodies: adrenaline, cortisol, oxytocin, dopamine. When people have a biological reaction to your values (pupils dilating, heartbeat accelerating, brain neurons synchronizing with yours), that's when you know your vision has truly landed.

How do you do that? By telling the right stories, which is the second component of Brandcasting.

2) Stories

A Visionizer's greatest influence comes through their ability to tell a story that captures attention, evokes emotions, and inspires action. A Brandcast allows you to illustrate your vision with real examples and inspiring outcomes through the power of potent storytelling. Most of all, it creates what storytelling science business expert Paul J. Zak calls your "founding myth."[2]

The founding myth story is what makes people rally around your big idea and want to help write the next chapter of the story.

There's an infinite number of stories that you could tell, but the most important stories to tell as part of your Brandcast are ones that convey authority, approachability, and association.

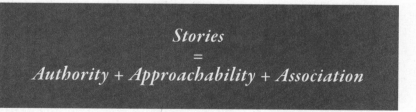

Stories
=
Authority + Approachability + Association

Brand Stories Determination

AUTHORITY	APPROACHABILITY	ASSOCIATION
Logical	Relational	Emotional
"We are using cutting-edge science / data to change the world." "The media has featured us for our innovations and solutions." "We have been refining our solutions since [year]."	"Here's our origin story. It all started back when . . ." "Our founder is just like you. She struggled with the same [insert void] that many people do." "Haven't you ever thought X? And wished there could be a better way? That's what our founder thought too, and what inspired them to create Y."	"Here's how you're the hero in our story." "Look at how we're solving this huge crisis [climate change, human rights, poverty, etc.] together." "See how the journey has solved a problem we all care about?"

This is not just motivational rah-rah, though.

Storytelling and its impact on our ability to rally around any idea is instinctual. As human beings, we are hardwired to digest information (and remember it for longer) when it's presented as a story.

When our brains encounter a good story, the neurochemical oxytocin is released, causing us to feel greater empathy.[3] Empathy is what drives us to join a cause; raise a hand and volunteer; help, serve, and give; and want to be part of something bigger than ourselves. It loudly exclaims, "We belong together!"

If you want a Unicorn Team to be effective, whoever owns the Visionizer role must tell effective stories to their fellow Unicorns, including the founding myth that's communicated in the Brandcast.

Now that you've identified your brand stories, it's time to tie them into what expectations for performance look like. These are what we call Meaningful Outcomes—as a result of living our values and telling our stories, this is how we will fulfill our purpose as a brand. This is the third component of the Visionizer's Brandcast.

3) Outcomes

Finding our purpose is the most exciting and most agonizing quest humans have.

The Unicorns who choose to work with you want to feel purposeful at work. While they may find a great sense of purpose at home or elsewhere in life, chances are they spend the majority of their waking hours working and want to feel purposeful doing it.

If you want to enroll the right Unicorns on your team, you have to tell them what success looks like individually and together. Exciting them with your values and stories isn't enough.

They want to know:

- What is the outcome we're working toward?

- What is expected of me individually and of the team?

- How will we measure success?

- How will we know if we are on track?

Underlying all of these questions are the deeper and often unspoken questions:

- As a team, are we actually doing something that matters?

- And if so, do my individual contributions actually make a difference?

Nobody wants to feel like they're toiling away at work and it's all pointless. Everyone wants to feel that their contributions matter and to see evidence that this is true.

The Outcomes part of the Brandcast allows people to see a very clear path from point A to point B, with measurements that show how their skills support the vision becoming real.

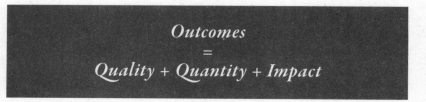

Outcomes
=
Quality + Quantity + Impact

Meaningful Outcomes (MO) Determination

QUALITY	QUANTITY	IMPACT
Standards	Reach	Legacy
"What is the promise we've made to our [clients / customers / community / the world / etc.]?" "What measurements tell us that our promise is being fulfilled?" "What happens when we don't produce the quality we expect?"	"How many people are we helping, and by when?" "What channels are speaking about our brand?" "What markets are we influencing?"	"What measurements tell us that we're impacting the future?" "What happens to the brand after the founders are gone?" "How did we make every market we entered better than it was before?"

People who want to add their magic and special skills to your Unicorn Team need to see where their contributions are making a difference. The Brandcast must communicate the expected outcomes they can bet on by being part of this team.

It's important not to confuse key performance indicators (KPIs) and objectives and key results (OKRs) with Meaningful Outcomes (MOs). KPIs and OKRs are the two prevailing goal-setting frameworks that many companies big and small use to set performance standards, but in a Brandcast, we are looking for more meta and macro commitments that the brand is making.

"What's our MO?" becomes the Visionizer's reminder to themselves and the other Unicorns why they're committed to the Big Idea.

Staying in "big thinking" is really important for a Visionizer, because for a Unicorn Team to assemble and do big things, they need to unite around the Values, Stories, and Outcomes communicated in the Brandcast.

BRANDCAST CASE STUDY

Gordy Bal is the founder of Conscious Thought Revolution (CTR), an investment fund that redeploys what he calls "Conscious Capital" to disruptive technologies, entrepreneurs, and media that are accelerating the evolution of human consciousness.

Bal is the *Wall Street Journal* best-selling author of *The New Millionaire's Playbook*, which includes seven rules to unlock a life where "everything is possible." (Are you sensing the Visionizer energy that Bal brings to the table?)

He wants people to understand that there are many different ways to invest in a company. You can invest cash. Or you can invest your thoughts, ideas, creativity, experiences, and professional skills as another form of "currency." He asserts that anyone can become an investor regardless of how much capital they have in the bank by using their mind as well as their money.

Portfolio companies that Bal has personally invested in include Bulletproof, Investabit, Good Money, PowerDot, HeroX, and Oura. You've probably heard of the Oura Ring, which tracks your sleep, activity, and readiness using light beams (infrared and red and green LEDs) and sensors to measure your respiratory rate, heart rate, blood oxygen levels, and body temperature and then gives you real-time data reported through its app.

In April 2022, Oura became what's known as a "unicorn" company, achieving over $1 billion in valuation. The Oura Ring helps users from NBA players to busy professionals to menopausal women understand what's happening in their bodies and how to optimize their health without the bulkiness of wrist devices like the Apple Watch or Fitbit. It's an elegant ring that comes in black, white, silver, or gold and looks just like an upscale piece of jewelry. You'd never guess it's a sophisticated body-scanning device.

I first heard Gordy Bal speak at a private mastermind event. In less than three minutes, he explained how he invested his skills to create SPVs—special purpose vehicles—to rally other investors to get behind the brands that fit their values and mission, and how everyday people could do the same. I was intrigued. He was the first person who spoke about venture capital in a way that helped me "get it."

At lunchtime, I sat next to him and asked, "What's next for you, Gordy? Have you ever thought about teaching people to create their own SPVs and investing like you've done? Because your three-minute talk helped me understand how to do that more clearly than I've ever understood it in my life—and I'm pretty sure there are others like me."

This unfolded into a deep conversation. We talked about how to shift the world so that wealth, power, and leadership are no longer exclusively reserved for the few people who graduate from prestigious Ivy League schools or who have private memberships to a golf club. We riffed on how other folks—people who have capital in the form of not just cash, but skills—could get into the investing game. As he shared the vision of where he wanted to go next, my Strategizer brain started whirling with ideas. I can't help it. I'm a Strategizing Visionizer (SV) Unicorn, after all. Bal is a Visionizing Mobilizer (VM). Together, the two of us check all the Unicorn boxes: Visionizer, Strategizer, and Mobilizer. We're a match made in heaven!

I told him, "If you want to bring this work to an even bigger audience, build a personal brand around it, and launch a new offer—I'm your huckleberry."

Right then and there, we did a quick Visionize > Strategize > Mobilize to evaluate if this idea was worth pursuing (remember the Navigate track in the Unicorn Innovation Model? It's the process for deciding which ideas to do) and confirmed that it was. We green-lit moving forward with the idea.

The first step to bringing it to life? Bal needed to create a Brandcast to communicate his vision with his team and other stakeholders to get them inspired.

Here's how we built Gordy Bal's Brandcast.

Values

What if everyone could be an investor, not just the wealthy elite who have a surplus of cash? What if billions of people could invest with their ideas and skills, with their "conscious capital," to build companies that change the world?

Bal saw the future (vision) as a place where the conditions that plague us—poverty, hunger, disease, climate change—could be solved by today's people.

In order to do so, we need to confront that the present reality is unacceptable (void) and ask ourselves what we can contribute to this future vision. Then we need to find solutions that are proven to outperform the past (violations) so that we can disrupt the status quo.

Stories

One of Bal's authority (logical) stories is the Oura Ring investment, proof that he has a nose for billion-dollar ideas. He's also a published author, lending further credibility and authority to his name.

For his approachability (relational) stories, Gordy is a husband and father, and with his beard, funky-colored glasses, and jaunty hats, he doesn't look like the typical "Silicon Valley tech bro in a hoodie" so often found in the venture capital space. He looks like (and is) a warm, friendly, and approachable guy.

His association (emotional) stories include those of the leaders he profiles in his book who are joining the conscious thought revolution. Remember how his very simple way of explaining how capital is distributed really helped me see how I belonged? That's how I associated myself with his ideas.

Outcomes

Bal's meaningful outcome is anchored in his mission statement: "To measurably impact 1 billion lives by 2030."[4]

To do this, Bal needs to find the Unicorns who are inspired by the idea of conscious capital and who want to be a part of this movement.

How could we test out this idea in a small and relatively risk-free way, similar to testing out new beverages in the Starbucks Innovation Lab? We decided the best container would be inviting 10 to 20 people to a private leadership retreat where Bal's frameworks could be taught and tweaked. At each private retreat, Bal could make a deep impact on each attendee. After the retreat, each person would return home and—like a missionary—spread the conscious capital gospel to their networks. The revolution would spread first to 20 people, then thousands, then millions and billions. This private leadership retreat would be the basis of how Bal could build his personal brand, present new offers, and grow his vision. The retreat would be the first strategic initiative, though not the last, as part of his larger plan.

We wrote out this Brandcast with Bal's Values, Stories, and Outcomes in less than a day. Now he had the language to galvanize his team and get them inspired about the future he envisioned. He had a set of stories that he could share with journalists, investors, retreat attendees, and other people. And he could sum up the outcome he wanted both long term (changing a billion lives) and short term (20 people attending his private retreat).

A vision without a Brandcast is useless. It's just airy thoughts in your head and a feeling in your heart. You need to write a Brandcast to pull the vision out of your head and put it into words that others can understand and get exhilarated about. Once you have a Brandcast, you can share the language in a variety of places—at an all-staff meeting, during your TED talk, during a podcast interview, in a one-on-one meeting with a potential investor—or even to reinvigorate your team if their motivation is waning and you want to remind them why where you're going matters. A Brandcast is a document that you can use over and over to enroll Unicorns into your vision.

EXERCISE

Create Your First Brandcast

Pick a great idea that you're excited about.

This idea could be an exciting new service you want to offer to your clients, a transformational event you want to host, or a brilliant way to upgrade an existing system within your organization.

Download the Brandcast template and start filling out the sections for your Values, Stories, and Outcomes. Get your free template here: https://UnicornTeamBook.com/Bonus.

Extra credit: share your Brandcast with your Unicorn Team—which may include employees, contractors, freelancers, consultants, coaches, advisors, investors, colleagues, or family and friends, depending on what phase of business you're in.

Upon hearing your Brandcast, notice how they respond. Is there one particular sentence that causes people's eyes to light up? Are there moments where they seem puzzled or uninterested? Did one story cause big emotions—tears, laughter, head-nodding? Tweak your Brandcast based on what's resonating the most strongly.

After hearing a rallying Brandcast, people feel invigorated, exhilarated, and inspired to swing into action. But . . . now what? Expressing the big vision is not enough. We need a sizzling-hot strategy to make it a reality. That's why the next communication tool is the Stratagem Session. Saddle up, Strategizer Unicorns, because the next chapter is all about you.

TOP TAKEAWAYS

- The Visionizer's number-one communication tool is called a Brandcast.
- A Brandcast includes three sections: Values, Stories, and Outcomes.
- An effective Brandcast signals to other Unicorns *why* lending their gifts, talents, skills, and magic to the mission is a very good decision on their part.
- By creating a Brandcast, you can magnetize the right Unicorns to want to join the cause and get your current team excited about your vision too.

CHAPTER 8

THE STRATAGEM SESSION

Thanks to the Brandcast, as a team, we can see the thrilling future we're rallying together to build. Now it's time for the Strategizer to translate the Brandcast into a road map of strategic decisions that will make the goals happen.

Teams are like toddlers. They need structure to function. A big idea with no strategy to support it is overwhelming and exhausting, making people have meltdowns like three-year-olds who have skipped their nap.

The Unicorn Innovation Model is all about bringing great ideas to life with astonishing speed and success. The point of this model is to bring the big idea to fruition with as little pressure, friction, and noise as possible. This requires building a brand culture where people are incentivized to be strategic finishers by way of a Stratagem.

The Unicorn Innovation Model

VSM Process		● VISIONIZE	▲ STRATEGIZE	■ MOBILIZE	
	Navigate How we make decisions together and choose the right idea to pursue	Ideastorm	DOIT	BEIT	
IDEATION **NEW** Launch brand-new initiatives	**Motivate** How we lead and the energy we bring to the team	V Types	S Types	M Types	**ITERATION** **BAU** Improve existing initiatives
		VV | VS | VM	SV | SS | SM	MV | MS | MM	
	Communicate How we get aligned, work on the right priorities together, and get things done at warp speed	Brandcast	Stratagem	Prototype	
		< ~ ~ ~ UNICORN ENERGY ~ ~ ~ >			

WHAT IS A STRATAGEM?

When you make a Stratagem, you're making a strategic plan, Unicorn style.

And when you gather with your team to create this plan, I call this a Stratagem Session.

Your Stratagem is your team's playbook to accomplish whatever you've set out to do, usually within a three-year horizon, including clear one-year goals and a quarterly adjustment to update what's working and what's not. A Stratagem Session is a way to ideate all the parts of the plan—the projects, initiatives, and campaigns necessary to make the great idea come to life quicker.

Stratagem Prep Work: Know Your Numbers

Results matter, and financial results are definitely required for a brand to grow and a business to thrive.

This isn't a book on how to make a P&L sheet or do financial forecasting. You should work with your financial Strategizers and Mobilizers to determine how much revenue your company needs to make and the profit margins you want to achieve. The Stratagem steps that follow are in service of achieving that profit goal.

Stratagem Step One: Get GIDDY

In my role as a strategic advisor for companies big and small, I've found there are really only five goals that matter for a company to thrive and for ideas to have the impact we want. These goals are Brandcast-agnostic, meaning these five goals work for any type of company or vision.

To make them easy to remember, I've turned them into the acronym GIDDY, as in, "Giddy-up and let's get moving, Unicorns!" And, "We're going to feel giddy with happiness because we're getting meaningful sh*t done."

The five goals are:

G = <u>G</u>row the business (reach, market, and sell more)

I = <u>I</u>mprove financial performance (run the business profitably and efficiently)

D = <u>D</u>eliver exceptional brand experience (fulfill the promises we make)

D = <u>D</u>iscover new ideas and innovation (make room for relevancy and competitive edge)

Y = <u>Y</u>ield better stakeholder results (improve the beneficiary's benefits—customers, staff, partners)

We plot these into a Stratagem like so:

Goals	Candidates	Decisions
G = Grow the business		
I = Improve financial performance		
D = Deliver exceptional brand experience		
D = Discover new ideas and innovation		
Y = Yield better stake- holder results		

You have the five goals in column one.

Next, come up with three candidates for each goal. In other words, three possible ways that each goal could be achieved. Think: "Here are three different ways we could achieve this particular goal . . ." Choose your three options based on past data, market trends, and your Unicorn instincts. Here's an example of what this can look like:

Goals	Candidates	Decisions
G = Grow the business	Initiative #1: Increase our leads database by 10% month over month (BAU) Initiative #2: Sell 2x more of our services every month (BAU) Initiative #3: Increase our social media conversions (BAU)	

Goals	Candidates	Decisions
I = Improve financial performance	Initiative #1: Increase our profit margin from 20% to 25% (BAU) Initiative #2: Eliminate 1 process that no longer helps us win (BAU) Initiative #3: Decrease the cost of our tech stack without affecting quality (BAU)	
D = Deliver exceptional brand experience	Initiative #1: Increase our customer brand score from X to Y (BAU) Initiative #2: Decrease the number of returns or amount of customer attrition (BAU) Initiative #3: Gain X new client case studies per month (BAU)	
D = Discover new ideas and innovation	Initiative #1: Implement AI efficiencies in our customer service department (NEW) Initiative #2: Create new product that supports our current services model (NEW) Initiative #3: Write a thought-leadership book that brings more authority to the company (NEW)	
Y = Yield better stakeholder results	Initiative #1: Update/revise policy on hybrid work (NEW) Initiative #2: Improve our employee satisfaction score (BAU) Initiative #3: Mentoring and succession planning (BAU)	

Notice how right after each initiative, I put BAU or NEW. BAU means "business as usual." This label is for ideas that are not exactly revolutionary or already have a process in place, but could use an upgrade and could absolutely help us achieve our goal. NEW means "new idea"—a departure from the norm and something we have not tried before.

BAU initiatives are keep-the-lights-on projects. These improvement projects are mission critical but don't usually involve big, sweeping changes internally or externally. Unless something dramatic changes, you shouldn't be breaking things that aren't broken. It's often the Mobilizer Unicorns who suggest BAU initiatives because they love to refine, refine, refine and get as close to perfection as humanly possible.

NEW initiatives are the innovative ideas that Visionizers and Strategizers typically bring to the table. These ideas ensure that we remain the market leader, introduce an exciting new offer, or change part of our internal culture dramatically. These NEW initiatives will most likely impact BAU, though, so the Stratagem should take that into consideration.

You have plotted out three candidates for each goal. Each of the candidates will compete for time, energy, and financial resources. Which ones should you and your team commit to doing? All of them? Just a few?

In an ideal world, we'd be able to do everything with no limitations. However, Unicorns live in the real world, and so we must prioritize. That's what we tackle next.

Stratagem Step Two: Prioritize What Matters

There's a saying in football: *Defense wins championships.*

Another one: *The best defense is a good offense.*

Old-school leadership books preach that "winning is everything," no matter the cost, with the dinosaur mentality to shut up, stop complaining, and get the job done. If you're physically, emotionally, or mentally crumbling apart under the strain, suck it up, because nobody wants to hear about it.

Fortunately, the world has changed for the better. Now we understand that work-life balance and self-care are required for Unicorns to produce their greatest work. Workplaces have shifted toward hybrid work, flexible structures, and empathizing with different family dynamics.

These are considerations you need to make if you want to recruit and retain top talent, the most Unicorn-y Unicorns of the bunch. If you don't factor these into your strategy, you're going to lose.

But let's be clear: while Unicorns do want flexibility, compassion, and respect at work, they also want to *win*. If anyone tells you that people don't care about winning, they don't understand human psychology. Winning doesn't mean hustle and grind; it means winning on your terms and feeling like your contribution is worth the time and trade-offs. When Unicorn Teams aren't winning, they will do what it takes to turn a sinking ship around.

When it comes to bringing a great idea to life, here are basic rules of strategy:

BAU = Defense	NEW = Offense

Remember those candidates that you put into your Stratagem chart? Now you need to decide which ones your team will actually do. Time to prioritize and categorize each candidate as yes, create, defer, or no in the Decisions column.

In your Candidates column, anything marked BAU is a default *yes*. These initiatives keep our lights on and have us moving forward on the right path. They are simply the defense we need to protect what we've built.

To be clear, if a BAU candidate creates organizational change that radically disrupts the current working process, it is not BAU. If it's a new way to do things, that means it's actually NEW, not BAU. For example, transforming your customer service department by implementing a highly complex AI interface usually affects a lot of people, process, and technology, excluding it from being a BAU candidate.

BAU initiatives may not always feel "sexy," but they're the steady and sensible needle movers that take a company from good to great. In some cases, BAU tasks can certainly be delegated to AI rather than a human being. This is great, because it frees up precious human-time to do what only humans can do: the NEW.

Okay, so what about the candidates marked as NEW? These are both offensive opportunities and also threats to BAU. Visionizers love NEW—and their passion for these ideas will be loud and contagious—but they aren't always great at understanding the trade-offs required to make their shiny NEW ideas happen. That's why making a Stratagem one-pager is so powerful. Once you've laid everything out in writing, it's easier to see "Wow, we probably can't do everything we'd like to do, because it's just too much." We have to be discerning and prioritize. This reality check can throw some cool water on the Visionizer's fire (in a good way).

Decisions have four identifiers:

YES	The strategic initiative is approved, and performance measurements that support it have already been created.
CREATE	The strategic initiative is 100% brand-new and approved for campaign development.
DEFER	The strategic initiative is not approved but moved to the next quarter or year for consideration.
NO	The strategic initiative is not approved and does not align with our Brandcast at this time.

Each decision needs to have an owner assigned. This can be a department, a dynamic duo, or one individual Unicorn who is taking ownership. Being an owner means you're responsible for seeing this through, all the way to the finish line. You don't get to take credit only if the initiative is a success or blame someone else if it is not. You have to own the results either way—which is scary but also exciting. In the following example, we see the decisions that have been made and their owners.

Goals	Candidates	Decisions
G = Grow the business	Initiative #1: Increase our leads database by 10% month over month (BAU) Initiative #2: Sell 2x more of our services every month (BAU) Initiative #3: Increase our social media conversions (BAU)	YES. Owner: Marketing YES. Owner: Sales YES. Owner: Marketing
I = Improve financial performance	Initiative #1: Increase our profit margin from 20% to 25% (BAU) Initiative #2: Eliminate 1 process that no longer helps us win (BAU) Initiative #3: Decrease the cost of our tech stack without affecting quality (BAU)	YES. Owner: Finance YES. Owner: Operations YES. Owner: Technology
D = Deliver exceptional brand experience	Initiative #1: Increase our customer brand score from X to Y (BAU) Initiative #2: Decrease the number of returns or amount of customer attrition (BAU) Initiative #3: Gain X new client case studies per month (BAU)	YES. Owner: Marketing YES. Owner: Operations YES. Owner: Sales
D = Discover new ideas and innovation	Initiative #1: Implement AI efficiencies in our customer service department (NEW) Initiative #2: Create new product that supports our current services model (NEW) Initiative #3: Write a thought-leadership book that brings more authority to the company (NEW)	CREATE. Owner: Operations CREATE. Owner: Marketing DEFER. Owner: Executive
Y = Yield better stakeholder results	Initiative #1: Update/revise policy on hybrid work (NEW) Initiative #2: Improve our employee satisfaction score (BAU) Initiative #3: Mentoring and succession planning (BAU)	CREATE. Owner: HR YES. Owner: HR YES. Owner: HR

For the rest of this book, we will focus on the NEW initiatives and how to get the right Unicorns rallied to make the offensive strategy work.

Stratagem Step Three: Develop Your NEW Campaigns

Your new initiative has been green-lit for creation. Now its success rides on the integration between the Strategizer and Mobilizer roles on your Unicorn Team.

You need a shared resource that defines the parameters of the new campaign and the players needed to achieve it. We call that the Campaign Playbook.

Each NEW initiative has a Campaign Playbook.

Remember, a Strategizer likes to try things, and they need a place for those tests to be documented and tracked. They also need autonomy so that they can create the most optimal environments for these tests to make the new idea succeed.

A Strategizer's greatest joy and fulfillment comes from asking the question:

WWHTBT?

What would have to be true (for that to happen)?

Strategizers tend to be comfortable with tweaking the strategy as it rolls out. They're the ones noticing what consumers respond to most strongly, how culture is shifting, what's in the news cycle, and the trends on everyone's minds. They understand that winning requires testing and adjusting. Mobilizers, on the other hand, don't necessarily love testing things. They like certainty and structure, and they desire with all of their being to *not* be responsible for something going wrong. Enter: the Campaign Playbook. This playbook contains all important information about a NEW initiative in one centralized place. It not only gives everyone clear direction, it also opens up an opportunity for the whole team to become more strategic, which is every Visionizer and Strategizer's dream come true.

The Campaign Playbook includes the following elements:

- Description of initiative
- Link to Brandcast
- Link to Stratagem
- Market trends
- Product development
- Customer journey
- Messaging guidelines
- Branding guidelines
- Budget and success criteria
- Unicorn Team resources
- Internal impact
- External impact
- Timeline anchors
- Technology guidelines
- Sustainable scale opportunities

Because the Campaign Playbook is a living document, with quite a bit of content and a lot of context involved, it would take up too many pages of this book to be useful. So we're just going to give it to you instead. Go to https://UnicornTeamBook.com/Bonus and get access to the Campaign Playbook template you can use and customize for your NEW initiatives.

STRATAGEM CASE STUDY

Remember Gordy Bal from Chapter 7? After we developed his Brandcast, we put his winning idea—the private leadership retreat on Conscious Capital Investing—into the strategic planning phase.

First, he and I did some work to define the Dream User for the retreat. We determined that the best leaders to invite were people who not only had currency in the form of cash, crypto, and other forms of capital, but even more importantly, had two other currencies: 1) a community of people who cared about solving the world's biggest problems, and 2) specific skills that would be valuable to an investable product.

After defining the Dream User, we set out to create the messaging to get these Dream Users to see the value of playing bigger in this way. The result: a Campaign Playbook for the private leadership retreat that was ready to be mobilized.

EXERCISE

Do Your First Stratagem Session

Download your Stratagem strategic plan here:

https://UnicornTeamBook.com/Bonus

Bring your team together. After reviewing the Brandcast and getting reinvigorated about the big idea and the future you want, fill out the Stratagem together.

Come up with candidates for each goal.

Discuss the potential rewards, risks, and trade-offs for each one.

Make a decision for each candidate: YES, CREATE, DEFER, or NO. And assign an owner for each one.

For any YES or CREATE candidates, create a Campaign Playbook to further outline the strategy that you'll deploy.

Congratulations! You just did a Stratagem Session.

Do this every quarter to determine (or recommit to) your priorities as a team.

Visionizers have the Brandcast. Strategizers have the Stratagem. Mobilizers have their own communication tool too, called the Prototyping Process. Prototyping is where the vision and strategy become real. It's where the website gets built, the copy gets written, the episode gets produced; where all the ethereal ideas become finished products that people can read, watch, hear, see, touch, taste, experience. Head to the next chapter to see how it works.

TOP TAKEAWAYS

- The Stratagem is a strategic plan with a Unicorn twist. It helps everyone understand the team's priorities: what we're doing now and why, what we're deferring and reconsidering later, and what we're not doing. If you're a Strategizer Unicorn, learn this tool and use it often.

- During a Stratagem Session, use **GIDDY**, which stands for the five goals of **G**row the business, **I**mprove financial performance, **D**eliver exceptional brand experience, **D**iscover new ideas and innovation, and **Y**ield better stakeholder results.

- For each goal, come up with one to three possible candidates. Each candidate should be labeled as BAU (business as usual, a simple improvement on something you're already doing) or NEW (brand-new, an idea that creates organizational and market change).

- BAU immediately gets the green light, assuming you're not radically changing current people, process, or technology.

- For each NEW item, decide if it's going to happen or be delayed until later, or if it's a hard no. Assign an owner to each initiative that's moving forward, and have a Strategizer Unicorn create the Campaign Playbook, or the owner's manual for the rest of the Unicorn Team to have a successful outcome.

CHAPTER 9

THE PROTOTYPING PROCESS

Every Visionizer should understand how to craft a Brandcast to express the values, stories, and outcomes that get the team fired up.

Every Strategizer should master the Stratagem so they can lead the team through the process of considering strategic initiatives and deciding which ones to do and when.

And every Mobilizer should learn how to do the Prototyping Process, which is the next communication tool we're going to cover.

There are many tools, processes, systems, and instruction manuals that Mobilizer Unicorns create and follow to make goals succeed. But to go from an average Mobilizer to a thoroughbred Unicorn, you need to show your WIP (work in progress) to confirm that you're on the right track.

The Unicorn Innovation Model

	VSM Process	● VISIONIZE	▲ STRATEGIZE	■ MOBILIZE	
IDEATION **NEW** Launch brand-new initiatives	**Navigate** How we make decisions together and choose the right idea to pursue	Ideastorm	DOIT	BEIT	**ITERATION** **BAU** Improve existing initiatives
	Motivate How we lead and the energy we bring to the team	V Types	S Types	M Types	
		VV | VS | VM	SV | SS | SM	MV | MS | MM	
	Communicate How we get aligned, work on the right priorities together, and get things done at warp speed	Brandcast	Stratagem	Prototype	
	< ~ ~ ~ UNICORN ENERGY ~ ~ ~ >				

THE PROTOTYPING PROCESS

Prototyping gives Mobilizers:

- Permission to take strategic action, not just wait for direction.

- An opportunity to provide insights and recommendations to make the initiative more successful, rather than just following orders.

- Confidence to be a leader on the team and to own their identity as a specialist, expert, or master craftsperson.

Remember, a Mobilizer's greatest fear is being wrong. This puts them in a naturally defensive state whenever there are issues, risks, or changes presented in an initiative. They'll spend more time defending why they aren't wrong instead of being part of the strategic solution to overcome it—and that wastes everyone's time. Mobilizers have no desire to waste anything. They revel in completion and order.

Every new initiative will encounter the predictable PFNs: pressure, friction, and noise.

PFNs either create drag (delay, cost, attrition) or flow (momentum, innovation, resolution). Mobilizers usually view dealing with PFNs as handling kryptonite, because they assume their ability to finish things will be interrupted. The truth is, Mobilizers have so much power to master PFNs and make a project go faster if they just use the Prototyping Process.

Prototyping allows Mobilizers to own their strategic interpretation of the Campaign Playbook in collaboration with the Visionizers and Strategizers, and solidifies their commitment to seeing it through in a way that is more valuable than just checking things off and calling things done.

PRODUCT PROTOTYPE VS. PROTOTYPING PROCESS

Before we continue, I want to describe the difference between a *product prototype* and the *Prototyping Process*.

A "product prototype" is standard lingo for a beta product that people put out there. It's an early version from which future versions are developed. Engineers and product developers often create these test versions of a new product, service, or device before officially releasing it.

The Prototyping Process is a communication tool in the Unicorn Innovation Model that gets us to the goal of achieving a well-delivered product prototype. It's the tool that helps not just the tech folks translate requirements, but other types of Mobilizers too—from administrative personnel to customer service and beyond. It's essentially the Mobilizer's way of checking in and saying, "This is my interpretation of the Campaign Playbook. I want to verify: Is this interpretation exactly right? Mostly there but not quite? Totally off? Let's discuss and get things aligned before I proceed with finishing the task." That way, the Mobilizer is not wasting time working on something that is ultimately unusable.

Let's jump into how it works.

Remember the elements of the Campaign Playbook? It contains all the important information about a NEW initiative in one handy location.

- Description of initiative
- Link to Brandcast
- Link to Stratagem
- Market trends
- Product development
- Customer journey
- Messaging guidelines
- Branding guidelines
- Budget and success criteria
- Unicorn Team resources
- Internal impact
- External impact
- Timeline anchors
- Technology guidelines
- Sustainable scale opportunities

Prototyping asks the Mobilizer to do a Visionize > Strategize > Mobilize treatment on the elements of the Campaign Playbook within a short time period and gets buy-in from the Strategizer.

IF YOU WANT YOUR TEAM TO READ
YOUR MIND, DO FIVE-TO-LIVE

Five-to-Live is a measurement that helps track the progress and growth of the Mobilizer role. Essentially it shows how you take up to five prototype "cracks" at interpreting the Brandcast and Stratagem accurately, within the timeframe given to them (usually one to three days). It's also a fail-safe for risk-averse Mobilizers that keeps the ball moving forward strategically.

The goal is for Mobilizers to interpret the strategy into action steps in five prototyping versions or less. When you make this part of your idea-to-implementation flow, your Mobilizers get better and better at "reading your mind" as a Visionizer or Strategizer, and do it in even less than five rounds at a time.

This means that they are seeking to get aligned agreement on their interpretation of the Campaign Playbook with as little friction, pressure, or noise as possible, while still hitting timelines and resource requirements and keeping the momentum of the project moving forward—instead of stalling out.

As someone who has worked with teams of all sizes, this one thing—the Prototyping Process—has reduced so much waste, conflict, and drama that it has literally saved millions in dollars and has helped to produce even more. It is a dreamy way to work with Mobilizers in a way that feels productive for everyone. *If there's one thing you implement in the Unicorn Innovation Model, this is it.*

The main question in the Prototyping Process is:

"Is this what you meant?"

Here are some examples of deliverables typically needed to complete the Campaign Playbook. These will vary depending on the type of industry you're in.

Campaign Playbook Element	Prototyping Process Deliverable
Customer journey	Mind map of customer experience Funnel design
Messaging guidelines	E-mail copy Paid advertising copy Social media copy
Branding guidelines	Campaign identity assets (web and print) UX design
Internal impact	Processes affected by the new idea

Let's say you're a product manager assigned to complete the customer journey deliverables in the Campaign Playbook.

Your Unicorn Leadership Type is Mobilizing Strategizer (MS), which means you are well suited to perform this Mobilizer role on your team. Your assignment is delivering the mind map of customer experience and overall funnel design of the campaign. You also need to get buy-in and approval from the Campaign Playbook owner (this is typically someone who is a Strategizer Unicorn).

You create the following mind map showing how the Dream User will experience the journey, starting with a quiz that they will take to see if the product/service is something that they will want to buy:[1]

Stage 1	Stage 2	Stage 3	Stage 4	Stage 5
Dream User starts quiz	Dream User submits quiz	Dream User requests sales call	Dream User makes decision	Yes—Fulfillment begins No—Follow-up sequence

* Based on Sixth Division's mind-mapping "The Experience" process.

And then you create the draft funnel design:[2]

Lead Source	Attention	Lead	Prospect	Client
Paid advertising	Push to quiz	Quiz opt-in web page	Quiz results page with invitation to sign up for sales call	Contract client and begin fulfillment

* Based on Sixth Division's funnel-mapping "The Playbook" process.

Note: This is a very simplistic depiction of a mind map and funnel, and this example serves to show you how Mobilizers create "drafts" to use as communication tools in the Five-to-Live process. Your company's way of doing this will vary.

During the Prototyping Process, you need to answer five fundamental questions to actively engage the Campaign Playbook owner while you are building the deliverables:

1. Is my interpretation of the vision and strategy accurate?

2. Is there anything I should know about the vision or strategy that I'm not currently aware of?

3. Is there a better question I'm not asking?

4. Does the Prototype get us the meaningful outcome (MO) we all want?

5. Do you co-sign this Prototype and can I move into implementation?

The key to success is embedding the Prototyping Process as part of the up-front strategic planning of any new initiative and reworking for error or misinterpretation during that time period instead of waiting for sh*t to hit the fan later in the implementation.

Prototyping also allows you to build more of a sustainable practice inside of your culture, empowering Mobilizers to see that it's healthy to take a few cracks at a solution instead of expecting it to be figured out perfectly on the first try (or expecting the Visionizer and Strategizer Unicorns to have all the answers). No one is better equipped to see the impact to the beneficiary than a Mobilizer. Often the Mobilizer role is the sentinel of the brand because they are usually closest to the people who will actually use it in the outside world.

This collaborative energy gets Mobilizers what they love most: the dopamine rush of getting stuff done and knowing they aren't alone in making sure it works well.

PROTOTYPING CASE STUDY

Back to our friend Gordy Bal and his big idea. After we got his Brandcast and Stratagem sorted, it was time to pull together Mobilizer Unicorns who could interpret the vision and strategy and make it happen.

When you think "private leadership retreat," you know you need someone in charge of logistics—an event planner who can source locations, keep an eye on the budget, and design the experience based on your vision.

We needed a strong Mobilizer to take on this role, which means someone with a MV, MS, or MM Unicorn Leadership Type. Before choosing someone for the job, we pulled together a few candidates and shared the Brandcast and Stratagem with each of them. We wanted to see if they could interpret the vision and strategy in an exciting way. We wanted a doer who saw themselves as an integral part of the brand experience we wanted to create, and who was excited to own it.

When we went through the interviews, one particular Unicorn stood out.

First, she was blown away by the Brandcast and Stratagem and by how much thought, care, and planning had already gone into the retreat. She wanted to be part of *this* kind of team. Her thorough understanding of the Brandcast and Stratagem would enable her to manifest the vision for the retreat and the strategic priorities much faster, as well as quote her services better and with more accuracy.

We offered her the contracted role and shared the Prototyping Process with her. We asked her to use the Prototyping Process to check in with Bal along the way, pausing at key points in the event planning process to confirm "Is this what you meant?" "Am I interpreting this correctly?" "What do you think about *this* concept?" "Ah, I see, nope, not quite right . . . okay, well, then how about *this* instead?" "Great! Do I have your co-sign on this before I proceed?" These Prototyping check-ins made the communication between them effortless and full of ease. She remarked how she'd never worked on a team that was so committed to winning . . . *ever.*

The private leadership retreat was a major success. Not just financially, but because it allowed Bal to fully live in his Visionizer role. After the first retreat, attendees said, "I have never in my life experienced something so transformational—and I really know how to invest at a level that I would have never known if I hadn't said yes."

Bal's retreat was just the first great idea—the one we wanted to test in our Innovation Lab before scaling it into something more—and now he was ready to build his new, evolved brand and could see with crystal clarity how to achieve his goal of impacting one billion lives by 2030.

Innovation doesn't have to be complicated. It just has to start with the right idea, brought to life by the right people, using the right process.

Prototyping means less wasted time, energy, and money caused by people misinterpreting the plan and fewer meltdowns with team members wondering, "Where did the communication go off the rails? This isn't what I meant *at all*." Prototyping also means happier Mobilizers who can confidently do what they love most: accomplish tasks with the highest level of excellence.

EXERCISE

Try the Prototyping Process

Ask a Mobilizer Unicorn on your team to try out the Prototyping Process.

Say to them, "Here is the Brandcast and Stratagem. You own [name of initiative that's been green-lit to proceed]. What do you think is the best way to get this initiative done? Show me a draft of your plan or concept."

Give them one to three days to put their draft together.

Review the draft with the Mobilizer.

Have the Mobilizer ask you five questions (page 165) so they can verify "Am I interpreting the vision and strategy correctly?" "Is this what you meant?"

If the interpretation is spot-on, excellent! The Mobilizer can proceed, implement the plan, and get everything done.

If the interpretation is way off the mark, discuss this together. Try using different wording to convey what you meant more clearly, or try using visuals to get your point across. Give the Mobilizer another chance at Prototyping so they can show you a revised draft. Do this until they provide a draft that you can both can co-sign.

YOUR THREE POWER TOOLS

You've learned three communication tools to help the people on your Unicorn Team work together fluidly and harmoniously:

Brandcast + Stratagem + Prototype

Once your Unicorn Team has been assembled and you're using these communication tools consistently, you'll notice less friction and more flow. But how can you ensure that your Unicorns feel appreciated—and generously compensated—and aren't tempted to leave the team? How can you create a Unicorn Team that is loyal, not fickle?

That's all coming up in the next chapter.

TOP TAKEAWAYS

- The Prototyping Process is a way to reduce the unhealthy pressure, friction, and noise that delay your ability to bring great ideas to life.

- There are five questions the Mobilizer Unicorn should ask during Prototyping. All these questions boil down to: "Is this what you meant?"

- Prototyping gives Mobilizers an opportunity to "show their work" and confirm that they're on the right track before proceeding with a project.

- Mobilizers love Prototyping because it allows them to confirm they are interpreting the vision and strategy correctly before investing tons of time and effort into completing it a certain way.

- Prototyping gives the Mobilizer the opportunity to interpret strategies and propose brilliant options rather than merely following orders.

CHAPTER 10

THE PERFORMANCE PULSE

Winning is measured on scoreboards, and most companies have some type of performance review process to tell the players on their team whether or not they are on the right track. But the traditional way of doing performance reviews needs an upgrade.

Introducing: the Performance Pulse.

This is how to give useful feedback to your staff the Unicorn Team way. With a Performance Pulse, you motivate individual stars to shine while in service of the company's Brandcast for any given year, season, or quarter.

Here's how it changes the game:

- The Performance Pulse links the person's individual values with the company's values so that they can see how their contributions are helping the company to win.

- Individual Unicorns will see that their time on the team is well spent and their work actually matters (because it does) and creates a sense of alignment. "My company cares about XYZ. I do too. We're synced up."

- When personal values and company values are linked, each Unicorn on the team feels a personal investment and ownership in the brand.

- The Performance Pulse also provides the opportunity for creativity with incentives that actually matter to the person. A higher salary is nice, but there are other rewards that have value too. The PP allows you to reward excellence in a personalized way, because (news flash) different things matter to different people.

If you're running a department or even if you're still a team of one (yes, you can do a Performance Pulse on yourself), the PP is a way for you to measure not just results, but the meaningful outcomes you've set out to achieve. It can transform the way your people see their part in the bigger vision of the company. And if you want to recruit winners and retain top talent for the long haul, adding it into your measurement systems is a must-do.

Should the Performance Pulse replace our current system of doing performance reviews? you may wonder.

Hard no.

It's *not* a replacement; it's a supplement and a monthly communication tool between the Boss Unicorn and their Employee (Contractor, Freelancer, whatever term is most appropriate) Unicorn.

Many organizations do a big performance review once a year and don't really talk about performance any other time—or, at least, not much. This leaves the employee feeling blindsided. They're thinking, "Wait, you were unhappy with my performance all this time? The whole year? Why didn't you say something sooner? You could have given me an opportunity to get things back on track." Or conversely, "Okay, thanks for the five-star ranking. If my performance is so exemplary, how come this is the first time you've acknowledged or thanked me all year long? A bonus earlier in the year sure would've been nice."

Having a conversation about performance once a year is simply not frequent enough. We need to check in more often. Research shows that when bosses and employees have regular, ongoing communication (instead of checking in only once in a blue moon), the employee is 87 percent less likely to quit.[1] Enter: the Performance Pulse.

Doing the Performance Pulse once a month helps your Unicorn understand where they can improve and, just as importantly, how they're already winning. The PP also provides an opportunity for your Unicorn to be rewarded in a way that's personally meaningful to them.

On top of retaining talent and reducing turnover costs, the real benefit of the Performance Pulse is that it keeps your Unicorn focused on the right priorities and getting the results that really move the needle for your team or company.

HOW TO DO A PERFORMANCE PULSE

Here's how the Performance Pulse works.

First, remember back in Chapter 8 when we talked about the Stratagem? During a Stratagem Session, you have a column with five goals, you come up with three options for each goal, you decide which of these options to do, and you assign an owner to each initiative.

Everything gets displayed in a chart with three columns: Goals, Candidates, and Decisions.

For this Performance Pulse example, let's choose *Initiative #2: Create a new product that supports our current services model (NEW).*

As you can see, the decision for that initiative is CREATE (meaning, "This is a brand-new initiative, not something we're already doing. So, let's create this!"), and the owner is Marketing. So, how is Marketing doing with this initiative? Absolutely crushing it? Not so much? Let's do a Performance Pulse to find out.

Goals	Candidates	Decisions
Discover new ideas and innovation	Initiative #1: Implement AI efficiencies in our customer service department (NEW) **Initiative #2: Create new product that supports our current services model (NEW)** Initiative #3: Write a thought-leadership book that brings more authority to the company (NEW)	CREATE. Owner: Operations **CREATE. Owner: Marketing** DEFER. Owner: Executive

Let's say a mental health company called Kindred Wellness (not its actual name but inspired by one of my clients) wants to create a product that's a natural extension of what the therapists and counselors in its current network already do. The number-one problem that Kindred's clients report is feeling lonely. Its clients say, "I want to be part of a community where I feel like I belong. But I don't know where to find my people." Kindred decides to launch a new product to meet this need.

Ryan from Marketing is the owner for this initiative. He's a product manager, and his Unicorn Leadership Type is Strategizing Mobilizer (SM). He is charged with the task of designing a new app that will combat loneliness and create safe ways to design "meaningful meet-ups" between local folks who want to be in "real-ationships" rather than "reel-ationships" (cultivating in-person connection over online-only connection).

"Souls by Kindred" becomes the working title of the initiative, and the Brandcast, Stratagem, and Prototyping Process begin for Ryan and his team.

They have one month to create the initial user-experience design, functionality, and requirements, and two more months to start prototyping development of the app features. They also have to establish branding considerations, create an end-user testing plan, and design the launch elements.

Ryan and his team simultaneously have to see where the initiative impacts current BAU operations like customer service and technology integrations and identify which team members are impacted so that they can enroll other internal influencers to support it, even if it affects their current jobs. Their goal is to get an initial designed app to show off at the next all-hands meeting so that they can enroll more internal support.

Ryan and his team understand the mission, but they need measurements to ensure they're on the right track.

Performance Pulse is a tool they can employ to get everyone transparently on the same page and give everyone a pulse of how healthy their progress is.

Ryan uses the Campaign Playbook to build the Performance Pulse, which looks like this:

Category [Pull these categories from the Campaign Playbook.]	Owner [The Unicorn Team member who is leading this initiative.]	Goal [The outcome you want to achieve.]	Personal Values [The owner's top three personal values.]	Values Linkage [The owner's interpretation of how their personal values align with brand values.]
Description of Initiative	Ryan, product manager	Build a working prototype for Souls by Kindred that can be demo'd internally within three months.	Innovation, Family, Impact	Souls by Kindred is an innovative way for us to solve the loneliness problem. It allows people to create better communication dynamics from stronger individual connections.
Link to Brandcast	Dr. Stacey, CEO of Kindred	Communicate Brandcast updates quarterly to entire organization.	Impact, Mental Health, Innovation	Souls by Kindred can reach more people and help create empowered, supportive connections through our investment in creating an algorithm and app for any time of day.

Category [Pull these categories from the Campaign Playbook.]	Owner [The Unicorn Team member who is leading this initiative.]	Goal [The outcome you want to achieve.]	Personal Values [The owner's top three personal values.]	Values Linkage [The owner's interpretation of how their personal values align with brand values.]
Link to Stratagem	Shaye, Ryan's manager	Assure that Performance Pulse is tied to overall company goals and measurements.	Organization, Creativity, Family	Souls by Kindred will give our clients a system to use that is based on our well-documented and proven intellectual property and help us spend time with the people that matter the most.
Market Trends	Ryan, product manager	Collect research that supports the prototyping assumptions within a set timeframe and due dates.	Innovation, Family, Impact	Souls by Kindred is an innovative way for us to solve the loneliness problem. It allows people to create better communication dynamics from stronger individual connections.
Product Development	Ryan, product manager	Work with business analysts and engineering to develop product specs, UX, and functionality within a set timeframe and due dates.	Innovation, Family, Impact	Souls by Kindred is an innovative way for us to solve the loneliness problem. It allows people to create better communication dynamics from stronger individual connections.

Category [Pull these categories from the Campaign Playbook.]	Owner [The Unicorn Team member who is leading this initiative.]	Goal [The outcome you want to achieve.]	Personal Values [The owner's top three personal values.]	Values Linkage [The owner's interpretation of how their personal values align with brand values.]
Customer Journey	Ryan, product manager	Work with business analysts and engineering to develop product specs, UX, and functionality within a set timeframe and due dates.	Innovation, Family, Impact	Souls by Kindred is an innovative way for us to solve the loneliness problem. It allows people to create better communication dynamics from stronger individual connections.
Messaging Guidelines	Chloe, marketing manager	Work with product manager to develop messaging and branding for product.	Creativity, Family, Fun	For Souls by Kindred to get lightning-in-a-bottle success, we must break through the noise using creative messaging and ways for clients to be proud to use the app.
Branding Guidelines	Reagan, branding agency contractor	Work with marketing manager to design visual branding of the app within a set timeframe and due dates.	Culture, Beauty, Creativity	Souls by Kindred is an app whose design is easy for people to recognize and whose logo and icon people are sharing everywhere.
Budget and Success Criteria	Joe, fractional CFO	Work with the executive team and product manager to set budget and P&L forecast for new product within a set timeframe and due dates.	Systems, Order, Family	Souls by Kindred has a forecasted growth that increases our revenue, which allows us to bring more impact and value to our end customers and grows a healthy company at the same time.

Category [Pull these categories from the Campaign Playbook.]	Owner [The Unicorn Team member who is leading this initiative.]	Goal [The outcome you want to achieve.]	Personal Values [The owner's top three personal values.]	Values Linkage [The owner's interpretation of how their personal values align with brand values.]
Unicorn Team Resources	Victoria, project manager	Work with the product manager to identify every team member to meet the performance goals of this initiative within a set timeframe and due dates.	Organization, Communication, Social Justice	Souls by Kindred will be an outcome that is the result of the right Unicorn Team resources coming together and communicating effectively to meet our goals together.
Internal Impact	Victoria, project manager	Work with product manager and Unicorn Team resources to identify any internal issues, risks, and changes that will affect the project's success within a set timeframe and due dates.	Organization, Communication, Social Justice	Souls by Kindred will be an outcome that is the result of the right Unicorn Team resources coming together and communicating effectively to meet our goals together.
External Impact	Chloe, marketing manager	Work with product manager and Unicorn Team resources to identify any external issues, risks, and changes that will affect the project's success within a set timeframe and due dates.	Creativity, Family, Fun	For Souls by Kindred to get lightning-in-a-bottle success, we must break through the noise using creative messaging and ways for clients to be proud to use the app.

Category [Pull these categories from the Campaign Playbook.]	Owner [The Unicorn Team member who is leading this initiative.]	Goal [The outcome you want to achieve.]	Personal Values [The owner's top three personal values.]	Values Linkage [The owner's interpretation of how their personal values align with brand values.]
Timeline Anchors	Victoria, project manager	Work with the product manager to solidify the timelines for performance goals of this initiative.	Organization, Communication, Social Justice	Souls by Kindred will be an outcome that is a result of the right Unicorn Team resources coming together and communicating effectively to meet our goals together.
Technology Guidelines	Brad, technology leader	Work with product manager and other Unicorn Team members to develop the engineering and coding plan and execution within a set timeframe and due dates.	Innovation, Technology, Impact	Souls by Kindred will be an app that's easy to use. The user experience will be simple and frictionless.
Sustainable Scale Opportunities	Craig, BAU internal owner	Work with the NEW initiatives team to map out any next-phase impacts and opportunities through the product launch phases so that there is as little disruption to BAU as possible and handoffs to BAU resources are as clear and efficient as possible.	Structure, Repetition, Sports	Clients who use Souls by Kindred will encounter the customer support, billing, and public communications they expect with excellence. Kindred will be on-brand every step of the way.

Make Team Members Actually *Care*

By identifying how their personal values link to the brand values, the Performance Pulse reminds each person why they're on the team to begin with. It's a tool for any of the Unicorn Leaders in the Owner column to remind themselves and other team members why they are here to bring this initiative to life regardless of those pesky PFNs—pressure, friction, and noise.

If you're in start-up mode, and you have only one person—yourself—to put in the Owner column, the Performance Pulse helps you see who you need to enlist, including outside contractors, part-time help, or even your kids, like I did, when I was first starting my own company. Or perhaps you need help from a mentor, coach, or consultant who has experience in an area on the list.

If you're an HR manager or other department lead who wants to integrate Performance Pulse into your current performance management process, link the key performance metrics (KPIs) or objectives and key results (OKRs) with the Performance Pulse so that your team members can see how their individual performance on a particular initiative supports the company's bigger financial and impact results.

Do a Performance Pulse Early and Often

Doing a Performance Pulse once a month is best practice. Every two weeks, maybe, when you're in the middle of a big launch. The Performance Pulse is a communication tool to continually check in on the energy and output of yourself and your team to determine "Are we on the right track?" This allows you to nip small issues in the bud before they turn into big nightmares. And it allows you to celebrate wins sooner and more often, instead of ordering a "Great job!" cake once a year.

If this makes you groan, don't think this requires an hour-long meeting or a drawn-out conversation. This quick, yet potent checkpoint shouldn't take more than 15 minutes. And it does not require you to grade your team members from 1 to 5, with most people getting a 3 (meets expectations), a tiny few getting a 4 (exceeds expectations), and maybe one person in a department getting a 5 (extraordinary results).

I remember when I had the responsibility of rating my own team members when I was part of a larger organization and feeling as if the choice of whom to give the few 4s and 5s to was like playing favorites with my own kids. Of course, there were objective measurements to follow, but let's be honest, there was a ton of subjectivity and politics at play.

Instead, the Performance Pulse empowers you (or whoever owns the initiative) to be a part of the dialogue in coordination with the direct managers who do the "formal" performance reviews. It flattens the hierarchy and informs you what matters to the individual Unicorns who are contributing to the meaningful outcome.

A GUIDE TO CREATIVE COMPENSATION

The standard company compensation and benefits—salary bands, bonus structures, promotions, health and retirement benefits, wellness perks, paid time off, and a host of other ways that team members are paid—are exactly that: standard.

My goal is to help you enlist a high-performing Unicorn Team to get big things done faster. If you have a small business, you can't always afford the top talent you want.

So, what are some creative means for compensation that you can discover through the Performance Pulse?

It all comes back to personal values.

Chloe, the marketing manager on the Souls by Kindred initiative, lists her personal values as Creativity, Family, and Fun. Here's her section of the Performance Pulse:

Category	Owner	Goal	Personal Values	Values Linkage
External Impact	Chloe, marketing manager	Work with product manager and Unicorn Team resources to identify any external issues, risks, and changes that will affect the project's success within a set timeframe and due dates.	Creativity, Family, Fun	For Souls by Kindred to get lightning-in-a-bottle success, we must break through the noise using creative messaging and ways for clients to be proud to use the app.

Chloe is crushing it. You want to reward her and inspire her to stay on the Unicorn Team for the long haul. However, at this exact moment, you don't have the budget to give her a big salary increase. So, what are some other rewards that would contribute to what she cares about in life? (Hint: look at her personal values again.)

Creativity: Allow Chloe to attend a workshop that supports her creative interests, paid in full by the company, and give her paid time off to attend it. Even if the workshop isn't directly related to her job or the company's products, trust that if the workshop sparks her creativity, it will directly or indirectly benefit the company in some way.

Family: Give Chloe tickets to Disney World (with a VIP tour upgrade) so that she and her family can enjoy a joyous weekend of magic and mouse ears and make memories together.

Fun: Make a choose-your-own-adventure list of 10 rewards she can pick from—an extra day off work, a gift certificate for a hot new brunch spot so she can treat her friends to eggs Benedict and mimosas, or that vintage typewriter she's been eyeing.

Or how about Craig, the BAU internal owner, whose personal values include Structure, Repetition, and Sports?

Category	Owner	Goal	Personal Values	Values Linkage
Sustainable Scale Opportunities	Craig, BAU internal owner	Work with the NEW initiatives team to map out any next-phase impacts and opportunities through the product launch phases so that there is as little disruption to BAU as possible and handoffs to BAU resources are as clear and efficient as possible.	**Structure, Repetition, Sports**	Clients who use Souls by Kindred will encounter the customer support, billing, and public communications they expect with excellence. Kindred will be on-brand every step of the way.

Craig is a guy who enjoys stability and predictability. I'd bet my bottom dollar that he's got a sports team that he roots for relentlessly and has a framed jersey in his man cave at home.

Craig's Creative Compensation could be two tickets to a home game of his favorite sports team or a gift card to the Container Store or Home Depot (a favorite of many Mobilizers everywhere), or just like for Chloe, a list of things he can choose from that would make him happy.

These rewards don't have to be expensive or lavish, but they do need to be intentional and aligned with each Unicorn's personal values.

Understand that these Creative Compensation incentives are *not* replacements for paying people well, giving out bonuses for extraordinary performance, or supporting their lives with benefits like 401(k) contributions. However, thoughtful rewards like the ones I just described can make a big difference in retaining your top Unicorns.

If you can't afford a salary for a full-time Unicorn you want to recruit, offer them equity in the company, a percentage of revenue, or profit sharing as an alternative paycheck. Or offer them the opportunity to get paid on commission for clients, customers, sponsors, investors, or donors that they bring in. "Bring us a client who signs a $50,000 contract, and you get ten percent in your pocket." That way, their compensation grows as the company grows, and you can get people who have real skills and experience to jump on board with your big idea.

The bottom line: don't assume that you can't recruit Unicorns onto your team just because you don't have a big budget to pay full-time salaries or offer significant raises yet. Do Creative Compensation to rally people around your idea and keep them motivated to be on the team. And for God's sake, don't give them a branded tote bag or water bottle as a special "treat." Not unless their personal values happen to be Boredom and Clutter.

Compensation Policies Need to Evolve

Codility is a provider of skill-evaluation software that approaches compensation from a human-centered lens.

Jason Medley, who was the chief people officer of the company, said, "The companies that are going to win are going to be more progressive early and not fighting what's happening." He added, "We really have to step back and be innovative and force ourselves to change."

Here's one innovative decision Codility made—and a perfect example of Creative Compensation.[2]

Leaders at Codility acknowledged that global warming is a real thing because . . . well, science. Each year, weather gets more volatile, natural disasters are on the rise, and in some locations, temperatures are spiking higher than ever. One consequence? Many of Codility's employees in swelteringly hot cities were struggling to be productive at work. Why? They were literally *just too hot* because they didn't have air-conditioning units when they worked from home. As we all know, it's no fun to sit in front of a computer screen when you're melting like a candle in hell.

So, what did Codility do? It paid for people's AC systems to be installed. Talk about Creative Compensation. Not only did a blast of frosty air help employees to be more productive during work hours, but it was a huge perk during nonwork hours too. Each time someone dialed the temperature down from 88 to 68 degrees Fahrenheit, they said a silent "thank you" to Codility for making it possible. This is just one excellent example of how to reward your team in a way that's both personal and meaningful. Now, that's very cool! (Pun intended.)

Investing in Intrapreneurship

My friend John Stix is the co-founder of Fibernetics, one of Canada's top five telecom and technology companies, and best-selling author of *Discover Your WHO*.

Stix told me about a Creative Compensation approach that motivates employees to think like entrepreneurs and build wealth by doing so. The concept is simple: when an employee has a brilliant idea for a new product, the company treats them like a "start-up founder" and invests in their idea.

Fibernetics calls this investment project Fibernetics Ventures, Inc. It's an in-house incubator that provides capital investment, office space, and logistical support (read: access to internal Strategizers and Mobilizers) to turn employees' big ideas into reality.

Beyond providing new revenue streams, the in-house seedlings have given Fibernetics employees a fresh incentive to stay with the company: equity in the new ventures they launch. This means that everyone—both the mother ship and the new start-ups—wins.

This initiative gave Stix and his Fibernetics co-founder, Jody Schnarr, both Visionizers, a powerful reminder of why they went into business in the first place.

"As we started getting bigger, going from a 10-person startup back in 2003 to 200 people in our organization, certain people didn't enjoy themselves as much any more," Schnarr shared with *Tech News*. "Cloud at Cost [one of the companies born from their in-house incubator] came from a couple of people who wanted to move on, but they were valuable friends, valuable employees . . . This way, we keep working together."

One of the Unicorns behind Cloud at Cost is John Cullen, who started working in the telecom wholesale division at Fibernetics during the start-up phase of the company. As Fibernetics grew into a stable enterprise, so did Cullen's urge to move on and start his own wholesale business. But Schnarr didn't want to lose him. "I told him, 'You know, you've always been a great employee; we've always worked well; why don't we do something together? I'll fund it,'" Schnarr recalled.[3]

Fibernetics isn't alone. Companies like Coca-Cola, Disney, Google, Mastercard, Microsoft, T-Mobile, Unilever, and Wells Fargo run their own business accelerators and incubators to bring start-ups in their industry into the mother ship.[4]

By investing in team members' ideas with cash, supplies, mentorship, and other resources, you can inspire them to stay and keep winning with you rather than skipping to greener pastures elsewhere.

Take a look at your brand values and ask yourself if you can build a company where new ideas can come from a place of "creationship" instead of competition. Can you give people a reason to stay and innovate with you instead of competing with you?

THE SCOREBOARD DOESN'T ALWAYS TELL THE WHOLE STORY

If you really knew me, you'd know I'm a huge football fan.

After I left the corporate world and started my own companies, I readily told people that the only brand that could make me come back into a traditional corporate structure was my favorite one in the whole wide world—and there is *no* close second—the San Francisco 49ers. If they offered me a job cutting their grass at the stadium, I wouldn't hesitate to say yes.

In our family, we bleed red and gold, and we've loved the 49ers since the beginning, even back when they sucked so bad, it was embarrassing to admit you were part of "the Faithful."

Football is big business (the NFL's annual profit is $2 billion[5]), and teams are brands that don't just get revenue from games and tickets sold. They get paid from merchandise and licensing too. The more successful the brand, the more potential it has to earn.

The 49ers had one of the lowest brand equity scores until January 10, 1979, when Bill Walsh, exiting head football coach at Stanford University, joined the franchise as head coach and general manager. In fact, Walsh took the lowest-paying head coaching position offered at that time because the 49ers couldn't afford to pay him a competitive salary.[6] But as a Visionizing Strategizer (VS), he was committed to his vision and had a strategy to get there. He just needed the right Mobilizers to execute.

For folks who are wondering why I'm sharing a story from the "late 1900s," as my elementary-school-aged son calls it, besides being a 49ers fanatic, I read Bill Walsh's book *The Score Takes Care of Itself*, an iconic leadership playbook, early on in my corporate career. It's still a tome that many managers use today to rally their teams to greatness.

While many football coaches believe that the whole point is to win, win, win every time, always, no matter the cost, collateral damage be damned, Walsh had a different point of view. His attitude? Failure isn't failure. It's training.

When Bill Walsh created the West Coast offense, he set the standard for how the game was played forevermore. It involved a short-run and short-pass game instead of one with long, sexy passes showcasing the strong arm of the team's superstar quarterback. While it's now considered the gold standard, at first people scoffed at him: *This is not football.*

The haters and trolls (imagine if they had social media back then) were supported by the fact that in the first two seasons with Walsh as head coach, the 49ers remained at the bottom of the division with an abysmal 8 wins and 24 losses. By the third season, though, they hit their stride with the Unicorn Team moves that Walsh made, getting key talent and constantly and repeatedly testing the West Coast offense. They were rewarded with football's greatest winning metric: the Vince Lombardi Super Bowl Trophy.

I still remember that Super Bowl Sunday, watching my mom and dad cry with joy. It's my earliest memory of really understanding how good being a winner feels. Chants of "We don't suck, we don't suck, we don't suck!" could be heard outside, because everyone in our neighborhood had just witnessed the dream come true too.

Bill Walsh brought the 49ers to their first Super Bowl win (and then three more, but who's counting—oh, wait, *I am*) with his Unicorns—Joe Montana, Dwight Clark, Ronnie Lott, and later Jerry Rice and Steve Young. The lineage of great coaches after him—including Mike Holmgren of the Green Bay Packers, Mike Tomlin of the Pittsburgh Steelers, Andy Reid of the Kansas City Chiefs, and Mike Shanahan of the Denver Broncos—all started using the Walsh West Coast offense as their new playbook for winning. Walsh disrupted how the game was played and was willing to test it in real time (the Prototyping Process) until he got the ultimate result he envisioned.

I think of other teams, like the Detroit Lions, who at the time of this writing are one of just 12 NFL teams that have never won the Super Bowl.[7] One could say the Lions are a "losing" team. But when it comes to fan loyalty, ticket sales, and cultural impact, they are indisputably winning.

The Lions have had superfans like musicians Aretha Franklin, Eminem, and Kid Rock and actors Tim Allen, Jeff Daniels, and Taylor Lautner.[8] When tickets for Lions games go on sale, fans snatch them up ferociously, even when they're not home games, traveling hours or even days to see their team play. Lions fans regularly fill 25 percent of the seats at opposing teams' stadiums, a higher percentage than 22 other NFL teams get.[9] I'd argue that this so-called "losing" team is actually a Unicorn Team that's already winning and poised for even greater success.

The team hails from the city of Detroit, storied for being the birthplace of the auto industry and Motown, and also for its gritty, resilient "born from fire" people and brands. The Lions understand the assignment. They live, breathe, eat, sleep, and sweat these values both on and off the field. They are grit personified. They're the underdog, and they know it—and they know that their Big Win is on the way. It's not a matter of "if" they'll win the Super Bowl, only "when." Once they do, their fans will erupt with a cry that's heard all the way on Mars.

Unicorn Teams, like the Detroit Lions, recognize that there are many pieces of data that indicate if you're on the winning path or not. Revenue doesn't tell the whole story. Neither do points on a scorecard. Unicorn Teams understand that there's a difference between a strategy that isn't working versus a strategy that *is* working and simply requires more time to unfold.

EXERCISE

Offer Creative Compensation

Think about a team member who is crushing it and deserves to be rewarded. (If you're a solo team of one, this person might be you.) Find out this person's top values, then brainstorm a form of Creative Compensation that they inspire. A few examples:

- If this person values Freedom, offer them a three-day weekend (hello, extra free time!).

- If they value Excellence, give them an award to honor their impeccable work.

- If they value Philanthropy, make a donation to their favorite charity.

- A value like Innovation or Entrepreneurship could be rewarded with providing funding to make an intriguing new business idea happen, and then you share the profits.

- If Competition is a top value, you could offer a big cash bonus once someone enrolls 10 new clients, and an even bigger bonus if they help the company to become the fastest-growing brand in the region.

Different Unicorns care about different things. The compensation that is highly motivating to one Unicorn may feel uninteresting to another. Design rewards based on personal values and watch your Unicorns sprint toward success.

Your Performance Pulse centers that data and makes your Unicorns care about outcomes, because their actions are tied to what they personally care about. Modeling creative solutions and compensation will be one of the reasons why great Unicorns will want to play bigger with you, and why they will stay for the long haul.

TOP TAKEAWAYS

- The Performance Pulse provides an opportunity for you to check in with a Unicorn on your team once a month (or more). It's not a replacement for the annual performance review; it's a supplement.

- The Performance Pulse helps the Unicorn see how their personal values link up with brand values, giving them a reason to care about the initiative they're working on.

- To motivate your Unicorn to care even more deeply, offer Creative Compensation in the form of equity, revenue sharing, or a reward that's connected to one of their top values so that the treat feels personalized and thoughtful, not generic.

- *Don't give up too quickly.* Just because one KPI is lower than expected doesn't mean the team is failing or that an individual Unicorn's performance is lackluster. Your Unicorn Team may be headed for massive success even if the numbers currently say otherwise. It's possible you have a winning strategy in place and simply need more time to achieve the desired results.

PART IV

CHALLENGES AND SOLUTIONS

The Unicorn Innovation Model

VSM Process	● VISIONIZE			▲ STRATEGIZE			■ MOBILIZE			
Navigate How we make decisions together and choose the right idea to pursue	Ideastorm			DOIT			BEIT			
Motivate How we lead and the energy we bring to the team	V Types			S Types			M Types			
	VV	VS	VM	SV	SS	SM	MV	MS	MM	
Communicate How we get aligned, work on the right priorities together, and get things done at warp speed	Brandcast			Stratagem			Prototype			

IDEATION NEW Launch brand-new initiatives

ITERATION BAU Improve existing initiatives

< ~ ~ ~ UNICORN ENERGY ~ ~ ~ >

"My Unicorn Team is rocking away, working to make the great idea a reality, but things aren't perfect. We're encountering challenges because humans are humans."

"One Unicorn made a costly mistake. Another is thinking about leaving the team. There's drama brewing. I shudder to think what they're saying about me in the group chat . . ."

"How can we handle the challenges that inevitably arise and turn setbacks into wins? Even better, how can we prevent issues from happening in the first place?"

In Part IV, we'll discuss how to handle conflict, transitions, and other tough stuff—the Unicorn Way. I want to help you avoid the friction, noise, and drama that all too often plagues ordinary teams.

We'll cover how to prevent many issues from happening in the first place, and how to nip issues in the bud if they show up within your team.

I'll also show you what causes Unicorns to feel unhappy at work and what causes them to leave for greener pastures (it's not always about financial compensation, and in fact, it rarely is). And how to inspire your best Unicorns to stay on your team for the long haul.

By anticipating challenges before they happen, you're being proactive, and you can keep your team in the flow state that I call Unicorn Energy.

Unicorn Energy is the energy of winning. We choose the right idea to pursue. We have the right blend of Visionizer, Strategizer, and Mobilizer energy on the team. We communicate impeccably with one another, and everyone is clear on their role and which piece of the project they get to own. And everything in the Unicorn Innovation Model comes together.

Unicorn Energy is the ultimate goal of this model. It's the place where people genuinely love collaborating together, where work feels energizing instead of draining, and where great ideas come to life with astonishing speed and success.

There are plenty of issues that can knock your team out of Unicorn Energy and into sluggish, unproductive, waste-of-everyone's-time energy. Let's discuss what these problems are and how to prevent and resolve them.

CHAPTER 11

WHEN THERE'S CONFLICT ON THE TEAM

I was humiliated . . . and pissed.

I had just flown 3,431 miles from California to Puerto Rico to attend a conference for women in business with 500 people in attendance. The conference was filled with women running seven-, eight-, and nine-figure companies who were determined to bring their big ideas to market quickly. It was a stellar opportunity for me to network, make an impact, and hopefully return home with tons of new clients.

I'd been invited to give a presentation alongside big-name speakers like Tabitha Brown (social media star and Emmy Award–winning TV host) and Ivy McGregor (Beyoncé's right-hand woman and executive director of her charity, BeyGOOD). Plus, my oldest daughter was flying out to see me onstage, and I wanted to make her proud. I needed to bring my A game and pour inspiration and actionable ideas into the audience.

This was not the moment to stumble. I needed to score perfect 10s across the board and stick the landing.

The trip was fraught with drama from the get-go, including lengthy flight delays and a migraine that felt unyieldingly cruel amidst the chaotic trek to get there. But I rallied, popping into the hotel gym at seven in the morning to walk on the treadmill and get my head together. When I delivered my presentation later that day, it went even better than expected. At the end of my talk, I told everyone, "Visit my website, enter your e-mail, and you'll get a free guide that you can use to implement what you just learned from me." Simple enough.

I got a major round of applause. Seated in the front row, my daughter was beaming.

Nailed it! . . . or so I thought.

What I didn't know but soon learned was that my website was malfunctioning.

Every time someone entered their e-mail, they got an error message—the Internet equivalent of a door slammed in their face. It's every entrepreneur's worst nightmare. Enthusiastic leads were trying to become paying clients, but they were getting blocked.

I messaged my tech team in a panic, but it took them three days to fix the issue. By then, we'd missed out on numerous opportunities and those leads were gone forever. What made this especially embarrassing was the fact that my topic was on how to create high-end experiences. I had preached onstage about elegance, excellence, and living your brand values, and this was the exact opposite—a hot mess.

After getting back to California, I called my Unicorn Team together. Turns out, the situation was even worse than I thought. It wasn't just one sign-up link that was broken—it was a systemic issue. Every single link throughout the entire site was broken, because all our websites had been hacked. This meant that not a single media appearance, podcast episode, interview, or article I'd written over the last 20 years was findable on my site. And apparently, this had been happening for *months.*

My stomach gnarled into a knot as I calculated thousands of potential clients being blocked from my mailing list, with millions in potential earnings lost. Not to mention how sloppy and embarrassing it looks when you claim to be a brand strategist and business expert, and your website isn't working.

"How did this happen?" I asked my team, taking deep breaths. To me, the company founder, this was an enormous problem. So why didn't anyone else seem as concerned as I was? Why hadn't this been solved months ago? What exactly was going on here?

No one had a satisfactory answer. Some folks got defensive. Others assured me, "We're working on it." But nobody (myself included) took ownership of the issue, apologized, or proposed a solution.

Confession: at this exact moment, I felt like I was having an out-of-body-experience, and my mind shifted to a doomsday scenario where I fantasized about firing everyone on my team (and I really, really love and respect my team). I wanted to shut down my business and start over from scratch. All of my hard work from the last two decades seemed to be spiraling down the toilet due to such an irritatingly small yet crucially important detail: *#^7!@* links!* I'm sure I'm not alone in having one of those internal-combustion moments; dealing with disappointment is part of the game.

But while it's tempting to point the finger at another person ("It's *your* fault this happened!"), I knew this wasn't an individual issue; it was a team issue. A team composed of numerous Unicorns, including me. I needed to own the part that I played in this tech meltdown, just as I needed my fellow Unicorns to claim responsibility too.

Having a Unicorn Team doesn't mean you live in a utopia, where everything goes perfectly and every single investment pays off. Links will break. Mistakes will happen. The difference is that instead of blaming others and avoiding the tough conversations you need to have, you can handle issues the Unicorn Way.

Own the brilliant contributions that you make. Own your mistakes too, and you will navigate conflict more successfully.

HANDLING CONFLICT

The Typical Way	The Unicorn Way
Assign blame to someone else. *"So-and-so really dropped the ball."*	Acknowledge that winning is a shared responsibility. *"The ball was dropped, and the area we need to work on is _____."*
Give an overly positive spin, no apology. *"There are no mistakes, only lessons and opportunities!"*	Apologize to fellow Unicorns when appropriate. *"This never should have happened. I made a mistake, and I own it."*
Follow orders exactly as instructed, no questions asked. *"The CEO said to do this, so that's what I did. I was just following their orders!" (Subtext: if it didn't work out, it's their fault, not mine!)*	Question orders and make appropriate recommendations. *"The CEO said XYZ, and I understand their reasoning; however, I see a better way to achieve this."*
Avoid difficult conversations. *"Maybe I'll bring it up . . . later."*	Embrace difficult conversations. *"By confronting this, we're going to figure it out faster, together."*
Choose Frankenstein or Band–Aid fixes instead of creating a real solution. *"We figured out a workaround for now. To really address the issue, we'd have to do XYZ, and that's not within the scope of my job."*	Solve the root cause and find a real and lasting solution. *"To solve the root cause of this issue, these are the decisions we need to make so that we don't encounter it again."*

Let's look at some of the most common conflicts that Unicorn Teams experience and their solutions. Each solution is based on one of the Unicorn Team Rules (page xxii).

Conflict #1: NEW vs. BAU

Business as Usual (BAU) refers to all the things your team currently does to bring revenue in the door and achieve other KPIs. The daily routine. The systems and processes that are already working pretty well or even extremely well. The deliverables that keep the lights on and the bills paid.

On a Unicorn Team, focusing on BAU initiatives feels to a Visionizer like tossing a cold, wet towel on their fire. While the Strategizer and Mobilizer folks work on refining the BAU and making it better and better, the Visionizer has already lost interest and wants to move on to something new. The Visionizer team member has a Big, Exciting, Wonderful, New Idea! This shiny object is alluring, sparkly, and has their full attention. They want to get going on it, yesterday.

This creates a difficult tension within the team. The Visionizer says, "Look at my Big New Idea! Isn't it amazing? Let's go!" Other team members think, *Whoa, wait a second—I already have a lot on my plate, and now you want me to do this new thing too? I don't have the bandwidth.* Conflict ensues, along with feelings of impatience (Visionizer) and resentment and overwhelm (Strategizer and Mobilizer). This is a common battle I call NEW vs. BAU.

Solution: Unicorn Team Rule #4

Remember Unicorn Team Rule #4: We win because we Visionize, Strategize, and Mobilize.

When there's a tension between Business as Usual and the Big New Idea, each Unicorn Team member has an important role to play.

Visionizer Unicorns: You need to recognize that your fellow Unicorns might be at max capacity. They may not have the ability to throw themselves into a brand-new project (no matter how thrilling it feels to you!) unless you're willing to give up something else. Accept there's going to be a trade-off. You can't have it all. But you can have what matters most.

Strategizer Unicorns: You need to help the Visionizer understand the trade-off more clearly. Help them see the benefits of doing this Big New Idea, as well as the cost in terms of time, energy, and money. Lay out the cold, hard facts. While this may feel like dumping frigid water on their exciting, hot idea, it's important and leads to better outcomes in the end.

Mobilizer Unicorns: You need to be courageous and speak up if you have concerns, see a better option, or simply can't do what's being asked because you're already maxed out and working full-time on other initiatives. Mobilizers have a tendency to become martyrs, thinking, *I'll do whatever the team assigns to me, even if it kills me.* Please don't do this. Your team needs your Mobilizer energy burning strong, not burning out. Rather than automatically complying (harboring resentment the entire time), you need to be a leader, not a follower. Use one of these phrases to push back and propose an alternative:

> "I hear what you're saying, and I agree that this new idea is exciting. However, I don't think we should do this right now—and here's why . . ."

> "I like the new idea; however, I don't think the strategy you're proposing is the best course of action. I think there's a better way to approach this. Let me show you what I'm thinking . . ."

> "I can do this new project, but only if we postpone one of my current projects until later. I can't do both at the same time."

We don't automatically say, "Yes! Let's do it!" just because someone happens to have a new, shiny idea. We Visionize > Strategize > Mobilize to make sure this idea:

- Aligns with the company values
- Leads to the outcome that we want
- Has been vetted alongside other candidates
- Has been evaluated to understand the benefits, risks, and trade-offs
- Is truly the best candidate to run with
- Can be assigned an owner who has the bandwidth to do it

Most things can be solved by applying the Visionize > Strategize > Mobilize process. We start here whenever deciding to do something new or change something that is already working.

Conflict #2: Unnecessary Delays Due to the "Approval Bottleneck"

Oftentimes on teams, there's a never-ending game of "tag, you're it" when it comes to getting approval.

The copywriter is waiting for the marketing director to approve their draft. The marketing director is waiting for the CFO to approve their budget. The CFO is waiting for the CEO to respond to their e-mail, and before you know it, every person on the Unicorn Team is saying, "I can't do XYZ until so-and-so gives me approval." Projects drag on unfinished for weeks, months, and years, stuck in a never-ending approval limbo. Then, just when it seems like the project will finally get in motion, uh-oh, the owner goes on vacation. Another two-week delay. The game of tag stalls once again.

What's really happening here? Whether consciously or not, each person on the team is thinking, *I don't want to make the final call. I want somebody else to decide what we're doing. Because if I decide and it doesn't work out, then it's my fault.*

It feels safer to wait for someone else to approve the budget, timeline, or plan rather than to make a courageous decision and own it. If the project turns out to be successful, it's easy to say, "I was part of making it happen." But if the project is unsuccessful, you can say, "Well, it was so-and-so's decision to do this, not mine."

Approval bottleneck is not the Unicorn Team way. On a Unicorn Team, everyone owns their role, including the decisions they need to make.

Solution: Unicorn Team Rule #5

Remember Unicorn Team Rule #5: We share the responsibility to succeed.

Being part of a Unicorn Team doesn't include "othering" when things don't go well and "centering" when things do. On a Unicorn Team, each person has to own their excellent decisions, their victories, their triumphs, and their mistakes too. Further, the team has to establish a culture where failing is *okay* and even *rewarded*. This is a radical shift for many teams and organizations.

Imagine saying, "We decided to XYZ. It didn't work out the way we expected. In the process we learned numerous lessons. Let's go through our top ten lessons together as a team." This is the Unicorn Way.

To prevent the "Tag, you're it!" pattern from continuing, point to the Campaign Playbook and commitments you've made as a team. Assert the importance of eliminating bottlenecks. Own your decision to either move forward after communicating a final timeline or stopping to avoid negatively affecting the meaningful outcome. Recommend a new, leaner approval process so that you and others don't have to encounter this irritating friction in the future.

Conflict #3: Staying Busy Doing the Wrong Things

You and your team may feel extremely busy. So much to do. Never enough time. But are you busy doing the *right* things?

I understand this predicament all too well. I once spent $150,000 trying to fix the way we were acquiring customers (our "funnel"), only to eventually realize that my team and I were trying to fix the wrong issue.

In digital marketing lingo, an online funnel is an automated e-mail system. It goes like this: the website visitor provides their e-mail address. This person immediately gets an e-mail saying, "Welcome!" and inside that e-mail, there's a valuable gift, such as a report, guide, video, audiobook sample, or discount code. After that, this person receives a series of follow-up e-mails to help them get better acquainted with the brand. They might receive an e-mail about the brand's origin story, the brand's mission, customer success stories, valuable tips and tools, and so on. Eventually, they receive an e-mail with a special offer—an opportunity to buy something. By this point, they're warmed up and ready to purchase! You've nurtured a relationship with this person, and now they're ready to act. You have "funneled" someone from being a curious website visitor, to a lead, to a paying customer.

E-mail funnels are pretty simple (almost every brand has some version), and when they're set up correctly, they perform astoundingly well.

I created a funnel for my own company that secured 400,000 leads. But hold your applause, because less than one percent of those people actually converted, or purchased anything. My

Unicorn Team and I went through all the possibilities. Was it the copywriting? Was it the number of e-mails in the series? Was there a tech glitch preventing people from purchasing?

"Maybe it's the offer," one Unicorn pointed out.

I wanted to smack my forehead onto my desk. We had spent copious amounts of time and six figures in cash trying to fix the e-mail funnel. Yet it had never occurred to us that the problem wasn't the funnel itself—it was the offer we were attempting to sell. The people signing up for this particular e-mail series did not want this particular offer.

Unicorns (particularly Mobilizers) love to get things done and feel the thrill of accomplishment. However, be careful. It's easy to stay busy doing the wrong things. Getting something done is not the same as getting the *right* thing done.

Solution: Unicorn Team Rule #2

Remember Unicorn Team Rule #2: We move fast, because we only work on the right hard things.

We fail faster because failing slowly kills culture and keeps us from getting value to the right people. This goes for everyone on your Unicorn Team.

If you're the Visionizer, your first job is to deliver the disappointment of what's happening in a dignified and honest manner. Saying "I'm disappointed" is not a bad thing. It gets across the truth of the negative impact on all of the team.

I gave my team a three-day turnaround to do research, provide a solution, and own the communication syncing around it. We updated our Performance Pulse and reporting requirements for the individuals working on this initiative too. Our Strategizer realized that the issue was undoing all the hard work we had done and was impacting our marketing and sales results, while our Mobilizer realized that they could own the fix and roll it out quickly without needing permission from some type of governance council.

Within three days, we had a viable solution: a brand-new offer that our data (and instincts) told us our audience would happily purchase. And purchase they did. Our conversion rate leapt from a piddly 1 percent to a whopping 20 percent.

HOW TO HAVE DIFFICULT CONVERSATIONS, THE UNICORN WAY

1) When describing an issue, say "we," "us," and "our"

There's a glaring typo in the newsletter. The CEO is giving a talk, and their slides are a mess. A client doesn't receive the deliverable on the promised date.

Whatever the snafu may be, avoid pointing the finger at one Unicorn. Instead, use words like *we, us, our,* and *as a team* to describe the issue. This language reinforces that it's a shared problem, not one person's problem.

"This is not very Unicorn Team of us."

"We can do better."

"What can each of us do to make sure this doesn't happen again?"

"What is our next right move?"

"As a team, we missed something here."

This language helps open the door for people to take more personal ownership when they understand they are part of a greater impact and domino effect.

2) Do a better postmortem review and ask Unicorns how to future-fix any breakdowns

A good practice for an any-sized organization is to have a session dedicated solely to reviewing what worked and what didn't, called a postmortem or after-action review (AAR). When discussing a project that did not go well or a chronic problem that keeps arising, invite each Unicorn to make a recommendation that will specifically help the team to avoid the same mistakes in the future. Make space for them to speak and be heard.

Regardless of whether their job title is CEO or intern or anything in between, each Unicorn's input is valuable. Go around the room or Zoom and ask:

"What do you think we should do differently next time?"

"What's your recommendation here?"

"Do you think there's a better way to achieve XYZ?"

"Let's take three days to research, generate ideas, and then report back. We can each share potential solutions."

Make sure someone is in charge of recording suggestions and seeing where to make improvements in the Stratagem and Prototyping Process. This is the part that actually matters most: whatever you document, you need to steward and consider in a future project. Otherwise, people will think the AAR process is a waste of time.

3) Ask to hear more

My client and friend Dr. Lynne Maureen Hurdle is known in the media as "the Conflict Closer." When big corporations have a team going through a major conflict that is costing them millions of dollars, they bring Dr. Hurdle in to help the team move through it. For more than 30 years, she has guided people through some of the toughest conversations of their lives.

When having a difficult conversation at work, at home, or anywhere else, Dr. Hurdle recommends using these eight words: "Is there anything more I need to know?"[1]

Ask that question. Pause. Allow your fellow Unicorns to share more, if needed. Too often, we rush through an uncomfortable conversation because we just want it to be over. These eight words provide an opportunity for team members to say whatever's been left unsaid.

Remember Unicorn Team Rule #6: We say what needs to be said, even when it's uncomfortable.

Reward Unicorns who are willing to speak the unsaid. Lean in to hard conversations with dignity and honesty.

There's a custom sports jersey I wear into the office that my kids got me for Christmas one year. It says across the back, "Jen Don't Lie"—meaning, "My mom will let you know if she feels like you're about to step into something really bad." I wear it proudly, because what that means is that you can count on me and my company to be completely honest when it comes to what could make your idea excellent and your brand the one to beat.

Think about a time when you had a big piece of green kale between your teeth and not one of the three colleagues you talked to right before you went onstage to do a big presentation told you. Yet wouldn't you have preferred they let you know?

Then why wouldn't you tell someone a strategy they were about to execute wouldn't work, if you knew it?

Try this: "Hey, Jen, that strategy has kale between its teeth!"

Now, that's a Unicorn Way of dealing with something awkward while being kind at the same time.

4) Take personal responsibility and apologize, when appropriate

On a Unicorn Team, every victory is a shared victory. Every mistake is a shared mistake. However, don't get it twisted. There are certainly moments when an individual apology is appropriate.

If you bungled something up and caused unnecessary strife for your teammates, say so. Own it. Try a statement like "XYZ happened, and I take responsibility for that. I'm sorry for causing stress for my team. Here's how I will make sure this doesn't happen again . . ."

You don't have to wring your hands and berate yourself, but you can calmly state what happened and how you'll take steps to address it. Then follow through and do what you promised to earn back people's trust.

Back in my corporate days, one time the CEO of the high-tech company I worked for hired a COO who was an absolute tyrant who got results through laying down an iron fist. It's important to note that we were making our performance goals and our investors were really happy—but the culture disintegrated and team performance started faltering. Unicorns started leaving. When our CEO realized that the new COO wasn't a culture fit, he removed him from the role and shared in his quarterly "state-of-the-business address" how important it was for all of us to be and live our values. He stated, "I made this change in service of that. I'm sorry for making the work environment nonoptimal for you, and I aim to do better." In other words, he owned his mistake and actually apologized. It was a power move that in many toxic work environments could have been seen as weak. Instead, it reinvigorated our commitment and gave us permission to own our own blunders too.

In our society, we often hear advice like "never apologize," or "stop saying 'I'm sorry' so much" (an admonishment that is often directed toward women). I respectfully disagree. There are times when "I'm sorry" is exactly what you should say, and when your team hears a sincere apology, it can neutralize some of the tension in the room. When you do so, you lead by example and show your fellow Unicorns that it's powerful to do the same.

That's how you resolve conflicts like a Unicorn Team.

But even if you're continually improving and leveling up as a team, that doesn't mean every single Unicorn will stick around forever. In the next chapter, I'll take you inside the mind of a Unicorn who is thinking about quitting. You'll see how you might be able to persuade this person to stay. Or, if that's not going to happen, how to navigate the transition gracefully and keep your team strong.

TOP TAKEAWAYS

- Every team experiences conflict. Unicorn Teams are no exception. Mistakes will happen. Launches occasionally flop. Not every decision will prove to be the right one.

- However, Unicorn Teams can recover from mistakes, learn, and move on faster than other teams do.

- When conflict arises, it's not one person's job to resolve it. Each Unicorn on the team has a role to play. Often the Visionizer needs to speak less and listen more; the Strategizer needs to help the Visionizer understand that every request they make comes with benefits, costs, and trade-offs; and the Mobilizer needs to speak up and make recommendations rather than merely follow orders.

- Saying "I'm sorry" is not a bad thing. Learn to own your wins *and* your mistakes. A sincere apology can defuse tension and change the energy in the room so that you can brainstorm solutions together and get back to winning.

CHAPTER 12

WHEN YOUR FAVORITE UNICORN WANTS TO QUIT

We live in a time in which there are infinitely endless ways to make a living. A Unicorn doesn't necessarily need to take a full-time position. They can start their own company. They can freelance. They can become a social media influencer and earn millions from paid sponsors. They've got options aplenty. Which means, if you want to attract the world's best, brightest, and most talented Unicorns, you've got to create a team that's worth belonging to.

Taking it personally when someone leaves the team isn't a good use of your energy. Redirect your energy and ask, "How can we be a place where Unicorns think twice about leaving?" and, "Would we be missed if our brand no longer existed?"

If you've done your job aligning a Unicorn's personal values with the core values of your brand, showing them how they are rewarded as a result (see Chapter 10), that's already a giant step. But it would be unrealistic to think that the Unicorn talent you've curated and nurtured hasn't been approached with other opportunities. Or maybe they're just seeking a change because a life event causes them to need something different. So, it is what it is.

Or is it?

Losing top talent is a big deal, and the numbers might make you gag.

THE COST OF LOSING YOUR UNICORNS

According to Gallup, $1 TRILLION dollars (yes, all caps—shouting required) is what businesses lose *every year* due to voluntary turnover, and that's just in the U.S. alone.[1]

When it comes to rare talent of the Unicorn variety, "voluntary turnover" is simply a nice way of saying, "You just lost the future."

Gulp.

I didn't intend to be so dismal, but there is hope, and best of all, you have the power to address it.

In the same Gallup study, 52 percent of voluntarily exiting employees say their manager or organization *could have done something* to prevent them from leaving their job.

You're already on the right track with protecting your future, and you're building a Unicorn Team culture. Sincere congratulations! You're already "doing something" to prevent attrition. And there's more you can do. But first, a cautionary tale.

Inside the Mind of a Unicorn Who's Preparing to Leave

Many years ago, I was working in a strategy and marketing leadership role at a large Fortune 50 publicly traded, blue-chip brand. We'll call them Corp X. I was a textbook intrapreneur—someone who thought creatively and expansively like an entrepreneur but genuinely wanted to bring new ideas to market by working inside of iconic brands I deeply admired.

Earlier in my career, one of my mentors (who was the president of one of the biggest advertising agencies in the world) gave me sage advice: "Jen, if you want to be someone who's seen as invaluable, take the projects no one wants. They won't be able to ignore you." That advice paid off so many times. I volunteered for the projects no one wanted to touch because they disrupted BAU activity. As a strong Strategizer, I could translate vision into mobilization like few others. I became known as the Go-to-Market Whisperer, the New Idea Alchemist, the Make the Impossible Possible Leader. And because I was a top producer, buzzing with ambition, Corp X management asked me to head up a new, game-changing service they wanted to offer.

With the right launch, this could be a revolutionary concept, and I was *all in*. If I could show my boss how much of a value-add I could be, then that promotion coming up could be mine. This was the step to get me into the C-suite, and then eventually a board seat. I had my eyes on the prize and was ready to dazzle. Whatever lofty hopes and expectations management had for me, I would exceed them all.

Like all of the initiatives I'd tackled before, this one was high stakes. The company was rebranding itself and spending millions on being seen as a technology leader instead of merely a telecommunications provider. It was an entirely new product suite—nothing smells more delicious than new revenue streams—and this wasn't just a nice-to-have, sexy new product. Its success was critical in replacing outdated technology that was on the verge of obsolescence.

There was a race to be first to market with a working product prototype, because our big competitor—the three-letter brand that was making acquisitions all over the country to gain this advantage—announced they were doing it too. But who would be first?

All the obstacles you can imagine—including lots of red tape, regulatory considerations, labor and union staff, and a very eager product-development department, not to mention itchy executives who wanted to take credit for a big win like this—were present. And I had to wrangle all of them with every strategy and tool I've shared with you so far. I showed my team how to Visionize > Strategize > Mobilize. We did a Brandcast. We made a Stratagem. We Prototyped. We Performance Pulse'd. I didn't use these terms yet, but I was creating intellectual property that I'd later be known for.

Fast-forward to the end: we crushed it. Our team of Unicorns created hundreds of millions of dollars and jobs for the company. Everyone got bonuses. There were acrylic trophies handed out at the all-hands meeting. I got the leadership award for Biggest Impact. That promotion I'd been eyeing with a half-million-a-year salary attached to it? I knew it was mine.

After we finished celebrating, my manager asked to have a meeting with me. This was it. The moment I'd worked so hard to create. I wore my best "professional" gray three-piece suit for the occasion, bringing every bit of the main-character energy I had. I walked into his office deciding to act gracious and thankful, surprised but not shocked. After all, I'd earned this.

My manager—we'll call him Ben—was sitting across from me, semireclining in his desk swivel chair, hands pressed together in a steeple.

"Jennifer, thank you for your work ethic. You hit your goals through your grit and coordination," he said with a wide, charismatic grin. "It's remarkable how you get teams to perform extraordinary things." He threw his arms up as if in prayer.

I sat straight-backed and poised. I would be calm and gracious, and accept my prize with dignity.

"You're going to continue to be an incredible asset to this organization under Ned's leadership in the new Strategy and Marketing Division. You two will make a great team."

My brain's processing speed slowed down. It took me a minute to realize I was being passed over. The promotion—*my* promotion—was being handed to someone else—who, unlike me, happened to play golf with my boss every weekend, a place I never really felt like I belonged anyway.

Suddenly my three-piece suit felt tight. Constricting. I was hot. Was this office stuffy?

Ned, who hadn't done much during the two years that I'd been getting this project off the ground, was the one leveling up. The type of effort he'd put in could best be described as standard. Average. Unremarkable. To give him credit, he was helping to keep the lights on, and that's mission critical. That's what BAU is, remember? But, wow. It stung.

I had just led my team to glory, delivering hundreds of millions of dollars to my employer on a sterling-silver, Unicorn-engraved platter. Ned, on the other hand? Not so much. Yet he was going to be my new boss.

And this, reader, is how you lose your top-performing Unicorn.

I mustered a tight-lipped smile, and in a low, clear voice, I thanked Ben for his mentorship and slowly rose to leave. When I got to the hallway, I realized the system I was in hadn't been made for me, that my ambition wasn't being met with the autonomy to write my own future. I began plotting my exit. Formerly, I would've done just about anything to help my employer win. But now? I would do just about anything to leave.

Nine months later, I handed in my resignation while contemplating a few options:

1. Start my own business. But what type of business? I didn't really know.

2. Get a recruiter and apply for another job, a bigger executive role where I would have more power and prestige inside of another brand.

3. Stay because the cost of leaving was also something to consider. I had a pony job with a badass team, the cross-functional respect of other department heads, a high-six-figure salary with a big bonus (and you know I achieved that bonus every damn year), a corner office with a disco ball hanging from the ceiling, and a parking spot with my name on it in the executive garage.

Despite having all of the trophies and triumphs to brag about and my identity being very much wrapped up in the culture there, you've guessed by now that I chose door #1.

It wasn't easy to do, and I don't recommend the entrepreneurial path for everyone. In fact, I believe that if more talented people worked in Unicorn Team environments, they might figure out that it's worth more to stay. But I also don't regret pursuing entrepreneurship, and I now get to use my superpowers to help people in a different way.

Why do Unicorns leave? They leave because they don't feel respected, appreciated, or rewarded appropriately for the contributions they've made. They leave when donkeys get promoted instead of the Unicorns who have earned the title. They also leave because they know they have plenty of other options, including becoming their own boss.

However, not every Unicorn longs to become an entrepreneur, and there are tons of talented people who sincerely want to be a part of something bigger than they can do on their own. These are your people. Send out the Unicorn signal to call them in and to inspire them to stay.

Don't forget your best tool to prevent Unicorns from leaving: the Performance Pulse. Do a PP early and often. I recommend doing a Performance Pulse once a month, *at minimum*, both to ensure that your Unicorn is on track and to reward them for excellence consistently.

That Gallup study that uncovered the staggering $1 trillion cost of losing your best folks? They also found that "over half of exiting employees say that in the three months before they left, neither their manager nor any other leader spoke with them about their job satisfaction or future with the organization."[2] Talk about a missed opportunity. This kind of loss is usually preventable, especially when you bake the Performance Pulse into your routine.

Remember: Values = Vision + Voids + Violations. Speak to the Unicorn's future, acknowledge their present contributions, and recognize their past experiences. A large corporation can absorb some Unicorn attrition, but a small- or medium-sized business can be destroyed by it.

When Team Members Are Ready for a New Role

Sometimes Unicorns want to quit the team. Other times, they don't necessarily want to jump ship, but they're hungry for a new role. They're evolving, perhaps turning into a new type of Unicorn, and they want a position that reflects this.

Take Sarah Paikai, who I introduced earlier as one of the core Unicorns on my team. Sarah had helped us become an eight-figure consulting company but found more joy in product delivery and fulfillment over the operational duties of hiring, training, financial forecasts, and P&L and revenue responsibility. She was the first Mobilizer on our team, and she eventually grew into the role of COO of my company, Master Brand Institute (MBI).

Sarah and I knew that the Unicorn Innovation Model had the potential to become its own business, separate from MBI. Bringing a whole new company into the world would require start-up energy and pull Sarah's attention (and mine) away from MBI. I welcomed this change, because I no longer wanted to run the company (I was happy to pass the reins over to Sarah) and was hungry for a new era in my career. I was ready to shift from well-paid consultant and CEO to thought leader, speaker, and author. I wanted to write more books that reached more people with the models we'd developed during our decade of working together. Change was afoot. This meant Sarah and I needed to reimagine what the most optimal Unicorn Team was—even if that meant our roles looked very different from what we had originally set up.

To navigate this transition, I needed to step more fully into my Visionizer energy, and Sarah needed to shift from being a Pure Mobilizer into more of a Strategizer role. We both found our stride in areas that we deeply wanted to dive into—beyond the traditional monikers of CEO and COO.

If there's one thing I hope you gain from this story, it's that *transition* is not a dirty word. When you (or another Unicorn) evolves into a new role, embrace it, and adjust the team to fill the gaps that this shift creates. It doesn't have to be all on you. In fact, it's better when it's not.

STAY, START, OR SABBATICAL?

Great leaders want people in their companies who *want* to be there. They also want people who are excited to be part of something significant and values driven. If you're not feeling aligned with your team or enthusiastic about the work you're doing, that's a real problem, and you need to confront it. Don't be afraid of what this contemplation uncovers. Allow yourself full permission to see what's possible.

If you're considering a job move to somewhere else (or if a Unicorn on your team is thinking about leaving), there are three choices:

- *Stay* inside of the company or brand you're currently at
- *Start* a new job somewhere else or with your own business
- *Sabbatical* by taking a break or leave of absence for a period of time

As you consider these options, here are 10 questions to ask yourself. I recommend taking time to answer them in a journal so you can see what reflects back to you.

1. What are the benefits of what I currently get to do?
2. Am I working on projects that are values driven for me personally?
3. Do I have the opportunity to contribute at the intersection of what I'm great at and also what I'm passionate about?
4. What's the cost of *Staying* in my current situation? (financial, emotional, mental, physical)
5. What's the cost of *Starting* a business of my own? (financial, emotional, mental, physical)
6. What's the cost of taking a *Sabbatical*? (financial, emotional, mental, physical)
7. Do I need to have a brave conversation before making my decision? With whom? About what?
8. What do I need in order to make the best and clearest decision? (This could be "a full night's sleep," "time to think it over," "more courage," etc.)

9. Will what I'm considering help me fully express my Unicorn Leadership Type?

10. If I'm considering quitting and doing something else instead, can I rally a Unicorn Team around my new idea? Who can help me make this move successfully?

Quitting my job was one of the scariest and best decisions I ever made. The same may be true for you. Or it may not.

Before you quit, thoroughly consider these 10 questions. I would place particular emphasis on the last question. If leaving is ultimately the right move, ask yourself, "Who can help me exit my current job / business / type of work and shift into my next era?" Surround yourself with people who want to see you happy, healthy, thriving, and living out your purpose.

TOP TAKEAWAYS

- Transition is not necessarily a bad thing. Sometimes a Unicorn needs to evolve into a new role on the team.

- The role you play on the team now may not be the role you play forever. For instance, someone whose Unicorn Leadership Type is Mobilizing Strategizer (MS) will be very comfortable in a Mobilizer role. But this person may need to put on their Strategizer hat as the brand evolves.

- When you're unhappy on a team, you must decide: *Stay, Start, or Sabbatical?* Stay inside of the company you're currently at; Start a new job somewhere else, or start your own business; Sabbatical by taking a break or leave of absence for a period of time.

- Only you can make the call. It's your life and career. Explore your stay, start, or sabbatical options thoroughly. Don't make a hasty decision.

- Ultimately, if you're unhappy on a team for a prolonged period of time, then you're holding the team back from being as successful as it could be. Part ways gracefully for the highest good of everyone involved . . . including you.

CHAPTER 13

WHEN A UNICORN IS AFRAID TO PLAY BIG

A great idea needs Visionizer energy first and foremost—to share the future vision, present void, and past violation so that others want to rally around it. A product or service that solves for this vision has a huge possibility of winning.

I'm really good at smelling a winner. I tell my clients that I can "smell the money," and I mean it literally. When someone describes an idea that has the potential to generate millions or billions, it's almost as if there's a scent in the air. I have a tingle up my spine and a thud in my chest, my eyes dilate, and I know: *"That's* the one." My instincts about where the market is going are rarely wrong.

I knew I needed to lean in to this money-sniffing superpower when I launched my own business.

While I eventually founded Master Brand Institute and was named one of *Forbes*'s top brand strategists, this wasn't actually the first company I started. My first business was a retail shop selling undergarments for women. While I'd built a personal brand as a rock star inside of the companies I'd worked for, this was my first foray into building my own company brand. It was a meteoric success. Until it wasn't. Here's how my first business was born and then died . . .

While I was still at Corp X and on a plane ride home from Dallas to Honolulu, something caught my attention.

Quite a few women stepping off the plane had the same carry-on bag. Pink with black-and-white stripes. Tissue paper peeking out of the top. An iconic logo on the side. I had one too. It was a bag from Victoria's Secret. In the late 2000s, carrying one was quite a status symbol.

For people who lived in Hawaii, it was more than that. We wanted a fun, sexy, and inspiring shopping experience, not one with the harsh fluorescent glare you'd find at Walmart. But we also wanted a store that you'd feel comfortable bringing your kids into (not a seedy "adult" shop in a sketchy area of town). Add the fantasy of the Victoria's Secret Angels and its multichannel marketing machine—retail, catalog, and online—and everyone felt proud to carry that pink, striped bag. But because Victoria's Secret didn't have any stores on-island, this meant booking a flight off-island to a city like Seattle, Los Angeles, or Las Vegas to shop, then toting your treasures back home with you.

On that fateful day at the airport, one by one, my Strategizer brain put all the pieces together.

- Women who live in Hawaii have limited options (really, none) when it comes to buying beautiful underwear. And (mostly) everyone wears underwear.

- They fly off-island to shop at Victoria's Secret but would probably love the option to shop closer to home.

- Victoria's Secret doesn't carry a diverse range of sizes. Their customers don't actually look like the models or mannequins, and if you were an XL or larger at that time, the options were nil.

- The products were pretty but not very comfortable then, especially for curvier bodies.

- What if I started a business to fill this void?

It was a "Eureka!" moment. I could create a new category in a market that Victoria's Secret had already opened up. I could apply my Unicorn skills to my own idea and bring it to life.

Once I decided I was handing in my resignation, I knew I had to get the strategy solid.

- *Financing:* I took a second mortgage on my house to open my first store and create inventory.

- *Research:* I poured through the SEC filings and found out that Victoria's Secret, a publicly traded company, had no plans to expand to Hawaii, Alaska, or any U.S. territories and definitely had no plans to go overseas. I decided to start in those markets and hoped to position the brand for acquisition by Victoria's Secret in the future.

- *Marketing:* I would do a local push to the media and ask my friends to tell people when the first store opened (I didn't have enough capital to do more than that).

- *Unicorn Team:* I couldn't afford to hire a team. I needed to be the V, the S, and the M. A one-woman show. I'd build an actual team later. Or so I told myself.

I enlisted my preteen kids to be my first "hired help," opened the first store, and quickly realized that my idea was a winner. We sold out everything in the first week, and the local media picked it up.

They started calling me "the UnderStyler." With the serendipitous timing of Oprah highlighting bra fitting as one of her favorite things and a new upstart undergarment company called Spanx by Sara Blakely, my fledgling company was soon poised for massive success.

But when you're running your own business, sometimes you're too close to see the bigger picture. Without the right team around you pointing out what you're not seeing, you can get in trouble really fast.

I needed someone who could drive logistics and inventory management, as well as manage the store staff. I kept telling myself,

I don't have the budget to hire more employees; it's better if I do it my-self. It would be too difficult to train someone to do this. I don't have time right now, so I'll just keep doing it. Underlying all of this? *Fear.* Fear of investing more money into my business to cover new salaries. Fear that I might fail and then have to lay people off. Fear of playing big and then winding up embarrassed and ashamed when my big vision didn't work out. Doing all the logistics and inventory management by myself felt safer. Hiring someone else felt too risky.

The problem? I'm not a strong Mobilizer. Never have been. I'm great at seeing where the winning idea goes and rallying the right doers to make it happen. But handling all the small but important details, completing the daily checklist, and bringing projects over the finish line have never been my top strengths. I needed a Mobilizer on my team but stubbornly refused to hire one. Rather than leaning in to the Strategizer superpowers that I'd honed during my corporate career and building a team to handle my low-fluency zones, I tried to do it all. That was my first fatal error.

Next error: I didn't believe I could afford the level of Mobilizer experience that I needed. Well, it was true. I couldn't afford a big shot, but I didn't even consider that anyone who had these skills would want to help me. I was so tangled in the muck of operational issues that I never paused to consider "Who is the right person to help me do this?" I should have been sharing my vision with anyone who would listen so that my *who* would show up. Instead, I was fixated on the *how.*

Hindsight is 20/20, and looking back, I should have come up with Creative Compensation options to entice a Mobilizer Unicorn to come on board. I couldn't offer a full-time salary with benefits (yet!), but I could have wooed a rock star Mobilizer by offering equity in the company, profit sharing, bonuses for hitting sales goals, free or discounted clothing, a joyful place to work where kids were welcome to hang out after school, flexible schedule . . . the list goes on and on. I wish Current Me could fly back in time to show Past Me the options I wasn't even remotely considering.

While our sales soared (hooray!), other parts of the business were crumbling. Because we offered size AAA all the way up to H, the largest available, our inventory was a real headache to manage and sourcing inventory was way more difficult with so many SKUs. I was determined to offer inclusive sizing beyond the usual size range, but mobilizing to deliver this to customers was becoming harder and harder for me to handle.

Despite the chaos happening behind the scenes, sales continued to explode, and in 2006 we opened five more stores. After a ringing endorsement from Oprah came in, and thanks to the market need and an excellent strategy, we easily hit seven figures. By 2007, we were poised for even more growth. Eight figures was tantalizingly close. But in retail, the operating expenses and payroll expenses tend to be high, while the profit margin is razor slim. I wasn't paying myself a legitimate salary, and I put everything back into the expansion of the brand.

By 2008, I was physically and mentally running on fumes. But customers loved us and forgave us for being out of their favorite products way too often. A mentor of mine told me it was time to start behaving like "the Jen who knew how to inspire people inside of a company to grow the business." He lovingly called me out: "Are you done doing this solo thinking that things are going to change? You are playing a losing game instead of a winning game."

He urged me, "Go back to what you know works, and fire yourself from sh*t you're not good at."

He was so right. And I knew it. But I had waited too long. The Great Recession was creeping in. Wallets were closing. The worst industries to be in at the time were real estate and retail. In September 2008, the U.S. lost 433,000 jobs. By November, 803,000 jobs. And in December, just in time for a grim holiday season, 661,000 jobs.[1] Suddenly, buying lacy underwear at more than $20 a pop was no longer a priority. My formerly bustling shops became disturbingly empty.

By 2009, without enough capital reserves in the bank and consumers' pockets bone dry, I had to close the business.

Depleted, exhausted, and broke, I moved myself and my two kids into my grandmother's house. I'd previously thought hiring a new store employee was too scary, but now I was in a truly scary situation.

For months, I sat on the front porch, watched the cane grass swaying in the wind, sipped green tea, barely ate, and thought long and hard about WTF had just happened. How did I go from corporate badass to broke and broken entrepreneur? How did I, a bona fide Unicorn, get things so wrong?

It was one of the lowest points in my entire life. What I couldn't see then, but see so clearly now, is that I had failed to surround myself with a winning team. By trying to do it all, I lost it all.

THE GIFTS OF HITTING ROCK BOTTOM

Most people (myself included) are afraid to play big. We say we want to do big things, but when the moment of truth arrives, we shy away from making the moves that we need to make. We postpone. We make excuses. We choose what feels safe and cheap and less risky.

I, for example, should have taken the leap to hire a real, legit manager for my specialty clothing business instead of cobbling together a crew composed of myself and my kids. Instead, I overextended myself and tried to do tasks I was terrible at doing, which led to my downfall. It was a painful lesson, but I learned it well.

Playing big doesn't always mean taking out an enormous business loan or raising millions from investors, although it can. Oftentimes playing big means being willing to rally a team around your idea instead of trying to carry the load on your own, even if being a one-person Unicorn Team feels like the "safe" option.

Hard transitions hurt, but when we're willing to confront what went wrong, we can learn more in one day than many learn in a decade. My key lesson: I was not a good student of my own work. I forgot that experienced mentors matter. That it's possible to assemble a Unicorn Team even if you have limited funds. That it's smart to ask colleagues and friends for help and to have conversations to troubleshoot the issues you're struggling to solve on your own.

Eventually, my 12-year-old daughter snapped me out of my funk. "Mom, you're Jen Kem. You can fix anything that you care about, and it's time to wake up now!" She was like a tiny Tony

Robbins, and damn it, she was right. It was time to get myself together and get back in the game. This Unicorn wasn't done fighting yet. It was time for a new business idea, a fresh start, and this time, a team to help me win.

This led me to launch the business now called the Master Brand Institute, where I offer my Strategizer skills to big brands in hot water who need a fixer and to smaller businesses who want to become legendary, culture-shaping brands. I didn't repeat the mistakes of the past, and this time, my Unicorn Team and I created sustainable success.

If I had operated differently way back when, would my specialty clothing brand still exist today? Quite possibly, yes. Interestingly, right when I was shutting down my five shops in Hawaii, another Unicorn in Texas was expanding her empire—doing the exact opposite of what I did at the exact same time. This is the story of how Kendra Scott became one of the wealthiest women on the planet.

FROM FAILED BUSINESS TO BILLIONAIRE

Kendra Scott's first entrepreneurial endeavor was the Hat Box, a tiny boutique that offered headwear she designed herself, inspired by her stepfather's cancer diagnosis and hair loss. After this business's disappointing closure, she reinvented herself and came up with a new concept: jewelry. Scott took $500 of her own money to start a wholesale jewelry business. Big, bold colors, dazzling crystals and gems, gold chains—it was the "everything's bigger in Texas" motto expressed in wearable art. Women went wild over it. That was in 2002. Fifteen years later, her brand was valued at $1 billion.

Scott never attended fashion design school. She just had an intrinsic desire to make beautiful things that she felt weren't readily available at approachable prices. She's what I would categorize as a very strong Mobilizer—someone who makes things. An artisan. A crafter. A doer. After she made the hard decision to close the Hat Box, she was surprised that customers reached out to her about how much they missed the jewelry she used to put in front of the register. Not the hats—the jewelry.

Ding! This was Scott's light-bulb moment. Inspired by her customer's desires and fueled by her creative interests in fashion, Scott started creating jewelry samples and going door-to-door to boutiques in Austin with her newborn baby boy in tow. She sold necklaces and bracelets out of an empty tea box to boutique owners. She was the designer, the maker, the salesperson, and the administrative assistant—a one-woman Unicorn Team who initially acted as Visionizer, Strategizer, and Mobilizer. At this point in her journey, I'd categorize her Unicorn Leadership Type as Mobilizing Visionizer (MV): heavy on the Mobilizer with a dash of Visionizer energy.

Yet, to realize her company's full potential as a retail store, it was time for her to step out of her comfort zone and into her Visionizer era by evolving from MV to VM. To do that, she needed to build a formidable Unicorn Team.

But that's not all.

She knew that they needed to be *all in* even when darkness was on the horizon. When the Great Recession of 2008 hit her store, Scott wanted to double down on her direct-to-consumer strategy both in store and online by launching the Color Bar, a new, innovative way of choosing jewelry where customers could mix and match semiprecious stones and charms to get more bang for their buck. The customer would now be the designer, maker, and Mobilizer. At the time, this in-store and e-commerce experience was the first of its kind.

To pull this off, the company had to move fast, and Scott asked her Unicorn Team if it would rally with her. And rally it did. Not only did Scott's retail store survive the recession, it had the biggest revenue growth it had ever experienced. It grew from $2 million to $20 million over the next four years.

Despite already making a pretty epic transition, Scott wasn't done. In 2011 she realized she needed a Strategic Mobilizer to help the business expand even further. Scott gave up her own salary (at least temporarily) to free up the funds to hire the next Unicorn she needed—Lon Weingart, one of the original strategic architects of the Starbucks brand penetration on every street corner.

Scott and Weingart got to work on expanding their retail and online footprint, all while investing in their rapidly growing Unicorn Team. In 2016, they moved into their state-of-the-art 43,500-square-foot facility including such perks as study rooms for kids who joined their parents after school, rooms for nursing mothers, a dog-friendly environment, and free yoga classes. Scott understood that if she kept her Unicorns happy, they would enthusiastically bring their genius to work every day and help the brand grow even bigger.

"When I became a mom and they handed me that little baby. I knew at that moment that nothing was more important than being able to be present for him. And if I could figure out a way to create a business that allowed not just me, but other men and women, to be present in their families and do what they love and be able to give back, that would be success. And that's what we've done," Scott told *Success* magazine.[2]

By 2016, Berkshire Partners wanted to invest in the Kendra Scott brand,[3] and their infusion of capital solidified the company into a $1 billion valuation.[4]

Scott still wasn't done Visionizing, though. During the pandemic of 2020, another major economic crisis loomed, and she transitioned to doing curbside ordering and pickup, as well as hosting jewelry parties online via Zoom with her customers to retain that sense of community that is so embedded in the Kendra Scott culture. The team worked quickly to develop tech-based tools so that customers could still play with fashion safely during quarantine. They even started doing "one-on-one clienteling." Store staffers also called customers to check in and let them know they were thinking of them and their families.

"My own core values have become the foundation of my company. Our pillars of Family, Fashion and Philanthropy have shaped my business, our culture and the decisions we make every day," Scott states.[5]

The company hires people, introduces new ideas, and makes new products based on these values. And with the capacity and resources to dream even bigger, she founded the Kendra Scott Women's Entrepreneurial Leadership Institute at the University of

Texas, something she wished had been available to her when she was starting out, and paying homage to the people who helped her believe in herself when she was a solo Unicorn.

WINNING IS EXHILARATING, BUT PAIN IS A GOOD MEDICINE

The contrast between my story and Kendra Scott's story is what the Unicorn Innovation Model helps to clarify. When I emerged from my own dark season after the Recession, I asked myself what I would do next. I licked my wounds and learned how to dream again, accepting that the pain of failure is really good medicine.

And with that medicine came fierce clarity.

At first, I worked for a huge corporation, leading a team that brought culture-shaping products to market with incredible speed. Then, I was the Unicorn that got away, quitting that job to launch my underwear business. As you know, this ended badly. But failure, no matter how abysmal, will never keep a true Unicorn down. Eventually I came to accept the pain of failure as really good medicine and realized I could go back to doing what I was best at—smelling the winners, translating vision into action, and assembling Unicorns in brands that I believed in.

Today, as one of the world's top brand strategists, I and my company—Master Brand Institute—have helped 400,000 Visionizers, Strategizers, and Mobilizers rally the right people around them to make their ideas a reality. Now I show companies how to build the kind of team I wish I'd originally had.

Full circle.

TOP TAKEAWAYS

- Most of us are afraid to play big. We claim we want to build million- and billion-dollar brands. But when faced with make-or-break moments, we usually choose to play small.

- Playing small can look like failing to bring the right people onto your team, insisting on doing everything alone, or refusing to invest (time, energy, money) into your idea even when it's what your idea requires.

- If you have a tendency to play small, surround yourself with Visionizer Unicorns who can show you how to play bigger. Let their visionary energy rub off on you and carry you to new heights.

CHAPTER 14

"OKAY, BUT WHAT ABOUT . . . ?"

Top Questions about Unicorn Teams

Here are the top questions that clients always ask me about Unicorn Teams.

Q: How many people should be on a Unicorn Team? Three? More?

It's possible to have a Unicorn Team with any number of people—100, 20, 10, 3, or even just 2.

The exact number of people doesn't matter. What matters is that you have people on the team who can confidently perform the Visionizer, Strategizer, and Mobilizer roles.

This can happen in a variety of ways. For instance, you could have a team of two people where the first person is the Visionizer and the second person acts as both Strategizer and Mobilizer. Or a team of 10 people with two Visionizers, one Strategizer, and seven Mobilizers. Or any other configuration.

"How many people do I need?" is the wrong question. A better question is *"Whom* do I need?" Is your current team missing Visionizer, Strategizer, or Mobilizer energy? Let this determine which type of Unicorn(s) you bring onto your team next.

Remember, too, that your Unicorn Team isn't limited to full-time employees. Your team can include part-time contractors, plus mentors, coaches, investors, friends, family, and colleagues.

Q: Should my team have one Visionizer, one Strategizer, and several Mobilizers? Is that the ideal ratio?

"Ideal ratio" is not a cut-and-dried formula—and it really depends on your business model. For most teams, yes, having one Visionizer, one Strategizer, and several Mobilizers who have different specialized skills is often a very good mix.

However, there are exceptions. For instance, say you run a brand advisory firm, as I do. This is a strategy-heavy field, so you may need numerous Strategizer Unicorns on your team in order to serve your clients.

Or consider a megabrand like Starbucks, where you might start an Innovation Lab and invite your Mobilizers to put on their Visionizer hats and generate new, groundbreaking product ideas. A few times a month, your Mobilizer Unicorns get to play in the lab and embody Visionizer energy.

Remember that Visionizer, Strategizer, and Mobilizer are roles that need to be performed, but it's not necessarily one person per role. On a very small team, one Unicorn might do two roles, at least for a while, and that's perfectly okay as long as they have the right strengths to do those roles well.

Q: I already have a system to delegate tasks to people on my team. Everyone knows what they should be doing. So, why do I need the Unicorn Team approach?

Even if your team is getting things done, that doesn't necessarily mean they're getting the *right* things done. And it doesn't necessarily mean that you have a culture that Unicorns want to stay loyal to.

There are plenty of highly "productive" teams filled with people who don't feel appreciated for their contributions, who dread going into work, and who anonymously post scathing one-star reviews on Glassdoor.

The Unicorn Innovation Model is a different way of building a team and working together. With a Unicorn Team, each person is treated with respect and regarded as a Unicorn in their own right.

Rather than "my role is more important than yours," the attitude is "each role is crucially important in order for us to win."

Your delegation system doesn't have to be replaced by adopting the Unicorn Innovation Model, though it can enhance and improve it, filling in the cracks between the standardized checklists and workflows you've already built.

Q: I work in a company that has established systems, processes, and ways of doing things. Can the Unicorn Innovation Model complement what we're already doing? Or do we have to stop doing everything we're doing, burn it all down, and replace it with the Unicorn Way?

The Unicorn Innovation Model is modular for this very reason—and fits into the working systems that you already use. Think of it like choosing to put premium instead of standard-grade fuel into your vehicle.

Let's say you have a hiring process that is working fairly well but could use an upgrade. Add the Unicorn Leadership Type Assessment (ULTA) into your current process. Ask a candidate to take the ULTA prior to their first job interview. Take a look at their results. Once you know their type, it will be easier to determine if this is the Unicorn that you need to bring on board.

Another example: your founder holds an all-staff meeting once a quarter. This is their opportunity to remind people about the future you're working to build together. Perhaps these all-staff meetings are "okay," but they're not particularly inspiring (plenty of yawns in the room). Encourage the founder to write a Brandcast (see Chapter 7) to communicate their vision even more powerfully and get people excited to be part of something bigger.

One more example. Next time you're feeling stuck at work and can't figure out a solution, get a few colleagues and say, "Let's VSM this together." *Visionize:* envision the future you want to move toward. *Strategize:* map out the journey from here to there. *Mobilize:* figure out the specific action steps, delegate tasks, and get moving.

You now have the Unicorn tools that you can plug into the systems you already use. You don't necessarily have to burn things down and start over from scratch. The Unicorn Innovation Model can complement what you're already doing.

Q: What if people on my team learn their Unicorn Leadership Type and then decide "Oh, that means I don't have to do XYZ anymore . . ."

The Unicorn Leadership Type Assessment (ULTA) is similar to DiSC, StrengthsFinder, and the Enneagram. All of these assessments, while different, paint pictures of your strengths and weaknesses.

When you get your results, you might feel a sense of clarity and relief. For instance, you may say, "Oh, I'm a Pure Visionizer! So *that's* why I love thinking about the big picture but struggle with tiny administrative details."

Your Unicorn Leadership Type shows the role you're best suited to play on your team. However, it is not a permission slip to shirk responsibilities. Everyone on the Unicorn Team needs to speak up when they have an idea or concern, take ownership of their work, and get things done. Whether you're a strong Visionizer, Strategizer, or Mobilizer, you have to actually finish the deliverables that you own, not just start them.

The deliverable you're responsible for will vary depending on your role. As a Visionizer, you might be responsible for wooing investors with deep pockets to fund the big idea. As a Strategizer, your responsibility might be to develop an influencer marketing strategy that builds demand for the product being sold. As a Mobilizer, you might be responsible for ensuring that the product actually works. Each Unicorn owns a piece of the team's success, and nobody gets to lie back on the couch and eat bonbons while others put in the work.

Q: When a Unicorn isn't performing at the level I know they can, do I need to be gentle? Give them tough love? Be harsh? What is the best approach?

Be direct, honest, and kind.

Tell this person, "You are an incredible [Visionizer / Strategizer / Mobilizer], but I'm not seeing XYZ right now. I know you're capable of doing this role, because I've seen you do it before."

Say, "XYZ isn't up to our Unicorn Team standards. I know we can do better. Take me through what happened so that we can be proactive and prevent this in the future."

Remember that this Unicorn is a human being.

Ask, "Is there anything that's making it difficult for you to do your best work?" Something at work or something at home (caregiving for a sick parent, nursing a new baby at three in the morning, chronic illness, burnout, etc.) might be impacting their quality of work. Ask, "How can I help?" If they say, "I don't know," propose one or two options. "What if we tried XYZ?"

Tone is everything. You can say, "We didn't reach our revenue goal this quarter . . ." in a calm, neutral tone or a frosty, hostile one.

Before having a conversation with a fellow Unicorn, have a conversation with *yourself.* Is there anything *you* could be doing better? Maybe you failed to communicate your vision clearly, failed to speak up and voice a concern, or something else. Take ownership of whatever you did or didn't do.

Try saying to your colleague, "I've been thinking about [name of project], and one thing I failed to do is XYZ." Start by owning your own mistakes. This may help your colleague to feel less defensive. Approach this as a conversation between equals—two Unicorns who want to figure out how to win—rather than one Unicorn reprimanding another.

Q: What if the Visionizer lays out a grand vision that they love, but nobody else on the team is excited about it?

It's the Visionizer's responsibility to communicate clearly so that other Unicorns get excited and buy into the big vision.

If the team isn't excited, it could be a values issue. Does this vision align with the brand values? How so? Help the Visionizer by saying, "Our core values are XYZ. Can you help me understand how this idea aligns with those values? I'm not seeing the connection. Tell me what you're thinking . . ."

It could be a timing issue. Perhaps it's a great idea but not the right time to do it, because the team is already at max capacity and there's no room for new projects right now. You can help the Visionizer by saying, "We can do this; however, that means XYZ will happen." Help them understand the cost and trade-offs that will occur alongside any benefit. Maybe there's another project that has to go onto the back burner or a consultant that needs to get hired. Is the new project still worth doing? And if so, why?

Q: We're doing the Unicorn Team approach, but something is not working. We're still not achieving the results that we want. What's up with that?

My advice: name the elephant in the room. Remember Unicorn Team Rule #6: We say what needs to be said, even when it's uncomfortable.

Is there something happening that nobody has been courageous enough to point out?

Perhaps none of your last 20 clients got excellent results, renewed their contracts, or recommended your services to the people in their networks. Something is broken. The team has been busy focusing on "other things" (social media strategy, e-mail funnels, revamping the product packaging) rather than focusing on what matters most. Or maybe everyone on the team is too afraid to say, "The offer we're selling isn't delivering the results that we promised, and that's why our clients are unhappy."

Ask every Unicorn on the team to be 100 percent honest.

"What do you think is preventing us from achieving our goals?"

"Why do you think we're struggling right now?"

"Is there something troubling you that you've been wanting to say?"

"Is there an 'elephant in the room' that we need to confront?"

Give each person space to think and respond. While this conversation may feel uncomfortable (naming the elephant usually is), it will illuminate what's misaligned and what to do about it. Feeling temporarily uncomfortable is the price you need to pay to win.

3, 2, 1 . . . WIN!

Play in Your Own Unicorn Innovation Lab

The best way to understand how the Unicorn Innovation Model works is to experience it for yourself.

Do this 15-minute exercise to take the concepts we've covered and apply them to a real-life problem you're dealing with.

EXERCISE

Unicorn Sprint

Think about a problem you're experiencing at work or in your personal life.

It doesn't have to be a serious life-or-death problem. It can be anything that is annoying, that keeps plaguing you, or that you wish was better.

Using the Unicorn Innovation Model, do critical thinking, come up with a viable solution, and move closer to the future you want.

Spend five minutes on each step in the process. This is a lightning-fast, 15-minute sprint.

1. Visionize

Spend five minutes thinking about *where* you want things to go.

Bonus points if your vision is wacky, weird, wild, or so big that most people think it's unrealistic. Come up with a vision that is not just 1 percent better than your current situation, but 1,000 percent better.

Your vision of the future might sound like "Presidents of countries call me for advice regularly," "I earn one million dollars every month," "Our children don't want screen time and beg us to bring them books from the library," or "We are the number-one most beloved and highest-rated workplace in the entire world."

2. Strategize

Once you have an exciting vision of the future that you desire, spend five minutes figuring out how to get from here to there.

Challenge yourself to come up with at least three different ways that you could get there. "To make this future a reality, we could do X, Y, or Z . . ."

Now you have three strategic initiatives to consider.

3. Mobilize

Pick one initiative and spend five minutes figuring out how to get it in motion quickly and actually get it done.

If you needed to complete this initiative in 100 days or less, who could help you pull this off? Who has the knowledge, skills, and strengths that you need? Who can bring this idea to life?

Break the initiative into a list of tasks. Next to each task, write the name of a friend, colleague, family member, freelancer, intern, employee, or another Unicorn who could get this specific thing done.

You can do this sprint by yourself, but even better, you can do it with a group. Assemble your Unicorn Team so that you can Visionize > Strategize > Mobilize together. See what you come up with in 15 minutes. You will be astonished.

CONCLUSION

My dad battled cancer for over 25 years, going through numerous rounds of chemotherapy, radiation, the whole grueling shebang.

After the first round of treatment, it seemed like the cancer was gone for good. But then, unfortunately, it returned. This pattern continued for decades. "The cancer is back." More chemo. "Now it's gone." A few months would pass. "Well, actually, now it's back again in a different form and a different part of the body." Over and over. My dad handled the ups and downs with incredible grace. Eventually, cancer was no longer a shocking event; it was BAU, business as usual, just something we dealt with continuously as a family.

Several years after his initial diagnosis, I lived in Hawaii, and Dad had moved back to the Philippines. We spent as much time together as we could, although making the trip to the Philippines grew increasingly difficult once I had three kids to take care of. It became harder to get on a plane and easier to say, "Maybe this summer," "Maybe at Christmas," "Maybe once things settle down at work," or "Maybe next year."

One day I woke up and felt a strange calling to go visit my dad. I couldn't explain where this intense yearning was coming from. Yes, the cancer had returned, but that wasn't particularly surprising, and his doctor seemed confident that he'd pull through once again. Dad's health was fairly good, all things considered. He certainly wasn't on death's door. Nevertheless, I knew I had to go. Not later. *Now.*

The timing could not have been worse. The older kids were in the middle of their school year. My baby son had just celebrated his first birthday. My workload was massive, with countless deliverables on my calendar. To pull this trip off, I would need to reschedule approximately a million commitments, and that's exactly what I did. I made the 12-hour flight (with all the children in tow) and spent two and a half precious weeks with my dad, sharing meals, laughing, and talking about the small matters of life and the big stuff too.

My dad had the mind of the comedian George Carlin—with brutally funny, sarcastic, dark humor—and the soul of an artist. As a young man, he had been a gifted painter, gotten a college degree in broadcasting, and had visions of moving to Los Angeles to work in the entertainment industry. At 21, he set his sights on LA. But by 25, he was a father, and everything changed.

My mom, then 22, pleaded with him to set aside his Hollywood dreams and get a stable and good-paying government job, like she had. It's what he needed to do for his family, she reasoned, and was the only sensible path forward. Out of devotion to her and his newborn child, he agreed. In the years that followed, more kids arrived, and the Hollywood dreams gradually faded away. Did he regret his decision? I never asked. But even though he chose a more conventional path, he never lost that rebellious spark.

As I sat with my dad on that trip, the conversation turned to my career. I told him how grateful I was to be doing meaningful work, how much I enjoyed working as a brand strategist, and how proud I was to be the primary breadwinner for my family.

When I was a little girl reading the daily newspaper with my grandma—my little legs swinging underneath the kitchen table in her Hawaiian plantation-style house—I saw headlines about big brands doing billion-dollar mergers, impacting millions of lives, and shaping culture. At age nine, I told my family that I wanted to be "general counsel for Coca-Cola" when I grew up, quoting a statement I'd seen in the paper. Even then, I wanted to play big and be part of a winning team—and my dad always believed that I could do it. Me, a Filipina girl from a rural island community with a withering sugarcane industry and very limited career options. Dad saw the bigness inside of me and celebrated it, rather than squashing it down.

In our household, Dad was the optimist and Mom was the realist. "I just don't want you to be disappointed," Mom often cautioned me when I described my outlandish goals. She spoke from a place of love, not wanting to see her daughter get trampled by the harsh world. She knew all too well that our society wasn't designed for girls like me to rise up, lead companies, and make millions.

Mom taught me that I needed to "be the best" at whatever I set out to do, because women who look like us have to work 10 times as hard to achieve half as much. She urged me to attain excellence, but also cautioned me not to aim too high. With her, I learned to keep quiet about my ambitions. But with Dad, I could be loud. "Pursue your vision," he always told me. "You're going to do big things." Whenever I talked about something I wanted to do, he'd respond with a huge smile, "Go f—ing do it, then."

"I'm thinking about making some new moves in my career," I told Dad on that trip.

He asked, "Like what?"

I told him about my new vision of creating a company called Master Brand Institute and hiring and building a team to scale from seven figures in annual revenue to eight. I would certify people in my methodologies so that thousands of people could teach the Unicorn Innovation Model rather than just me. I could be a role model for women in business, particularly women of color, and write a best-selling book on business and leadership that would sit alongside the classics like *Good to Great* by Jim Collins, *Outliers* by Malcolm Gladwell, and *Purple Cow* by Seth Godin. On the Mount Rushmore of authors, I wanted to carve out a place for my name and face, and for everyone who looks like me, so that people could see that there were choices and other interesting perspectives.

As I described my next-level life to my dad, his face brightened. He had one question for me:

"What are you waiting for?"

That trip was the last time I saw my dad. He died just five weeks later, when his health took a rapid nosedive and he passed away abruptly. I am thankful that I listened to my instincts and went to visit him when I did. And I'm profoundly grateful for those five powerful words he spoke to me: "What are you waiting for?"

Reader, I want to leave you with that same question:

What are you waiting for . . . really?

You have a great idea that could improve your department, company, community, industry, or the world. Or maybe the next idea you didn't know was brewing inside you is now bubbling up to the surface because of what you've learned in this book.

You are the innovator that we've been waiting for. We need your ideas. And you're the human to do it.

Find the people who have the strengths that you lack. Surround yourself with excellence. Working as a team, you can do more, faster, and with less friction and stress.

The Unicorns you seek are looking for you too. Go forth, find each other, and win.

GLOSSARY

Brand—A brand is what you're known for. There are three main types of brands: Personal Brand, Offer Brand, and Company Brand. When a brand becomes wildly successful, I call it a Unicorn Brand, because it's rare and exceptional.

Brandcast—The Brandcast is the Visionizer's main communication tool. Creating a Brandcast helps you take a big, lofty idea and put it into words that others understand and can rally behind. See Chapter 7 for instructions.

Business as Usual (BAU)—BAU refers to initiatives that have already been implemented and work pretty well but could use an upgrade. Examples: human resources performance management, accounting systems, or current products that are already generating revenue.

Innovation—*Innovation* means bringing something new into the world. This can be a brand-new idea that is revolutionary and does not exist yet (ideation) or an upgrade on an existing idea (iteration). Humans are the source of all innovation.

Intrapreneur—A person who thinks and behaves like an entrepreneur but doesn't necessarily want to found their own company. They work inside an organization (typically as an employee) and use their entrepreneurial spirit to help the company achieve great things.

Mobilizer—On a Unicorn Team, the person in the Mobilizer role takes each piece of the strategy and gets tasks finished. Mobilizer energy is all about getting it done and closing the loop.

Performance Pulse—The Performance Pulse is a monthly check-in between the Boss Unicorn and another Unicorn on the team. It helps both people stay in regular communication instead of talking about performance only once a year.

Prototyping—Prototyping is the Mobilizer's main communication tool. It helps you show your work in progress to your team and confirm that you're on the right track before proceeding.

Stratagem—The Stratagem is the Strategizer's main communication tool. It helps you map out five business goals, come up with three options to achieve each goal, and decide which options to do. You also assign an owner to each initiative—the person who's going to lead the project and make sure it gets done.

Strategizer—On a Unicorn Team, the person in the Strategizer role takes the big visionary idea and comes up with a strategy to get from here to there.

Unicorn Energy—The ultimate goal of the Unicorn Innovation Model, this is the flow state of winning, the energy of success, the vibe in the room when the right people are working on the right priorities. When great ideas come to life quickly, it's because the team has tapped into Unicorn Energy.

Unicorn Leadership Type—Take the Unicorn Leadership Type Assessment (ULTA) to find out your Unicorn Leadership Type. There are nine types. To play big and win in business, surround yourself with Unicorns whose types are different from your own—people who excel in areas where you struggle.

Unicorn Team—A team of people who rally around a great idea and make it happen with astonishing speed and success. The team must include people who can perform the Visionizer, Strategizer, and Mobilizer roles.

Values Driven—When a team is values driven, it makes decisions based on values—not what's trendy right now, not what's happening in the economy at the moment, not what the latest consultant advises, etc. It is what the most sustainable, long-lasting, and legendary brands embody as part of their culture.

Visionizer—On a Unicorn Team, the person in the Visionizer role comes up with the big idea, the ambitious goal, the future we want to create. This person sees what is possible before others do.

ACKNOWLEDGMENTS

I felt strongly that writing a book about rallying the right people around your big ideas so that you can change the world was the one I needed to do first, and getting to the finish line means it's time to properly thank the Unicorns who made this book possible. I hope that I do this last bit justice, because there are so many people to thank and acknowledge. Be sure to read the last paragraph, because its words are specifically for you, the reader.

On the surface, this is a business book written for leaders about brand, innovation, and leadership. But really, it's a collection of wisdom and best practices that are based on my real-life experiences and influences that just so happened to create success while I was doing work-related things. So, the first people I need to acknowledge are those that have truly shaped the way I look at the world and how I still navigate all of it, starting way back from the very beginning.

First, I want to thank my grandparents, Leon and Generosa Valbuena, who left everything behind in their province in the Philippines to create a life of opportunity for me and our entire family. To do that they faced grueling, hot days in the sugarcane plantation fields of Waialua, Hawaii, making 39 cents an hour, to build a home and become a place where every descendant in our ancestral line thereafter was able to create abundance and favor through their modeling and sacrifice. Grandma Generosa, you gave me the business section of the newspaper every morning while you ate your peanut butter toast and had Lipton hot tea, encouraging me to read it, because you said that one day, I'd know what to do with it. Well, you were right. You didn't realize how much of an innovator you were and that you actually taught me how to think like a leader because of the way you problem-solved everything while always making time for affection and attention while you juggled everything and made it look natural. This book is a love letter to the ultimate Visionizer > Strategizer > Mobilizer of our family—YOU.

Thank you also for giving life to Anita Rose, who is the bravest, strongest, and most committed human I know—and just so happens to have given birth to me. Thank you, Mom, for being the rock to my unstoppable, (sometimes) raging river—I know you didn't fully know what to do with my energy and curiosity, but what I know for sure is that you never gave up on me, no matter what, and that the gift of education and work ethic was your love language. With the support of you, Uncle Arthur, Uncle Henry, and Aunty Gwen—and our collective family, including Bernard, Eric, Michelle, Jimmy, Sheila, Chris, Abbey, and all of our kiddos, uncles, aunties, and cousins—you gave me the confidence to shine and face any adversity with courage and resilience. I love you, Mom.

To my dad, Michael Kem: you are still the smartest, wittiest, and most creative person that I trusted with my biggest dreams— and even though you're no longer here to give me sage advice or a famous Kem clapback, your spirit and belief in me were with me the entire time I was writing this book. You were the perfectly imperfect representative of how to not take crap from anyone while reminding me that people are fallible and still worthy of forgiveness and love. Most of all, you helped me choose myself when I found myself questioning everything and anything. You were a safe place to listen and hear me when I was in my fiercest storms. Whenever I'm enjoying a piping-hot black coffee at the breakfast table, I hear you saying, "What are you waiting for, Jenny?" And I want you to know: your little girl did it! Also, thank you for the eyebrows. I miss you, Dad.

Mikaela, I didn't fully believe in unicorns until you were born. You are joy. You are inspiring. You are talented. You are generous. You are a beautiful role model for friendship and integrity. You are one of my greatest teachers, my mini-me, my muse. The immense pride I have in calling you my daughter is hard to put into words, but know this: everything you and your siblings have is because you set the pace and set it well. You get me. I'm literally in awe of who you are and the natural leader that you've become. Your passion is infectious. And you made this book better with your creative gifts and ability to put pictures and illustrations around my words in the most perfect way. I feel so lucky to be your mom.

Jordan, you are such a model for autonomy and independence. I look to you when the world feels void of discernment, because you always show me that having the biggest heart while maintaining beautiful boundaries at the same time is possible. Who knew a daughter would be so good at mentoring their own mother in that? You do that so impeccably. Your smile, laughter, and hugs are the absolute best. You are the most delightful and fun friend. I love how you share your obsession of Japan and anime and make me obsessed with them too. Traveling with you and geeking out on new books, shows, and movies are some of my favorite ways we spend time together. Your creative abilities astound me. You show me that quality matters above all. I feel so proud to be your mom.

Noah, my miracle baby boy—you have made our lives richer and more fun than I could have ever imagined. Your natural curiosity, your sweet heart for fairness and inclusion and love of books and art just make me smile from ear to ear. I wake up every day thinking about how happy I am that you are here and how you teach us how to stay vibrant and healthy and present. The way you've already written your own comic books and built Lego cities and make the best birthday cards—while you also apply focus and discipline to your love of jiu jitsu and sports—is so awesome. And who knew how much you would love to sing and perform? Being here and witnessing how you think and grow and approach everything with an energetic life force that lights up everything around you brightens my world. Don't ever lose that spark. Every day you surprise and delight us. I feel so blessed to be your mom.

To my husband and partner in life and business, Nathan J. Francisco: 30 years in the making, and who knew that the Unicorn I was really looking for was you? You are the ultimate masterful Mobilizer in our crazy, beautiful life, and it just wouldn't work without you. Your belief in me, your ability to use your hands

and heart in the service of what our big dreams and goals are together, your yin to my yang . . . sharing everything together—the
good, bad, and magical—is the most gratifying relationship I've
ever experienced. And your parenting skills—I knew you were surprised at how good you are at being a dad, but I never was. The
way the kids can depend on you being there makes me the lucki-
est woman alive. Thank you for also letting me come home with
new dogs from the rescue once in a while, and for loving them as
much as they deserve. Our adventure has just started, and for the
rest of my life, I look forward to how much more of the world we
will see and savor together. You had me at "I'm a 49ers fan." You
are so appreciated, and I don't tell you that enough but want you
to know that I'm thinking it every single moment. I love you to the
moon and back.

To Sarah Paikai, the ultimate ride-or-die Unicorn, the one
who helped me make space for this book more than anyone: we
are 'ohana forever. Yes, you have made sure that the operations of
Master Brand Inc. work, and work so well that we've helped and
made millions together the past decade. Your loyalty, intuition,
systems mind, creativity, and integrity make you the best "work
wife" in the world. Your heart, kindness, patience, generosity,
openness, acceptance of who I am, and love of travel and shopping and discovering new things make you one of my best friends
in the world, which is a gift that makes all the effort we've made
so worth it. Who knew that in a tiny nonprofit meeting room so
many years ago that our story would turn into one of the best relationships I've ever had (and one of the longest lasting). You have
said yes to me even when you weren't sure where we were headed,
but you trusted us and this, and I feel like I must have done something right to have you show up in my life when you did. You are
an amazing mom, wife, and leader. I want to thank Landen and
your kids for letting me borrow you to help make the world a better place. Whatever happens next, I know you'll always be the first
one I entrust with my vision and that you'll know exactly what to
do. I'm excited about our next chapter together. Also, thank you
for bringing Kajana Movery into not just the business, but our chosen family as well. Kajana, you've been a godsend. Even though

you're a Seahawks fan, that hasn't dampened my gratitude for what you've brought to our company and our clients. ☺

To our extended Unicorn Team at Master Brand Inc. and our accompanying brands, you are the heartbeat of the business, and thank you for growing with us and being a stand for the Unicorn Team way of life. There are so many names to mention who've worked with us over the years, so to honor you I would love for you to write your name here: _____. Every contributor, whether you were full-time staff, a part-time contractor, or a vendor, your name deserves recognition—it would be impossible to list all of you without inadvertently leaving someone off, and I want you to know you are seen and remembered. It doesn't matter how long you were on the team; building a ship like this takes incredible spirit, work ethic, and commitment. I honor you and thank you so much.

To every client who's ever worked with us, at any level and at any time—my body of work is available in book form because you were an important part of making it so. I've had the honor of being the Strategizer inside of your brands and businesses, working with you on the fun and the tough stuff, advising your teams on how to translate your vision into reality, and having the fortune of being behind-the-scenes on some of the most game-changing go-to-market launches in the history of business. Thank you for your investment of time, energy, and money, and for sharing your work with the world.

To Shaye Maeda, thank you for always being there for me and for being a model for strength and smarts inside of our corporate career together, and for continuing to be one of my best friends in life. When I was deciding to leave the corporate world, you were the one I trusted the most with my fears and excitement, and you never wavered in your belief in what more I had to say and teach and serve up next in pursuing my path as a business owner, consultant, and entrepreneur. Our personal and professional development paths are united forever. The corporate world is lucky to have a Unicorn like you leading the way. Ryan, Jeff, Bobby, Spero, and Fiona—you probably don't realize how much impact you've had on my postcorporate career. You're the best damn product marketing and strategy team ever assembled, and it's because of our work together that the Unicorn Innovation Model exists at all. It's rare to have had the pleasure to work with a group of Unicorns like you, and I'm grateful to share your contributions inside of a framework that I know will help so many others recreate the magic we made together.

When I was 11 years old, I wrote the first chapter of a book I named *Vision on a Subway*, a tale about a girl named Paige who left her country home to find success in the big city—New York City—and made her first friend on a subway ride from Brooklyn to Manhattan. My plan was to share their subsequent adventures in the chapters that followed. Although 11-year-old me didn't really even know much about subways, or NYC for that matter, it was the tiny library in my hometown on the North Shore of Oahu where I learned about other places in the world, and the Big Apple seemed like the right place to set the scene. Almost 40 years later, I'm grateful that *Unicorn Team* is here and that I've kept the silent promise I made to my childhood author heroes Judy Blume and Beverly Cleary.

The part about friends in my "first book," though?

They came true, in the form of my sQuad besties in life and business. Jadah Sellner, thank you for going first and helping us all navigate putting on our "author pants." The amount of time you spent generously sharing with me how you've accomplished writing your two best-selling books is priceless. But what I'm most grateful for is how you reminded me and reinstalled my desire to be an author when disappointment and setbacks made me question everything. You have had my back the entire way through, and our hot-tub hot seats were some of my favorite parts of this book journey. You're the first person I call when I know someone will rally with me, especially if being part of an experience together is the game plan. You also travel like a boss with a magical Mary Poppins carry-on that we all still believe cannot be real, but you're just mystical like that. You've also taught me how to be in a healthy, reciprocal friendship better than anyone. I love you.

Nicole Walters, thank you for modeling what persistence and consistency look like—whether life was smooth or turbulent in any of our lives, you always had time for a reassuring remembrance ("Jen Kem, you are Jen Kem!")—and for being a powerful story-teller and believer in the highest good. I look to you when I need to remind myself that I'm going to make it, no matter what. You're also one of my favorite shopping buddies (and we have had some of the best jaunts around the world!)—whether we're window-shopping or getting wild in the actual store, our conversations light me up. Our friendship is one that is so deep and beautiful, and I thank God for your presence in my life every day. You get me. Plus, the skin-care tips are on point, always. I know when we're 100 years old, we'll look the same, thanks to you. Your surprise trip to see me to support my book still stirs feelings in me that I'll never forget. I love you.

Nikki Elledge Brown, thank you for your word nerdery and perfect use of metaphors and delightful insights that always have me tearing up from both nostalgia and laughter. You have taught me to savor every single moment and to "lock in" the memories of this journey, and you make me feel important and seen and loved as your friend. Our early days of taking walks near the Pearl Harbor shoreline sowed seeds that have now become harvest, and it makes me emotional just thinking about how the simplest things can make the biggest impact, because you model that for me all the time. I could listen to you talk all day and so appreciate how you make time for me, and I still think your beautiful, cinnamon-sugar hair needs its own book and show because she is next level and we're all not worthy. You are values-driven magic. I love you.

Writing this book, navigating the publishing world, and making it align with my own goals and dreams wouldn't be pos-sible without finding experienced people to help me through it all. Thank you to Farnoosh Torabi, whose first workshop, Book to Brand, helped me decide if it was a path for me and is where I met Meg Stevenson, who helped me get the initial book proposal completed and introduced me to my book agents, Kim Perel and Margaret Danko at High Line Literary. To my publisher, Hay House/Penguin Random House: thank you to editorial director Melody Guy, who believed in and acquired the book; my executive editor, Lisa Cheng, who provided such thoughtful and detailed edits to make the book more clear, consistent, and beneficial to the reader; as well as the entire publishing and marketing team alongside.

The most important thing to me in writing *Unicorn Team* was that it would be an immensely helpful book that people would actually read, finish, recommend, and use—frequently. If any part of this book accomplished that, it's because of the keen mentorship of Anjanette "AJ" Harper and her world-class program for authors called Top Three. AJ, you helped me write the book of my dreams, mostly because you reminded me that writing for the reader first is always the way. You believed in me and this book, and I'm so grateful.

Years ago, when I was visionizing this book coming to life, I had one person in mind that I wanted to be my writing partner and editor—and secretly prayed that one day, she would say yes when the timing was right and the stars were aligned. Alexandra Franzen, I'm forever grateful that you said yes to this project, fully taking on my ginormous vision, listening deeply to what I wanted to create, and then going all in on using the Unicorn Team way of writing this book with me. You are a masterful Mobilizer with the extra Strategizer glue that took that vision and helped me transform it into the masterpiece I dreamed of. We made legendary Unicorn Energy together: mission accomplished! You are a genius, you really see me, and you know how to focus my energy into the areas that matter most. You're also a master of snacks and introduced me to my new favorite coffee shop, which gives me even more excuses to visit you and your beautiful family often. Our collaboration and friendship is one I will always treasure. Alex, thank you for playing big and winning with me, and I can't wait to do it again.

To SARK, thank you for being a mentor and showing me that a creative life is a good life. It's an honor to be a part of such a life-giving relationship with someone I've admired since the first day I picked up your book in Borders Bookstore 20 years ago. You and your beloved husband, David, are dear friends, and I feel so lucky to have you in my corner. I love you both.

To Seth Godin and Sally Hogshead, who graciously gave their insights and experiences and were so helpful in how I approached the book. You both also shared precious gold: what to look out for and what really mattered, which ultimately was about creating a quality, useful book that people would be happy to share. I'm so grateful for your generosity and thank you for producing excellent work that other authors like me can refer to and learn from. To other authors whose books I admire and share frequently, thank you for opening the door and leading the way with quality and consistency.

To the test readers who read the early drafts of this book and gave suggestions: Alice Lima, Auret Esselen, Beth Nydick, Cathryn Castle Garcia, Danielle Cohen, Dr. Doroteya Vladimirova, Elisha Ward, Jackie VanCampen, Jadah Sellner, Kaitlyn Chock, Kali Bell, Karin Goldmann, Kirsty Mac, Krystin Morgan, Lauryn Shields, Lori L. Cangilla, Marisa Mohi, Mary Beth (MB) Huwe, Penelope Jane Smith, Selena Soo, Stefanie Schram, Tina Forsyth, Tonia Winchester—thank you for taking the time to provide feedback early on so we could make this book the winner we wanted it to be.

To my friends and clients and colleagues and mentors and other leaders who are sharing the Unicorn Team way of life far and wide, including my publicity team, speaker and event agent, the Femmefluence network, my book-launch posse, masterminds I've been part of past and present, and the group of Unicorns who raised their hands high to sing praise or recommend it to their own companies and communities during the prelaunch and launch of the book, a deep bow of gratitude to you. To Giovanni Marsico, thank you for introducing me to so many epic, good humans who are featured in this book through the magic you've created at Archangel. To Joana Galvao and the team at GIF Studios, thank you for bringing my aesthetic vision to life with the Unicorn Team company branding and book cover; I'm so in love with what we came up with. To Regina Anaejionu, thank you for helping me sort these big ideas into potent articles, stories, and pieces—you have been the perfect thought partner for me to organize how I want to share this book with the world. To Selena Soo, thank you for being not just an inspiring catalyst for so many and for being the embodiment of rich relationships better than anyone I know, but for how personally invested you've been in supporting this book. Our friendship means the world to me.

To Rory Vaden and the entire team at Brand Builders, thank you for being the other side of the publishing coin for me—helping me strategize how to share this book and its work far and wide though the power of my personal brand and to fulfill my wish to make it not just a bestseller, but a perennial seller that keeps helping people way beyond its launch date. Your guidance is top-notch, and your friendship is such a blessing. To Chris Winfield and Jen Gottlieb, thank you for sharing the good word and best people to know so that this book has the biggest impact it can have.

To the Unicorns who were featured in this book, who inspired me to share their stories because of the way they visionized, strategized, and mobilized their ideas into life and changed the world, including Tracey Franklin, Rosalind Brewer, the *Hadestown* team, Bruce Cardenas, Rachel Rodgers, John Stix, Gordy Bal, the San Francisco 49ers, Kendra Scott, Melanie Perkins, and the other personal and company brands highlighted herein—your real-life experiences will help countless others, and we're all grateful for that. Please keep innovating and showing the way.

Finally, to you, the Unicorns who are reading this book, for those who are recommending it to others, and especially to those that are using it to create more integration not separation, creating your own innovation labs and embodying this way of leading and learning together, I admire you. Thank you for being committed to a world where we can improve the way we live, solve the problems that keep us apart, create the brands we want to be part of and rally around, and truly understand that to innovate is innately human. You are the answer.

BOOK CLUB DISCUSSION GUIDE

Want to read *Unicorn Team* in your book club? Or discuss the book with your business partner, your team at work, your friends, or another group? Use these questions to spark conversation.

Unicorn Team explains how to take great ideas and bring them to life. A major theme in this book is "playing big." What does playing big mean to you at this moment in your life and career?

What does "winning" mean to you, and who are the people who can help you win? Come up with at least two people whom you could bring onto your Unicorn Team. (Remember that these people could be friends, colleagues, mentors, coaches, freelancers, employees, etc.)

Do you have a great idea that you're excited about? What is it? Or are you searching for a great idea that you can be part of?

Did you take the Unicorn Leadership Type Assessment (ULTA)? What is your Unicorn Leadership Type? Does it feel accurate to you?

Can you remember a time when you were part of a very successful team? Who played the Visionizer role on that particular team? Strategizer? Mobilizer?

Can you remember a time when you were part of a dysfunctional or ineffective team? Do you think this team was missing a Visionizer, Strategizer, Mobilizer, or several roles? Or was there something else going on that caused this team to struggle?

Do a Visionize > Strategize > Mobilize exercise with your book club. Have one person Visionize and share an idea that feels visionary and audacious. As a team, Strategize to figure out the moves to make it happen. Then Mobilize and figure out, who are the people you'd need to recruit to pull this off? Who could get each task done?

What part of the book resonated the most, and why? Was there any part of this book that you disagreed with? Which part, and why?

Would you describe yourself as a Unicorn? The best of the best; the most elite, excellent, sought-after person in your field? If not, how could you become a Unicorn? What would need to happen?

Did you have an aha moment while reading this book? What was it?

WORK WITH US

Do you want to bring the Unicorn Innovation Model inside of your company, unlock what's possible for how people see and choose your brand, and fully unleash the innovative capabilities of your team? We help you bring great ideas to life with astonishing speed and success. Want to work with us or one of our Certified Unicorn Team Advisors? Visit www.UnicornTeam.co. Fill out the application and we'll point you toward the option that's best for you.

Newer Companies	We can help you: Assemble your first Unicorn Team Find your great idea and bring it to market quickly Use the Unicorn Innovation Model to build an iconic brand
Established Companies	We can help you: Diagnose why your current team is struggling and what to do about it Create a Unicorn Innovation Lab inside of your company Become the market leader and most legendary brand in your category

Certifications

We offer two certifications—one for individuals and one for companies.

As an individual, become a Certified Unicorn Team™ Advisor. Master the model so you can teach, consult, and advise the

Unicorn Way to your clients, colleagues, seminar attendees, and more—with access to our entire strategic templates and tools.

As a company, proudly display the Certified Unicorn Team seal on your website and other brand assets. Show the world that yours is a company worth working for, that it rewards people in meaningful ways for their contributions, and that it has a culture of innovation where Unicorns come together to play big and win.

ENDNOTES

Author's Note

1. "Kendra Scott," University of Texas at Austin, Kendra Scott Women's Entrepreneurial Leadership Institute, n.d., https://kswelinstitute .utexas.edu/about/kendra-scott/.

2. Katie Friel, "Kendra Scott Wants to Change the Game for Women in Business—Starting with UT Students," *Alcalde*, January–February 2020, https://alcalde.texasexes.org/2020/01/kendra-scott-wants-to -change-the-game-for-women-in-business-starting-with-ut-students/.

3. "Following $1B Exit, Quest Nutrition Co-Founders Ron and Shannan Penna Spend $14.6M for Pair of California Homes," American Luxury, February 29, 2020, https://www.amlu.com/2020/02/29 /following-1b-exit-quest-nutrition-co-founders-ron-and-shannan -penna-spend-14-6m-for-pair-of-california-homes/.

4. "About Us," KetoPet, n.d., https://www.ketopetsanctuary.com /pages/about-us.

5. "About Us," BetterHelp, n.d., https://www.betterhelp.com/about/.

Introduction

1. "Hard Hit Southern California to Receive 5,000 Body Bags and 60 Morgue Trucks," *Guardian*, December 16, 2020, World section, https://www.theguardian.com/world/2020/dec/15/california -coronavirus-deaths-body-bags-morgue.

2. Michelle Llamas, "Pfizer," Drugwatch.com, last modified July 9, 2024, https://www.drugwatch.com/manufacturers/pfizer/.

3. *Pfizer Inc. 2019 Financial Report*, Securities and Exchange Commission, n.d., https://www.sec.gov/Archives/edgar/data/78003/000007800320000014/pfe-exhibit13x12312019.htm.

4. Kelly Servick, "This Mysterious $2 Billion Biotech Is Revealing the Secrets behind Its New Drugs and Vaccines," *Science*, March 25, 2020, https://www.science.org/content/article/mysterious-2-billion-biotech-revealing-secrets-behind-its-new-drugs-and-vaccines.

5. "Moderna Completes Application to U.S. Food and Drug Administration for Emergency Use Authorization of Omicron-Targeting Bivalent Covid-19 Booster Vaccine, mRNA-1273.222," Moderna, August 23, 2022, https://investors.modernatx.com/news/news-details/2022/Moderna-Completes-Application-To-U.S.-Food-And-Drug-Administration-For-Emergency-Use-Authorization-Of-Omicron-Targeting-Bivalent-Covid-19-Booster-Vaccine-mRNA-1273.222/default.aspx.

6. "Vaccine Research and Development: How Can COVID-19 Vaccine Development Be Done Quickly and Safely?," Johns Hopkins University and Medicine Coronavirus Resource Center, n.d., https://coronavirus.jhu.edu/vaccines/timeline.

7. Jon Cohen, "'Absolutely Remarkable': No One Who Got Moderna's Vaccine in Trial Developed Severe COVID-19," *Science*, November 30, 2020, https://www.science.org/content/article/absolutely-remarkable-no-one-who-got-modernas-vaccine-trial-developed-severe-covid-19.

8. McKenzie Sadeghi, "Fact Check: Dolly Parton Helped Fund Moderna's COVID-19 Vaccine Research," *USA Today*, November 21, 2020, https://www.usatoday.com/story/news/factcheck/2020/11/21/fact-check-dolly-parton-donated-modernas-covid-19-vaccine-studies/6373339002/.

9. "Spikevax (Previously COVID-19 Vaccine Moderna)," European Medicines Agency, updated April 7, 2024, https://www.ema.europa.eu/en/medicines/human/EPAR/spikevax-previously-covid-19-vaccine-moderna.

10. Matej Mikulic, "Moderna's Revenue 2016–2023," Statista, May 22, 2024, https://www.statista.com/statistics/1107794/revenue-and-net-income-moderna-inc/.

11. Catherine Clifford, "How the Moderna Covid-19 mRNA Vaccine Was Made So Quickly," CNBC, July 3, 2021, https://www.cnbc.com/2021/07/03/how-moderna-made-its-mrna-covid-vaccine-so-quickly-noubar-afeyan.html.

12. MeiMei Fox, "How Moderna's CHRO Helped the Company Rapidly Develop and Launch a Covid Vaccine," *Forbes*, July 19, 2022, https://www.forbes.com/sites/meimeifox/2022/07/19/how-modernas-chro-helped-the-company-rapidly-develop-and-launch-a-covid-vaccine.

13. "Our Mission & Values," Moderna, n.d., https://www.modernatx.com/en-US/about-us/our-mission.

Chapter 1

1. "BetterHelp Founder on Risking Everything to Bootstrap," Mixergy, March 30, 2016, https://mixergy.com/interviews/betterhelp-with-alon-matas/.

2. "I don't know if I had clinical depression or *[sic]* feeling really, really down." From "BetterHelp Founder on Risking Everything to Bootstrap."

3. Danielle Dresden, "We Tested BetterHelp: Is It Worth It and Our Editors' Experience," *Medical News Today*, updated June 26, 2024, https://www.medicalnewstoday.com/articles/betterhelp-reviews.

4. Laura Lovett, "Teladoc's BetterHelp Comes Back Down to Earth after Years of 'Hyper-Growth'," Behavioral Health Business, February 22, 2023, https://bhbusiness.com/2023/02/22/teladocs-betterhelp-comes-back-down-to-earth-after-years-of-hyper-growth/.

5. Sarah Fader, "Virtual Therapy Is the New Now: An Interview with Alon Matas, Founder of BetterHelp," Good Men Project, February 21, 2019, https://goodmenproject.com/featured-content/virtual-therapy-is-the-new-now-an-interview-with-alon-matas-founder-of-betterhelp/.

6. "BetterHelp Customer Service: Quick Answers to Your Questions," BetterHelp, updated April 23, 2024, https://www.betterhelp.com /advice/general/betterhelp-customer-service-quick-answers-to-your-questions/#.

7. "Verizon Communications Inc. (VZ)," Stock Analysis, updated August 2, 2024, 19:20 UTC, https://stockanalysis.com/stocks/vz /statistics/.

8. "Howard Schultz," Starbucks.com, n.d., https://stories.starbucks .com/leadership/howard-schultz/.

9. "Why You Need a Third Place (and How to Find One)," *The Jordan Harbinger Show*, April 2, 2018, https://www.jordanharbinger.com /why-you-need-a-third-place-and-how-to-find-one/.

10. Jennifer Warnick, "Inside the Tryer Center, the Starbucks Lab Where Anything Is Possible," Starbucks.com, June 11, 2019, https://stories .starbucks.com/stories/2019/inside-the-tryer-center-the-starbucks -lab-where-anything-is-possible/.

11. "Rosalind 'Roz' Brewer," Starbucks.com, n.d., https://archive .starbucks.com/record/rosalind-roz-brewer.

12. Beth Kowitt, "How Starbucks Got Its Buzz Back," *Fortune*, September 24, 2019, https://fortune.com/longform/starbucks-coo-roz-brewer -sales-retail/.

13. Nathaniel Meyersohn, "It's Iced Coffee Season All Year Now," CNN Business, August 7, 2023, https://www.cnn.com/2023/08/07 /business/cold-drinks-coffee-tea-starbucks/index.html.

14. Rosalind Brewer, "Trailer: Rosalind Brewer Teaches Business Innovation," MasterClass.com, n.d., https://www.masterclass.com /classes/rosalind-brewer-teaches-business-innovation.

15. Meghan McCarron, "What Exactly Are Starbucks's Egg Bites? An Investigation," Eater, September 6, 2019, https://www.eater.com /2019/9/6/20841290/starbucks-egg-bites-review.

16. Kate Taylor, "The Unicorn Frappuccino Infuriated Baristas—But It Was One of Starbucks' Best Decisions in a Long Time," *Business Insider*, April 24, 2017, https://www.businessinsider.in/The -Unicorn-Frappuccino-infuriated-baristas-but-it-was-one-of -Starbucks-best-decisions-in-a-long-time/articleshow/58351447.cms.

Chapter 2

1. Molly Haskell, "Dreams of Starting Over: Molly Haskell on Barbara Stanwyck," British Film Institute, July 16, 2021, https://www.bfi.org.uk/sight-and-sound/features/molly-haskell-barbara-stanwyck.

2. Emily Sernaker, "The Ms. Q&A: What Led Anaïs Mitchell to Hadestown," *Ms.*, September 2, 2019, https://msmagazine.com/2019/09/02/the-ms-qa-what-led-anais-mitchell-to-hadestown/.

3. "The Local Story of Hadestown: From Vermont to Somerville to Broadway," WERS.org, January 6, 2022, https://wers.org/the-local-story-of-hadestown/.

4. "About," DaleFranzen.com, n.d., https://dalefranzen.com/about-1.

5. "Mara Isaacs Bio," Broadway World, n.d., https://www.broadwayworld.com/people/Mara-Isaacs/#bio.

6. "Broadway Investing Basics," Broadway Investor's Club, n.d., https://www.investingbroadway.com/broadway-investing-basics.

7. Jesse Green, "Review: The Metamorphosis of 'Hadestown,' from Cool to Gorgeous," *The New York Times*, April 18, 2019, https://www.nytimes.com/2019/04/17/theater/hadestown-review-broadway-anais-mitchell.html.

8. Lin-Manuel Miranda (@Lin_Manuel), "We saw Hadestown. Y'all." Twitter, April 22, 2019, 2:27 P.M., https://twitter.com/Lin_Manuel/status/1120439090695016448.

9. Greg Evans, "Broadway's Tony-Winning 'Hadestown' Recoups $11.5M Investment," Deadline, November 11, 2019, https://deadline.com/2019/11/hadestown-recoup-investment-broadway-1202782727/.

10. "Hadestown Broadway Grosses," Broadway World, n.d., https://www.broadwayworld.com/grosses/HADESTOWN.

11. "Box Office History for Fifty Shades of Grey Movies," The Numbers, n.d., https://www.the-numbers.com/movies/franchise/Fifty-Shades-of-Grey#tab=summary.

12. Jeff Rumage and Hal Koss, "How Long Should You Stay at a Job?" Built In, updated October 10, 2023, https://builtin.com/career-development/how-long-should-you-stay-at-a-job#.

13. "Bruce Cardenas of Quest Nutrition Explains Why This Forward Thinking Food Company Is a Celebrity Favorite," Press Pass LA, October 13, 2016, https://www.presspassla.com/bruce-cardenas -quest-nutrition-explains-forward-thinking-food-company-celebrity -favorite/.

14. "Get in the Kitchen with the Creator of Quest Bars," Muscle and Fitness, n.d., https://www.muscleandfitness.com/muscle-fitness -hers/hers-features/get-kitchen-creator-quest-bars/.

15. "Our Story," Quest Nutrition, n.d., https://www.questnutrition.com /pages/about-quest.

16. Sam Danley, "Simply Good Foods Completes Acquisition of Quest Nutrition," *Food Business News*, November 8, 2019, https://www .foodbusinessnews.net/articles/14854-simply-good-foods -completes-acquisition-of-quest-nutrition.

Chapter 3

1. "The DoorDash Story," Medium, October 4, 2013, https://medium .com/@DoorDash/the-doordash-story-b370c2bb1e5f.

2. "The DoorDash Story."

Chapter 4

1. "The Difference between a Plan and a Strategy," May 3, 2023, in *HBR on Strategy*, podcast, https://hbr.org/podcast/2023/05/the-difference -between-a-plan-and-a-strategy.

Chapter 5

1. Warren Cassell Jr., "Who Is Martha Stewart?" Investopedia, updated May 28, 2024, https://www.investopedia.com/articles /professionals/071415/how-martha-stewart-built-media-empire.asp.

Chapter 6

1. Alex Konrad, "Canva Uncovered: How a Young Australian Kitesurfer Built a $3.2 Billion (Profitable!) Startup Phenom," *Forbes*, December 11, 2019, https://www.forbes.com/sites/alexkonrad/2019/12/11/inside-canva-profitable-3-billion-startup-phenom/.

2. Julia Faria, "Disney: Brand Value 2020–2024," Statista, June 26, 2024, https://www.statista.com/statistics/1324425/disney-brand-value/.

3. "Walt Disney's Right-Hand Man, Theme Park Designer Dies," CBS News, July 28, 2017, https://www.cbsnews.com/losangeles/news/disney-theme-park-marty-sklar/.

4. "Richard Branson," *Forbes*, updated August 2, 2024, https://www.forbes.com/profile/richard-branson.

5. Lisette Voytko-Best, "The World's 10 Highest-Paid Entertainers," *Forbes*, February 13, 2023, updated November 22, 2023, https://www.forbes.com/sites/lisettevoytko/2023/02/13/the-worlds-top-10-highest-paid-entertainers-of-2022/.

6. Hiranmayi Srinivasan, "Taylor Swift Is a Billionaire—Swift's Net Worth and Business Empire Explained," Investopedia, updated October 26, 2023, https://www.investopedia.com/taylor-swift-earnings-7373918.

7. Amy Coval, "Six Connecticut Billionaires Make Forbes 400 List of Wealthiest Americans for 2023," *CT Insider*, updated October 5, 2023, https://www.ctinsider.com/news/article/ct-billionaries-forbes-400-list-2023-18406567.php.

8. Ray Dalio, *Principles: Life and Work* (New York: Simon & Schuster, 2017).

9. Yuval Atsmon, "Why Bad Strategy Is a Social Contagion," McKinsey, November 2, 2022, https://www.mckinsey.com/capabilities/strategy-and-corporate-finance/our-insights/why-bad-strategy-is-a-social-contagion.

10. "U.S. Business: The Men on the Cover: Advertising," *Time*, October 12, 1962, https://content.time.com/time/subscriber/article/0,33009,829288-6,00.html.

11. Lynsey Eidell, "Why Did Martha Stewart Go to Prison? A Look Back at Her 2004 Fraud Case," *People*, January 28, 2024, https://people.com /martha-stewart-fraud-case-prison-sentence-look-back-8550277.

12. Elyse Moody, "Martha Reimagined and Updated Her Bedford Home during the Pandemic—Take a Look Inside," Martha Stewart, February 18, 2021, https://www.marthastewart.com/8061492 /martha-stewart-bedford-home-tour-pandemic-updates.

13. Jenn Selby, "Emma Watson Named as UN Women Goodwill Ambassador," *Independent*, July 10, 2014, https://www.independent .co.uk/news/people/emma-watson-appointed-un-women-goodwill -ambassador-9590993.html.

14. Anna Bryan, "COP26: Harry Potter Actress Emma Watson Hosts Panel Event, Attended by Greta Thunberg, at Glasgow Climate Change Summit," *Scotsman*, November 4, 2021, https://www .scotsman.com/news/environment/cop26-emma-watson-hosts -panel-event-at-glasgow-summit-3445690.

15. Jamal Collier, "Who Is Toni Kukoc? 5 Things to Know about the 3rd-Leading Scorer during the Chicago Bulls' Second 3-Peat," *Chicago Tribune*, May 16, 2021, https://www.chicagotribune.com/2020/05/03 /who-is-toni-kukoc-5-things-to-know-about-the-3rd-leading-scorer -during-the-chicago-bulls-second-3-peat/.

Chapter 7

1. Simon Sinek, "How Great Leaders Inspire Action," TED.com, September 2009, https://www.ted.com/talks/simon_sinek_how _great_leaders_inspire_action/transcript.

2. Paul J. Zak, "Why Your Brain Loves Good Storytelling," *Harvard Business Review*, October 28, 2014, https://hbr.org/2014/10/why -your-brain-loves-good-storytelling.

3. Paul J. Zak, "Why Inspiring Stories Make Us React: The Neuroscience of Narrative," *Cerebrum* 2015 (January–Fe bruary 2015): 2, https:// www.ncbi.nlm.nih.gov/pmc/articles/PMC4445577/.

4. "Mission," CTR.com, n.d., https://ctr.com/#mission.

Chapter 9

1. "Our Programs," SixthDivision, https://www.sixthdivision.com/programs/.

2. "Our Programs," SixthDivision.

Chapter 10

1. *Communication in the Workplace Statistics 2024*, Pumble, n.d., https://pumble.com/learn/communication/communication-statistics/#Benefit_3_Effective_communication_increases_retention.

2. Dale Buss, "12 New Approaches to Compensation," SHRM.org, February 14, 2022, https://www.shrm.org/executive-network/insights/12-new-approaches-to-compensation.

3. Anthony Reinhart, "Cloud at Cost Injects Fibernetics with Startup Energy," Communitech, October 16, 2014, https://communitech.ca/technews/cloud-at-cost-injects-fibernetics-with-startup-energy.html.

4. Elaine Pofeldt, "The New Intrapreneurs," *Columbia Business Magazine*, November 17, 2023, https://magazine.business.columbia.edu/ws-24/new-intrapreneurs.

5. "How the NFL Turned Football into a Billion-Dollar Business," Bison and Bird, n.d., https://www.teambisonandbird.com/post/nfl-business#:~:text=NFL%20Revenues,for%20tickets%20and%20television%20rights.

6. Bill Walsh, Steve Jamison, and Craig Walsh, *The Score Takes Care of Itself: My Philosophy of Leadership* (New York: Portfolio, 2014).

7. Bryan Murphy, "Have the Lions Ever Won a Super Bowl? A (Brief) History of Detroit's Big Game Appearances," *Sporting News*, January 28, 2024, https://www.sportingnews.com/us/nfl/news/lions-won-super-bowl-history-detroit/c50df3236ead87b7adf1296e#:~:text=The%20Lions%20are%20one%20of,games%20between%201935%20and%201957.

8. Michelle Ganley, "11 of the Detroit Lions' Most Famous Fans," Click On Detroit, September 7, 2018, updated September 9, 2021, https://www.clickondetroit.com/sports/2018/09/07/11-of-the-detroit-lions-most-famous-fans/; Dan Treacy, "Who Are the Lions' Biggest Celebrity Fans? Eminem, Taylor Lautner, Ninja and More Cheering on Detroit," *Sporting News*, January 27, 2024, https://www.sportingnews.com/us/nfl/news/lions-celebrity-fans-eminem-taylor-lautner-ninja/ba774c51c8fd1c338043a3a5.

9. Dave Boucher and Dana Afana, "'Emotions Are High' as Detroit Lions Fans Travel for Historic Game against 49ers," *Detroit Free Press*, January 26, 2024, https://www.freep.com/story/sports/nfl/lions/2024/01/26/detroit-lions-san-francisco-49ers-fans-game-playoffs-crackman-tickets-nfc-champions/72339045007/.

Chapter 11

1. Lynne Maureen Hurdle, "It's the High Conflict Season," Dr. Lynne Maureen Hurdle, December 13, 2023, https://lynnemaureenhurdle.com/its-the-high-conflict-season/.

Chapter 12

1. "The True Cost of Employee Attrition," Peoplelogic, n.d., https://peoplelogic.ai/blog/the-true-cost-of-employee-attrition#:~:text=According%20to%20Gallup%2C%20U.S.%20businesses,companies%20are%20struggling%20to%20get.

2. Misti Aaronson, "Resilience and Grit | Stay Conversations | Inequity," SHIFT, October 29, 2021, https://www.shiftthework.com/blog/resilience-stay-conversations-inequity.

Chapter 13

1. Kimberly Amadeo, "The Bureau of Labor Statistics' (BLS) Monthly Jobs Report," *Balance*, updated December 2, 2022, https://www.thebalancemoney.com/jobs-report-monthly-employment-growth-statistics-3305732.

2. Amy Anderson, "Meet Kendra Scott, Homemade Millionaire," *Success*, March 7, 2016, updated April 11, 2016, https://www.success .com/meet-kendra-scott-homemade-millionaire/.

3. "Kendra Scott," Berkshire Partners, n.d., https://berkshirepartners .com/portfolio-companies/kendra-scott/.

4. John Jannarone and Karen E. Roman, "A Beacon in Affordable Luxury: Kendra Scott CEO Tom Nolan Elevates the Jewelry Unicorn and Its Customers," Yahoo Finance, October 6, 2023, https://finance .yahoo.com/news/beacon-affordable-luxury-kendra-scott -155305172.html.

5. Elana Lyn Gross, "How Kendra Scott Built a Billion-Dollar Jewelry Company," *Forbes*, March 1, 2018, updated March 2, 2018, https:// www.forbes.com/sites/elanagross/2018/03/01/how-kendra-scott -built-a-billion-dollar-jewelry-company/.

INDEX

ABOUT THE AUTHOR

Jen Kem was named a Top Brand Strategist by *Forbes,* is the master-mind behind many innovations that have changed your life, and led the team that invented streaming video technology. As a brand futurist, writer, and speaker, she has appeared on CBS, NBC, and Fox News, and in *Entrepreneur, Fast Company,* and *Inc.*

Kem is the secret-weapon strategist that top brands like the Oprah Winfrey Network, Blue Cross Blue Shield, Microsoft, Coca-Cola, Verizon, and Oracle call when they want to launch new offers into the marketplace at lightning speed. Her client roster also includes dozens of *New York Times* best-selling authors, keynote speakers, and thought leaders who use her Unicorn Innovation Model to bring great ideas to life and rally the right people around them.

In addition to helping her clients make billions, Kem is an entrepreneur and investor. She's the founder of Master Brand Institute, the top consulting and training firm for thought leaders, executives, and personal brands; runs a private-equity club that funds technology and wellness ideas that benefit women and children; and owns a vineyard and farm that produces wine named in honor of her grandmother Generosa.

Kem writes a newsletter that reaches 400,000 readers, sharing insights on how to rally the right people around your idea, create a winning team, get big things done faster, and build an iconic brand that shapes the way we live and innovates the legacies we want to leave behind.

A proud Filipina American originally from Hawaii, she now lives in the San Francisco Bay Area with her husband, kids, three wild French bulldogs, and one very smart Jack Russell terrier.

www.TheJenKem.com

Hay House Titles of Related Interest

THE SHIFT, the movie,
starring Dr. Wayne W. Dyer
(available as an online streaming video)
www.hayhouse.com/the-shift-movie

***

HIGH PERFORMANCE HABITS: How Extraordinary People Become That Way, by Brendon Burchard

BE SEEN: Find Your Voice. Build Your Brand. Live Your Dream.,
by Jen Gottlieb

GRAVITAS: The 8 Strengths That Redefine Confidence, by Lisa Sun

THE NEW MILLIONAIRE'S PLAYBOOK: 7 Keys to Unlock Freedom, Purpose, and Abundance, by Gordy Bal

WHAT'S IN IT FOR THEM?: 9 Genius Networking Principles to Get What You Want by Helping Others Get What They Want,
by Joe Polish

WORTHY: How to Believe You Are Enough and Transform Your Life,
by Jamie Kern Lima

All of the above are available at your local bookstore
or may be ordered by visiting:

Hay House USA: www.hayhouse.com°
Hay House Australia: www.hayhouse.com.au
Hay House UK: www.hayhouse.co.uk
Hay House India: www.hayhouse.co.in

***

We hope you enjoyed this Hay House book. If you'd like to receive our online catalog featuring additional information on Hay House books and products, or if you'd like to find out more about the Hay Foundation, please contact:

Hay House LLC, P.O. Box 5100, Carlsbad, CA 92018-5100
(760) 431-7695 or (800) 654-5126
www.hayhouse.com® • www.hayfoundation.org

———

Published in Australia by:
Hay House Australia Publishing Pty Ltd
18/36 Ralph St., Alexandria NSW 2015
Phone: +61 (02) 9669 4299
www.hayhouse.com.au

Published in the United Kingdom by:
Hay House UK Ltd
1st Floor, Crawford Corner,
91–93 Baker Street, London W1U 6QQ
Phone: +44 (0)20 3927 7290
www.hayhouse.co.uk

Published in India by:
Hay House Publishers (India) Pvt Ltd
Muskaan Complex, Plot No. 3,
B-2, Vasant Kunj, New Delhi 110 070
Phone: +91 11 41761620
www.hayhouse.co.in

———

Let Your Soul Grow

Experience life-changing transformation—one video at a time—with guidance from the world's leading experts.

www.healyourlifeplus.com